【學科能力測驗、指定科目考試適用】

U0092777

指考篇章・閱測秘技

王靖賢

學歷／國立臺灣師範大學英語研究所碩士
經歷／建國中學

蘇文賢

學歷／國立臺灣師範大學教育研究所碩士
經歷／基隆高中

三民書局

國家圖書館出版品預行編目資料

指考篇章‧閱測秘技／王靖賢,蘇文賢編著.－－
初版一刷.－－臺北市: 三民, 2018
面；　公分.－－(英語Make Me High系列)

ISBN 978-957-14-6361-2　(平裝)

1.英語教學 2.讀本 3.中等教育

524.38　　　　　　　　　　　　　106022645

© 指考篇章‧閱測秘技

編 著 者	王靖賢　蘇文賢
責任編輯	黃菀晨
美術設計	郭雅萍
封面設計	廖文心
內頁設計	廖文心
發 行 人	劉振強
著作財產權人	三民書局股份有限公司
發 行 所	三民書局股份有限公司
	地址　臺北市復興北路386號
	電話　(02)25006600
	郵撥帳號　0009998-5
門 市 部	(復北店)臺北市復興北路386號
	(重南店)臺北市重慶南路一段61號
出版日期	初版一刷　2018年1月
編 號	S 804520

行政院新聞局登記證局版臺業字第○二○○號

有著作權‧不准侵害

ISBN　978-957-14-6361-2　(平裝)

http://www.sanmin.com.tw　三民網路書店

序

英語 Make Me High 系列的理想在於超越，在於創新。

這是時代的精神，也是我們出版的動力；

這是教育的目的，也是我們進步的執著。

針對英語這種國際語言的全球化趨勢，

我們設計了此套功能取向的英語學習叢書。

面對英語，不會徬徨不再迷惘，學習的心徹底沸騰，

心情好 High！

實戰模擬，掌握先機知己知彼，百戰不殆決勝未來，

分數更 High！

選擇優質的英語學習叢書，才能激發學習的強烈動機；

興趣盎然便不會畏懼艱難，自信心要自己大聲說出來。

本書如良師指引循循善誘，如益友相互鼓勵攜手成長。

展書輕閱，您將發現…

學習英語原來也可以這麼 High！

給讀者的話

　　閱讀測驗是大考英文中分數佔很重的題型。同學們除了平常應多閱讀英文文章外，也應該針對不同的閱讀測驗題型來練習，並且使用各種閱讀策略技巧，以提升答題效率。本書指考篇章・閱測秘技針對此概念，提供閱讀測驗的解題技巧與策略解說，並且也提供了許多例子和大量的練習題，能夠讓學生應試時更有信心並且從容地面對大考試題。

　　本書包含了理論篇和題目篇。理論篇仔細地分析應試時該如何針對不同的題目類別使用不同的閱讀策略。題目篇則有二十篇閱讀測驗文章，並附上詳盡的解析，讓學生可以在家輕鬆學習，全面地掌握閱讀測驗，在各種英文考試中攻無不克，百戰百勝。

王靖賢

　　在大學指考英文科測驗當中，可以看出偏重考生閱讀能力的趨勢，因此，閱讀的能力將會是得分的重大關鍵。而在各類題型中，許多考生常對「篇章結構」題型感到困擾，因為要找出正確答案，考生不但要能夠讀懂文章，還必須能夠看出文章的敘述脈絡以及各種語氣的連貫性，若平常沒有充分練習，在考試中將不易得分。

　　針對此種困境，本書《指考篇章・閱測秘技》不但仔細說明作者如何在文章中利用各種技巧來達成語意的連貫性，也提出各種解題關鍵與線索，提供實際範例與詳盡說明。考生在讀完本書所提供的各種解題秘技，並做完書中豐富的練習題後，一定能迅速找出文章中的各種線索、理解文章脈絡與邏輯，輕鬆克服「篇章結構」的挑戰！

蘇文賢

指考篇章・閱測秘技

G O

篇章結構
理論篇

解鎖秘技

文章中的句子並非隨意拼湊組合而成，而是作者為了要清楚地傳達心中的想法和理念，依循一定的章法與邏輯來組織文章，才能讓讀者瞭解文章內容。因此，為了達到這個目的，句子與句子之間必須有清楚的邏輯關係，才能使文章結構清晰、條理分明。根據這樣的脈絡，在寫篇章結構的題型時，我們所要考慮的，就是空格內所選的句子必須和前後句在邏輯上連貫、並且能夠產生一致的意義。

篇章結構之必備技能 ▶▶

◈ 必備技能 1 (required skill 1)：快速掌握段落結構

在閱讀文章的過程當中，盡量快速地掌握整體文章段落的結構，並且瞭解整篇文章的概念。這樣就不難在篇章結構這個題型中獲取高分。

◈ 必備技能 2 (required skill 2)：連貫性的要素

在掌握文章段落的結構後，若想要選出正確的答案，還必須認識在文章中為了達到連貫性而出現的要素。此種要素可再細分為以下兩種：

(1) 意義的連貫性 (coherence)：也就是句子的順序，會以合乎某種邏輯的次序加以安排。

(2) 文字語氣的連貫性 (cohesion)：意即藉由一定的語言形式 (language form)，使句子的語氣達到連貫且順暢的狀態。

◈ 必備技能 3 (required skill 3)：邏輯思考

平常在閱讀文章時，應該要訓練自己的邏輯思考能力。所謂的邏輯思考能力，是指能夠依據線索而推敲出文章發展過程之因果關係的能力。如果具備了正確且敏銳的邏輯思考能力，那麼在寫篇章結構這個題型時，就能夠迅速、準確地找出句子間的關係，並且找出正確答案。這也是在寫本題型時最重要且不可或缺的能力。

◈ 必備技能 4 (required skill 4)：瞭解文章中的語言形式

為了使文章句子間及段落間的起承轉合等更為流暢與連貫，作者通常會在文章中使用各種不同的語言形式 (包括轉折詞、連接詞、代名詞、同義詞、以及關鍵字的重複等等)，若能快速地辨識出這些語言形式，就能更明確地理解文章的脈絡與次序，進而找到正確答案。

篇章結構─攻略 ▶▶

在寫篇章結構的題目時，可依循以下三個步驟，以更快速地掌握整篇文章並找到正確答案。

◈ Step 1：先閱讀提供的選項

在寫篇章結構時，應該先閱讀選項中的句子，對這些選項有大致的瞭解之後，再開始瀏覽文章。

◈ Step 2：瀏覽文章

大略瀏覽整篇文章，對整體架構與段落大意有基本概念。

◈ Step 3：仔細閱讀並找出文章中的邏輯與相關線索

開始仔細閱讀文章，尤其是在空格的前後句子。找出這些句子與選項中句子之間的邏輯關係，並在文字之間尋找線索或指示詞，像是轉折詞、代名詞、同義詞等等，以確認選出的答案是否符合文章邏輯與發展脈絡。

模擬戰 ↓ A

以下為一篇難易適中的文章，可按照先前所提過的答題步驟來測試一下自己的能力。在文章後面的戰略分析會詳細地說明如何尋找線索，和一些技巧的細節。在接下來的 unit 2 和 unit 3 會更加詳細的說明。

Today, it is becoming increasingly likely that we will be able to bring extinct species back to life. ___1___ In fact, since it is impossible for us to accurately forecast what might happen if we do, many people have taken a cautious and critical approach to bringing extinct species back to life.

Critics of reviving extinct species often bring up the passenger pigeon as an example of the possible disasters that might result. Before they became extinct, passenger pigeons were very common. ___2___ They were very noisy when they flapped their wings, and when they migrated, they would black out the sun. Perhaps this is why, a hundred years ago, these birds began to be hunted on such a massive scale. ___3___

If these birds were brought back to life, people wonder where they would live, since many of their old habitats have disappeared. ___4___ As well, their consumption of seeds might damage trees or cause their growth to slow.

___5___ From this example, it seems clear that we would do well to proceed with caution when it comes to reviving extinct species.

(A) People also worry that they might crowd out other birds and animals.

(B) In fact, one flock of these birds was usually made up of billions of passenger pigeons.

(C) Scientists have been trying hard to find a feasible way to bring passenger pigeons back to life.

(D) However, some people wonder if reviving extinct species is really such a good idea.

(E) The case of the passenger pigeon is just one example of the possible effects of bringing extinct species back to life.

(F) As a result, passenger pigeons vanished.

1. _____ 2. _____ 3. _____ 4. _____ 5. _____

⚠️ 戰略分析

1. D

邏輯 第一句提到人們愈來愈有可能使已滅絕的物種復活，而在下一句則提到人們對此事的態度為 cautious and critical approach，語氣從一開始的樂觀，到後來的謹慎小心，出現了轉折，因此 (D) 選項中的 However 這個轉折詞正可發揮此作用。

重複 在第一句和下一句、以及 (D) 選項中都重複提到 extinct species。

同義詞 在第一句和下一句提到的 bring ... back to life，與 (D) 選項中的 revive 為同義詞，故可知 (D) 為正確答案。

2. B

邏輯 本段以已滅絕的物種 passenger pigeons (旅鴿) 為例。前一句提到，在旅鴿滅絕之前，曾經非常普遍。而下一句提到當旅鴿遷徙時，they would black out the sun (他們遮蔽了太陽使天空變暗)，由此可知其數量極為龐大。而在所有選項中，只有 (B) 選項提到與數量相關的詞，也就是 billions，故為承接前後句的銜接句子。

舉例 在前一句提到旅鴿極為普遍，為了進一步說明到何種地步，此處舉出實際的例子，也就是一群旅鴿通常由幾十億隻所組成。此處 billions 表示數量極為龐大，正好呼應前一句的 very common。

代名詞 (B) 選項中的 these birds，指的是前一句的 they 和 passenger pigeons。

3. F

邏輯 前一句提到了旅鴿被獵殺，並且是 on such a massive scale (大規模)。我們從第一段的內容得知旅鴿已經滅絕，故可合理推測此處在解釋因果關係。

轉折詞 透過邏輯分析得知此處說明一種因果關係，而在 (F) 選項中的 as a result 這個轉折詞正是說明某事所造成的後果。

用字 (F) 選項中的 vanished (消失) 表達了前一句 be hunted on such a massive scale 所造成的後果。

4. A

邏輯 從本題的前後兩句可知，本段在討論如果讓旅鴿重新復活可能帶來的問題。前一句提到 where they would live，以及 their old habitats have disappeared，這些都是令人擔心的地方。下一句則提到旅鴿可能會破壞生態的行為。此種擔心的口吻與 (A) 選項一致，因為 (A) 選項裡提及 worry 一字，並且也提到其他物種生存的危機，因此可知 (A) 為正確答案。

代名詞 由句意來判斷，(A) 選項的 they 指的是前一句的 these birds，也就是旅鴿。

用字 本段都在討論如果旅鴿復活可能產生的問題，本段用了許多較為負面的字，像是 disappeared、damage、slow 等，與 (A) 選項的 worry、crowd out 等用字相呼應。

5. E

邏輯 本題為文章的最後一段，通常會對前述的論點進行總結。由 (E) 選項提到的 just one example of the possible effects 可知，這句話為前面文章的結論句，故答案選 (E)。

重複 在 (E) 選項和下一句都重複提到 example 這個字，可見這兩句是利用重複使用 example 來達成語意的一致與連貫性，故 (E) 選項為正確答案。

至於 (C) 選項，後面提到了 bring passenger pigeons back to life，似乎與第 1 題的前後句相呼應，但是在第一段只提出讓滅絕的生物復活的廣泛概念，並未具體提出以旅鴿當作例子，故不適合作為第 1 題的答案。雖然旅鴿的例子也出現在第二、三段，但並未提及科學家努力使牠們復活，因此 (C) 選項為多餘的，故非正解。

模擬戰 ↓ B

以下這篇文章的難度稍高，但條理清晰，脈絡順暢，是值得克服的挑戰。現在就來測試對於篇章結構的掌握程度吧！

You've probably heard of Saint Valentine. Perhaps you know that Father Christmas is also called Santa Claus which stands for Saint Nicholas. But what exactly is a "saint"?

_____1_____ After they died, people began to pray to their spirits and asked them to help in some way. Often, their bodies were preserved and worshipped. Some saints were believed to have supernatural powers even when they were alive.

_____2_____ In fact, in order to become a saint, a person had to have performed at least one miracle.

Not all Christians believe in saints. When the Christian church broke up into several different branches several centuries ago, some Christians rejected the idea of saints. _____3_____ Despite this, the Catholic church, which is the largest Christian church, not only still believes in saints, but even continues to create new ones.

For example, Pope John Paul II, who died in 2005, became a saint in 2014. The process of becoming a saint is called canonization. _____4_____ Their role is to find flaws in the person's character, reasons why the person should not be named a saint. _____5_____

Although not everyone believes in the religion aspects today, the idea of saints still forms an important part of the traditional culture of countries that have practiced Christianity.

(A) When it occurs, investigators are sent to study the life of the candidate for sainthood.

(B) Saints were men or women who were considered especially holy when they were alive.

(C) They claimed it had been taken from pre-Christian religions and was not part of true Christianity.

(D) Throughout history, many religious people have become saints and been highly respected.

(E) When they used their magical abilities to help people, it was called a "miracle."

(F) Because of this negative approach, they are called "Devil's Advocates."

1. _____ 2. _____ 3. _____ 4. _____ 5. _____

篇章結構‧理論篇

1. B

邏輯 第一段最後一句，作者提問 What exactly is a "saint"?，由此可合理推論此為必要回答的問題。而 (B) 選項的主詞正是 saints (聖人)，後面提及的 men or women who were considered. . . ，正是對於 saints 的說明，因此可知 (B) 為正確答案。

重複 saint 在第一段最後一句，以及 (B) 選項中都有出現，可知是重複的關鍵字，為答題的重要線索。

時間順序 在 (B) 選項的最後提到了 when they were alive，而下一句一開始提到了 After they died，很明顯地具有時間順序，亦是答題的線索。

2. E

邏輯 前一句提到有些聖人在世時，也被認為有 supernatural powers (超自然力量)，下一句則提到要成為聖人的條件之一，是至少要展現出一次的奇蹟。因此可以得知此處在討論聖人所具備的神奇力量，而 (E) 選項也提到 used their magical abilities to help people，來承接前後句意，故為正解。

同義詞 在前一句的 supernatural powers 與 (E) 選項中的 magical abilities (魔法般的能力) 可視為是同義詞，為答題線索。

重複 (E) 選項與下一句裡面都提到 miracle 這個字，是極為關鍵的線索。

3. C

邏輯 從本段的主題句 Not all Christians believe in saints 可知，本段主題為關於反對「聖人」的想法之意見。在 (C) 選項中提到「聖人」這樣的概念並不算是真正基督教義的一部分，與本段主題相呼應，故為正確答案。

代名詞 (C) 選項中的 They 所指涉的對象為前一句的 some Christians。而下一句中的指示代名詞 this，則指的是 (C) 選項這整件事。這兩個代名詞所指涉的對象環環相扣，故可知 (C) 為正確答案。

4. A

邏輯 前一句提到 canonization 就是 the process of becoming a saint，由此可以推測接下來應該要解釋這個 process。而在 (A) 選項中的 investigators (調查者)、study (研究)、candidate (候選人)，都可以聯想到與 canonization 的過程有關。

代名詞 在前一句裡的 canonization (封為聖人) 是重要線索，在 (A) 選項裡有代名詞 it，後面加上動詞 occurs，可推論出此處的 it 所指涉的是 canonization。除此之外，在下一句裡提到代名詞的所有格 their，其指涉對象亦可回推 (A) 選項中的 investigators。由此可知，it 和 their 所指涉的對象依序層遞，使語意連貫，故 (A) 為承接前後句的正確答案。

5. F

邏輯 在空格的前一句提到了 flaws in the person's character、why the person should not be named a saint，此為舉出反面事例或否證式的做法。此處語意與 (F) 選項中的 negative 一字相呼應，故 (F) 為正確答案。

代名詞 (F) 選項中的代名詞 they，所指涉的對象與前一句裡的 their 是相同的。

換句話說 (F) 選項裡的 this negative approach，表達了前面提到的 find flaws in the person's character、why the person should not be named a saint。而這正是一種換句話說的手法，也是相當重要的答題線索。

至於 (D) 選項，其敘述的主題為 saints，乍看之下似乎與第 1 題或第 2 題的主題相呼應，但是第 1 題的句子是承接上一段的最後一句問句而來的，因此必須先說明 saints 的定義，而 (D) 並未說明此點，故不適合作為第 1 題的答案。而第 2 題，雖然主題也在討論聖人，但是重點在於聖人生前所具有的神奇力量與奇蹟，與 (D) 所提到的內容不合，故 (D) 也不適合作為正確答案。

Unit 2 意義的連貫性
Coherence

解鎖秘技

所謂意義的連貫性，指的是句子與句子之間邏輯次序的安排。為了讓讀者能更清楚瞭解文章所要傳達的意思，因此依據文章主題內容的不同，作者會選擇適合的邏輯安排次序，而此種次序本身就是一種表達連貫性的方式。換句話說，文章中句子的安排方式與先後次序，會依循著一定的發展脈絡而呈現出來。常見的邏輯次序安排方式如下：

⑴ 先描述所觀察到的現象，接著談到該現象可能造成的問題或影響，最後再提出解決之道。
⑵ 按照時間順序來敘述事件和說明過程，而此種方式可分為依時間發展先後順序的順敘法，以及時間發展次序由後往前的倒敘法。
⑶ 按照空間順序來描述人、事、物或是地點，在次序上的安排可以由遠到近或近到遠。
⑷ 依照推理次序來描述因果關係，可以先描述原因，然後再說明結果，也可以先說明結果，然後再解釋其原因。
⑸ 在說明理由或提出細節來解釋或推理時，其順序可從簡單到複雜、從廣泛籠統到具體明確、從比較不重要到最重要或是從比較不明顯到最明顯等。

EXAMPLE

邏輯順序：現象 → 問題 → 解決之道

Day in, day out children in Africa work with dangerous tools and sometimes black out under the harsh sun in order to provide the cocoa around the world. Out if economic necessity, their families disregard their education, but it creates a cycle of poverty that is nearly impossible to break. One increasingly popular solution to this problem is the fair-trade chocolate campaign.

大解密

在這段文字中，作者先提出了非洲兒童在惡劣環境中工作的現象，然後再點出造成此種現象的真正問題是這些兒童都來自於貧困的家庭，最後則提出這個問題的解決方法之一就是推動巧克力的公平貿易活動。

EXAMPLE

時間順序：先 → 後

After breaking into the house, the thief looked around the house to ensure it was safe. Next, he found the safe, opened it and stole the money inside.

大解密

在本例中，動作的描述順序是依照時間的發展，並且也用了轉折詞 next (接著) 來使兩句的連接更為順暢，同時也加強了時間順序的感受。

EXAMPLE

因果關係：第一句為原因，第二句為結果

On September 21, 1999, a huge earthquake hit Taiwan all of a sudden. This disaster claimed more than 2,000 lives.

大解密

在這個例子裡，第一句提到了 1999 年的 921 大地震，第二句則提到這起地震造成超過 2,000 人死亡，是典型因果關係的敘述。

篇章結構・理論篇

11

邏輯次序：廣泛籠統 → 具體明確

Generally speaking, most of us use computers with little concern about cybercrime. If one knew the true risks, one might be more shocked. In 2011, approximately 41 adults became victims of cybercrime every second.

大解密 ?

在本段文字裡，一開始先提到大多數人對於網路犯罪幾乎都漠不關心，然後再提到網路犯罪的超高發生率，也就是每一秒竟高達 41 名成人淪為網路犯罪的受害者。此種方式是先提到一個大概念，然後再具體地說明，是寫作時常採用的邏輯次序。

EXAMPLE

以下這篇文章所談的是如何建立個人的自尊，讓我們以這篇文章為例。作者於文章中先以一般大眾對於自尊的看法作為開頭，再針對文章主題——如何建立個人的自尊，來提出具體的作法及建議。(畫底線的 2、5、7、10、14 句為題幹中挖空的空格)

(1)Some people feel they are what they own, what they buy or what they wear. (2)But there are ways of building self-esteem that involve little or no money being spent.

(3)The quality of your appearance is, of course, more often determined by your body than by the clothes that cover it. (4)So if you can't afford to buy the latest designer gear, get fit instead. (5)Studies have shown that regular exercise improves our sense of self-esteem.

(6)Self-esteem can also be based on accomplishment. (7)So, find something you like and become good at it. (8)In the end, your skills will impress others and inspire a healthy pride in yourself.

(9)Another way of enhancing your self-image is to set yourself goals for the future. (10)These should be ambitious but realistic. (11)"Become a Jedi Knight" may be going too far! (12)As you gradually achieve the targets you have set, you will experience a sense of purpose and satisfaction.

(13)Whenever you're suffering from self-doubt, it can be helpful to remind yourself of why you're special. (14)<u>Draw up a list of your best features.</u>

(15)A deep sense of self-confidence is not built upon the clothes you're wearing, but something more substantial and long-lasting.

大解密

一、主題句

本篇文章的主題句是第 2 句。在第 1 句中提到有些人認為他們的所有物、購買的商品或是穿著的衣物才能代表自己，但第 2 句則推翻此論點，並提出有許多建立自尊的方法幾乎是不需花費金錢的。我們可以從此句推敲文章的脈絡，也就是作者接下來會針對這個主題提出具體的說明。

二、邏輯順序

就本文而言，其邏輯順序是從一個廣泛籠統的概念 (ways of building self-esteem) 出發，然後接著在第 3、6、9、13 句裡再提出較具體的概念並舉例論述，以下是文中提及的四個具體觀念的簡要解析：

⑴ 第一點為自尊通常來自於你的身材，而不是外在的穿著 (第 3 句)。
   接著作者說明運動的重要性並舉出研究的結果來支持此說法 (第 4、5 句)。

⑵ 第二點為自尊也可以來自於成就 (第 6 句)。 因此我們應該找到自己喜歡且擅長的事 (第 7 句)。如此一來，最後別人將會對我們的能力印象深刻，而我們也會培養出健全的自尊心 (第 8 句)。

⑶ 第三點是為自己的未來訂下目標 (第 9 句)。 但是這些目標必須要遠大並且可實踐的 (第 10 句)。作者接著舉出一個不切實際的目標為例 (第 11 句)，然後說明在逐步完成目標時所體會到的滿足感 (第 12 句)。

⑷ 第四點則是鼓勵讀者找到自己與眾不同之處 (第 13 句)， 並列出自己最棒的特質 (第 14 句)，此種方式也有助於提升自尊。

三、結論句

本文的最後再次強調自尊並非建立在穿著， 而是某個更為實質且長久的事物 (第 15 句)。不但呼應了前面所提出的論點，也為本文作了總結。本文的架構清楚，銜接順暢，是一篇條理分明的文章，故在答題時，只要注意空格在段落的主題與邏輯順序，就可以輕鬆地找出答案。

解鎖秘技

在安排文章的句子順序時，除了要依照清楚的邏輯脈絡之外，句子間的語氣也必須順暢地銜接在一起，要達到這個目的，就必須依賴一定的語言形式才行，其中包括轉折詞、代名詞、同義詞、關鍵字的重複等等，而這些就是寫篇章結構時所要找的線索。

◈ 線索 1：轉折詞 (transitional words or phrases)

轉折詞的作用在於承接上下兩個句子或段落，使語氣的銜接更為順暢，有助於達成句子和段落之間的連貫性。常見的轉折詞包括 for example (例如)；on the one hand (一方面)、on the other hand (另一方面)；in addition、besides、moreover、what's more (除此之外)；in other words (換句話說)；however、nevertheless (然而)；therefore、thus、as a result (因此、結果)；in fact、actually (事實上)；to begin with (首先)；finally、in the end、at last (最後、終於)；in a word、in a nutshell、in short (簡而言之) 等。在英文中，轉折詞的數量龐大且豐富，平時除了多翻閱寫作與文法相關書籍來瞭解各種轉折詞之外，也可以從文章中觀察作者使用各種轉折詞的時機與情況。

EXAMPLE

Expressions referring to animals come from a variety of sources. For example, to "cry wolf" means to give a false alarm, and it comes from one of Aesop's fables with this title. And "crocodile tears" means to show insincere sympathy and fake tears. It comes from ancient anecdote.

大解密

for example(例如) 是用來針對前面所提出的論點，提供相關的例子與佐證以進行更詳細的具體說明。在本例中，前一句提到與動物有關的表達方式有各種不同的來源，為了進一步說明此論點，下一句則用 for example 帶出 "cry wolf" 及 "crocodile tears" 為例，使讀者對文中的 a variety of sources 有更明確的概念。

EXAMPLE

    A celebrity both on and off the court, LeBron James' fame probably exceeds that of just about any other athlete. <u>As a result</u>, the Cleveland Cavaliers forward has endorsement contracts for companies like Nike, McDonalds, Coca-Cola, and Upper Deck, among others.

大解密 ？

在表達因果關係時，as a result 是相當重要的轉折詞，用以表示某件事或某個動作所造成的結果。在本例中，前一句提到 NBA 球星 LeBron James 的知名度很可能遠超過其他運動員，而後一句則用 as a result 來表達此事所造成的結果，也就是他得到了許多品牌代言的機會。

EXAMPLE

    Mandy used to be a shopaholic. She couldn't resist latest clothes and fancy high heels. However, she made up her mind to spend money wisely after her baby was born.

大解密 ？

however 是個很常見的轉折詞，意思為「然而」，常常當作是重要的解題線索。在本例中，第一句提到 Mandy 原為購物狂，她無法抗拒最新款的衣服和花俏的高跟鞋。然而，孩子出世的原因，讓她下定決心要謹慎地花錢。

◈ 線索 2：代名詞 (pronouns)

寫文章時，運用代名詞是達成連貫性最簡單的方法。雖然代名詞在文章中相對而言比較不明顯，但是對於理解文意而言，辨識出代名詞所指涉的對象是非常重要的。而在作答篇章結構時，代名詞也是極為重要的關鍵線索，因此千萬不能小看代名詞，它們有時甚至可以發揮「小兵立大功」的作用呢！

常見的代名詞如下：

人稱代名詞：

主格：I, you, he, she, it, we, they

受格：me, you, him, her, them, us

所有格：my, your, his, her, their, our, its

所有代名詞：mine, yours, his, hers, theirs, ours, its

指示代名詞：this, that, these, those, such, so

不定代名詞：one, both, all, some, each, another, the other, others

EXAMPLE

The hunchback character, Quasimodo, has the terrible misfortune of looking like a monster. His face is ugly, **he** has a huge bump growing on his back, and **he** can barely speak.

大解密 ?

第一句提到在鐘樓怪人這本小說裡的主角 Quasimodo 的不幸，而下一句裡的代名詞 he 所指的對象正是 Quasimodo。

EXAMPLE

Animal idioms are very common and can be useful in making one's language more colorful. However, avoid over-using **them**. Before using a colorful animal idiom, consider your audience and make sure the expression would be understood and appropriate.

大解密

第一句裡提到了 animal idioms (與動物相關的慣用語)，而下一句裡的代名詞 them 所指的正是 animal idioms。

EXAMPLE

Gangsters use viruses and innovative scams to steal passport, driver's license, or credit card numbers. **This** is facilitated by the proliferation of online banking and shopping.

大解密 ?

指示代名詞 this 可以用來指涉前面已經提過的敘述或是說明。在這個例子當中，this 所指涉的就是前面的整個句子。

◈ 線索 3：同義詞 (synonyms) 或換句話說 (in other words)

在文章中有時會重複提到某個人、事、物，但如果不運用同義詞的話，會使得文章缺乏變化並顯得單調。因此，作者通常會以不同的同義詞來指稱同一個人、事、物。同樣地，為了避免文章枯燥單調，作者除了運用同義詞之外，也會以不同的說法來表達出同樣的意思。而這些同義詞或是換句話說的句子亦是相當重要的解題線索。

EXAMPLE

Many popular expressions like animal idioms can make one's expression more colorful. Without a doubt, these can be difficult to understand unless you are accustomed to hearing them.

大解密 ?

在這個例子裡，many popular expressions 和 animal idioms 是同義詞。一般而言，作者為了使文章更生動、更有變化性，通常會在文章中使用同義詞，而這也是在答題時可以善加利用的線索。

If a choking victim is conscious, however, you should obtain <u>consent</u> before beginning CPR. <u>A quick nod of their head to indicate "yes"</u> is sufficient.

大解密 ❓

在本例中，第二句的主詞 A quick nod of their head to indicate "yes" 也是在說明第一句提到的 consent，這正是一種「換句話說」的手法，也就是以不同的字詞來解釋或說明前面提過的某個事物或概念。

⊕ 線索 4：重複 (repetitions)

有時候為了要達成文章的連貫性，作者會在句子裡重複關鍵字，這也是我們能夠加以利用的線索。

Using <u>CPR</u> can save a life when a person's breathing or heartbeat has stopped. Along with cases of cardiac arrest, <u>CPR</u> is most commonly employed in emergencies.

大解密 ❓

第一句中提到了使用 CPR 可以拯救他人的生命，而在第二句的後半段又再次提到，發生心搏停止的緊急狀況時，CPR 是最常使用的方法。可知作者利用重複關鍵字的技巧來表達出 CPR 的重要性。

Some critics believe that the <u>selfie</u> is a form of expression that will become a lasting form of art. Historians are eager for the collection of artifacts that <u>selfie</u>-taking inevitably produces. What is clear is that <u>selfie</u>-takers are in love with their own image, no matter what the background is.

大解密 ?

在這個例子中，每一句都重覆提到 selfie (自拍) 這個字，而作者就是利用此關鍵字來達成語氣的連貫性與一致性。

篇章結構
題目篇

詳解請參閱解析本 p.

Hot Dogs

In the late 19th century, many immigrants sailed from Europe to the U.S. They were poor and desperate. ___1___ But not every one of them had the professional skills to find a job. Naturally, using the only skill they had, some of them opened restaurants to serve their own fellow immigrants.

___2___ One of the items he offered was Frankfurt sausage. In order to better serve his customers, he provided a pair of gloves for them. ___3___ The owner soon discovered that many customers took the gloves away when they left. The cost of washing these gloves was also very expensive. ___4___ Was there any way to protect the customers from burning their hands while eating without the use of gloves?

___5___ He baked longer buns and placed the sausage, by then known as frankfurters, in the middle. His customers were satisfied with this new idea and that is how the famous "hot dog" was born.

(A) He thought day and night in order to find a solution to the problem.

(B) The sausage he offered was so delicious that it was always sold out soon.

(C) In 1904, a German immigrant opened a small restaurant in St. Louis.

(D) Finally, he came up with a marvelous idea.

(E) In this way, when his customers were eating the hot sausage, their hands would not be burned.

(F) They came to America looking for a better life.

1. _____ 2. _____ 3. _____ 4. _____ 5. _____

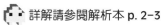

Sky Lanterns

The launching of sky lanterns in Pingshi is becoming one of the most famous folk activities during the traditional Chinese Lantern Festival. Sky lanterns, also called Kong Ming lanterns, can be traced back to the Three Kingdoms era. ___1___ But why do people in Pingshi launch sky lanterns for the festival instead of hanging up regular ones?

In the Qing Dynasty, settlers came from Fujian Province to Pingshi. Times were extremely hard for them. ___2___ At this time every year, the women, children, and elderly of Pingshi would go to the mountains to hide, carrying their valuables with them. ___3___ On seeing this message, their fellow villagers would start to come back home. ___4___

Nowadays, however, sky lanterns are used to convey people's wishes to Heaven. ___5___ Next year during the festival why not come to Pingshi to witness this unique and fascinating folk activity?

(A) From this arose the custom of launching sky lanterns.

(B) Kong Ming lanterns were used to be a signal to warn people that the area was dangerous.

(C) At the end of the festival, the men guarding their homes would send lanterns skyward to signal all was safe and at peace.

(D) Isn't it amazing to see one lantern after another floating up into the night sky, each bearing its own small wish?

(E) During the New Year's holidays, bandit gangs would come to the village to rob people.

(F) In those times armies employed them as signaling devices.

1. _____ 2. _____ 3. _____ 4. _____ 5. _____

A New Way to Improve the Ability to Learn

While music enjoys a long history in improving health, it is only in recent decades that music has been used to improve the ability to learn. Dr. Georgi Lozanov, a Bulgarian psychiatrist and educator, noticed that many patients coming to him were suffering from a common, but unnamed disease. ___1___ Lozanov therefore began to experiment with various techniques to improve the learning experience. ___2___ Dr. Lozanov reasoned that if music can take the pain out of surgery, surely it can take the pain out of learning. ___3___ Information is then read to them while classical music plays in the background. However, not all forms of classical music are suitable. ___4___ Although applicable to all branches of learning, Dr. Lozanov's technique has been especially effective in language learning. ___5___ Small wonder that in the West Dr. Lozanov's method is called "Super Learning."

(A) His techniques have been proven successful in teaching young kids how to read efficiently.

(B) It is reported that some classes are able to learn 400 new words a day using his method.

(C) He then found that their disease was caused by poor teaching methods and terrible learning experience.

(D) Students are first taught how to relax.

(E) One of these was listening to music.

(F) Only a special type known as Baroque music is effective.

1. _____ 2. _____ 3. _____ 4. _____ 5. _____

Get!

詳解請參閱解析本 p. 4-5

Guide Dogs

Guide dogs help blind or visually impaired people get around. ___1___ Most guide dog schools train golden retrievers, Labrador retrievers, and German shepherds. ___2___

The first guide dog was a German shepherd called Buddy. Buddy's owner, Mrs. Dorothy Eustis, who lived in Switzerland, was originally training German shepherds for the police. ___3___ Hearing about this article, Morris Frank, a young blind American, wrote a letter to her. He wrote, "Thousands of blind people like me hate being dependent on others. Help me and I will help them. Train me and I will bring back my dog and show people here how a blind man can be completely independent." ___4___

When Frank and Buddy returned home, they traveled all over the country to promote the training and use of guide dogs. In 1929, Mrs. Eustis went to the United States. ___5___ The school brought to its students the hope of gaining a new independence. Today "The Seeing Eye" is still in operation in Morristown, New Jersey.

(A) Eustis hoped to help more blind people so she cooperated with Frank to set up a foundation.

(B) With the help of Frank and Buddy, she established the first guide dog school "The Seeing Eye" in Nashville, Tennessee.

(C) But not all dogs can be trained to perform the task.

(D) That letter led Frank to stay in Switzerland for five weeks learning to be guided by Buddy.

(E) These three breeds are much more intelligent, obedient, friendly, and energetic.

(F) Then in 1927, Mrs. Eustis wrote a newspaper article about how dogs were trained in Germany to help blind war veterans.

1. _____ 2. _____ 3. _____ 4. _____ 5. _____

Dr. Martin Luther King Jr.

Although in 1865 the Civil War finally freed black slaves in the South, people of color continued to be treated as inferiors. ___1___ In 1955, Dr. Martin Luther King Jr. led 500,000 of them to protest against the city bus system. They refused to ride on the buses until the company changed its policy, which required African-Americans to sit in the back. ___2___ The peaceful protest had finally succeeded.

___3___ He traveled to deliver speeches and preached his philosophy of nonviolent resistance. ___4___ Arrested for breaking discriminatory laws, he went to jail dozens of times. He became an inspiration around the world for people to protest peacefully against unjust laws. ___5___ However, four years later, tragedy struck when this hero who loved peace and freedom was taken from those who loved and admired him: he was assassinated while attending a conference for civil rights in Memphis, Tennessee.

(A) He urged African-Americans to use nonviolent sit-ins, marches, and demonstrations to gain full freedom and equality.

(B) The boycott lasted for one year until the Supreme Court finally ruled that segregation on buses was illegal.

(C) They didn't begin to demand their rights as American citizens until almost a century later.

(D) In 1964 Dr. King was awarded the Nobel Peace Prize in recognition of his achievements.

(E) After this success, Dr. King decided to use his nonviolent tactics in efforts to change other discriminatory laws.

(F) After receiving the prize, he kept working even harder to make everyone treated equally in the U.S.

1. _____   2. _____   3. _____   4. _____   5. _____

詳解請參閱解析本 p. 6-7

The Amazing Elephant

When it comes to an elephant, you probably think of its trunk, big ears, tusks or huge size. ___1___ For example, when an elephant dies, other elephants come and stand around the dead elephant and run the tips of their trunks over its body. They sometimes use their trunks to pick up the bones or tusks of elephants that died some time before and pass them around the group. These odd activities can go on for about four hours a day, and last five to six days. ___2___

The elephant group or family structure is very organized. ___3___ The females, however, stay with the group all their lives. The leader of the group is the oldest female and she is also the director of their activities. She warns of danger by calling to the other elephants. ___4___

As you can see, the elephant is a very interesting animal. But the elephant population is decreasing fast, mostly because so many are killed for their ivory tusks. In addition to this, the areas in which elephants live and breed are continually taken to make more room for cities, homes and farms. ___5___ What a sad, sad thought!

(A) No one really knows the reason for these rituals, but they show us that elephants must have emotions and feelings.

(B) When the males reach an age of about fourteen or fifteen, they are ready to mate and leave the family group.

(C) The females are mainly responsible for taking care of young elephants.

(D) Besides having a long trunk and sharp tusks, its behavior is amazing.

(E) Unless action is taken soon, the elephant may one day become extinct and will take its place next to the dinosaur.

(F) This call signals the group to gather around the youngest members to protect them.

1. _____ 2. _____ 3. _____ 4. _____ 5. _____

Do You Want to Take a Gap Year?

Traditionally, after most students graduate from high school, they directly go on to a college or a university. ____1____ They are taking a "gap year" first, before continuing on to post-secondary school.

Simply put, a gap year is a period of time off between high school and college. ____2____ It is usually one-year long, and it is sometimes also called a "sabbatical". The purpose of a gap year is to give students time to explore. ____3____ Some simply backpack through different countries while others may get a job and work in one place for months at a time.

It is believed that gap years first started in the United Kingdom. However, more and more students from different countries, including Canada, Australia and even Taiwan choose to have gap years.

Gap years have become so popular that some people are now taking more than one of them! For example, today, when some young people change jobs, they may also take some time off to travel before starting their next job. ____4____ It is becoming more accepted in the working world today.

If you plan to take a gap year yourself, there are a few things you can do before you begin. ____5____ Next, be sure to do some advance planning. This includes making a budget—making sure you have enough money for the year. Finally, have fun! After all, a gap year is a time to explore and learn, outside of school and in the real world!

(A) This has come to be called a "career break".
(B) First, do research and try to seek advice from others who have taken a gap year.
(C) It can also be a break between college and graduate school.
(D) Gap years help people find who they truly are.
(E) Most take this opportunity to travel to other parts of the world.
(F) Some students, however, have decided to take a different path.

1. _____ 2. _____ 3. _____ 4. _____ 5. _____

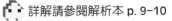

Move the Body to Remove the Fat

Are you afraid of getting overweight? Do you want to look more attractive? For many, both answers will be "yes"; but very often people find it difficult to lose excess fat. Trying to eat less is one solution, but the feeling of hunger can be really unbearable. ___1___ Another solution people may consider is liposuction, a form of surgery, which removes fat from a particular area of the body. ___2___

Taking exercise is probably the best way to keep slim. ___3___ Indeed, everyone can afford to lose weight by engaging in the most common forms of aerobic exercise, such as walking and jogging. Sports like weightlifting are also excellent.

___4___ In the beginning, you are likely to feel exhausted after exercise, but over time you certainly will get used to it and discover the profits of working out regularly. You will feel not only physically stronger but mentally happier and more confident. ___5___ Why not get started right now and discover the amazing "positive exercise cycle" yourself?

(A) Healthy, pain-free and definitely inexpensive, this solution should be suitable for all people.

(B) Even worse, you might suffer from anorexia, an illness in which a person refuses to eat enough and becomes thinner and thinner.

(C) Certainly these changes will further encourage you to go on in the right direction.

(D) However, this option is expensive and sometimes unsafe since all surgical treatments more or less involve risks.

(E) Moreover, more and more people now tend to do plastic surgery to make themselves look prettier.

(F) Taking exercise will benefit you, even if you are not overweight.

1. _____ 2. _____ 3. _____ 4. _____ 5. _____

The Problem with Stress

In today's society, stress has become a widespread problem affecting people of all ages. We have all experienced stress, perhaps from pressure at school, work, family related problems or even from driving in city traffic. ___1___ However, too much stress can actually make a person physically sick or even cause death.

___2___ The group was split into two sub-groups; one of people who were under stress and were not so happy in their lives, the other of people who were generally happy. The outcome is that people in the first group developed illnesses while those in the second remained healthy. Further evidence of the relationship between stress and its physical effect on us has been found in studies of people whose loved ones had died. ___3___ If this situation had continued for a long period, these people would have been more likely to become sick and even die earlier as a result.

So, what can we do to avoid stress and stay healthy? ___4___ We can reduce stress in our lives by choosing how we react to things. Another important factor is our lifestyle. ___5___

(A) By making sure we eat properly and get enough exercise, we can be assured of a longer and happier stress-free life.

(B) Their immune systems, which depend on white blood cells vital in fighting against disease in the body, did not work properly.

(C) Sometimes a little pressure can help us to get more done in our lives.

(D) Experts in the field of stress management advise us that the key is to stay positive.

(E) As is known to everyone, stress can make us feel blue or depressed, and even greatly reduce our productivity.

(F) A study designed to find out how stress can cause illness was carried out on a number of people who all carried a common virus in their bodies.

1. _____ 2. _____ 3. _____ 4. _____ 5. _____

Why Were the Greek Temples Really Built?

Every year, thousands of international tourists visit Greece. Some come for the food or shopping, while many others come for the history and culture. ___1___ However, travelers to Greece might be surprised to learn that there may be a mysterious reason why these temples were actually built so many years ago.

___2___ They were not meeting places, as some mistakenly believe, since people usually met and performed rituals outside of the temples. ___3___

Recently, however, a new theory has been proposed. ___4___ It is interesting to note that when many of the important ancient Greece temples are looked at on a map, they form perfect isosceles triangles. This could mean that the Ancient Greeks had a greater understanding of astronomy than we had previously believed. ___5___

Although some people believe more evidence must be show to prove this new theory, one thing is certain: if you travel to Greece, you should be sure to visit the ancient temples. No matter why they were really built, they are definitely worth seeing.

(A) Some people believe that the ancient Greek temples were actually built to line up with the planets in the sky above.

(B) This is especially true of Greece's ancient temples, which are on most every visitor's must-see list.

(C) Greek is the origin of the western culture and every visitor would like to see the Great statues of the ancient Gods in the temples.

(D) For many years, it was believed that Greek temples were built to house statues of the ancient Greek gods.

(E) Rather, their main purpose was to store and protect important statues and offerings.

(F) Interestingly, most temples were usually built to point to where the sun would rise on the days that the gods of these temples were celebrated.

1. _____ 2. _____ 3. _____ 4. _____ 5. _____

Freestyle Basketball

Street basketball is a very open and free-flowing game. It gives people the opportunity to test their creativity, and to stretch their physical limits. _____1_____ Some children even start playing the sport in kindergarten. Unlike in professional basketball, a streetball player's career can last decades. _____2_____

In this version of basketball, usually only one side of the court is used, and there is no precise schedule. _____3_____ The number of participants in each team may range from two one defender and one attacker (known as one-on-one) to full teams of five.

Street basketball has come a long way since the 1940s in New York City, spreading across hundreds of cities worldwide. _____4_____ It became especially popular when a team of players from New York started traveling the United States and competing against local streetballers. The matches were taped and those tapes have turned into a popular show on the international sports channel ESPN.

_____5_____ Whether you are young or old, male or female, short or tall, when it's time to step onto the court, nothing else but your passion for the game matters.

(A) That's because the game doesn't require much training and energy and is played for fun.

(B) It has grown from a game into a culture that has its own group of followers.

(C) The rules are simple and it can be played by people of all ages, from 5 to 65.

(D) The reason street basketball is so powerful is that everyone can play it.

(E) Even NBA players like to play street basketball to interact with their fans.

(F) Participants may play ten games in one day, or one game in ten days.

1. _____ 2. _____ 3. _____ 4. _____ 5. _____

The Pros and Cons of Nuclear Energy

These days, everyone seems to be worried about global warming. As a result, many people want to replace traditional fossil fuels with alternative energy sources, such as the wind and sun. Some people, however, say that nuclear power is already providing us with an established source of energy.

Nuclear power does have several advantages. ___1___ In addition, it is highly reliable, compared with solar and wind power. What's more, after a nuclear power plant has been set up, it costs very little to keep it running. Finally, nuclear power plants need only a small amount of fuel to produce a very large amount of power.

Yet, despite the advantages of nuclear power, there are some disadvantages as well. First, a nuclear power plant needs uranium, which must be mined. ___2___ In addition, once uranium has been used, it becomes radioactive. Besides, there is only a limited amount of uranium in the world. ___3___ To make matters worse, the mining and transportation of it can be very costly. ___4___ Finally, it takes several years and a lot of money to build just one nuclear power plant.

It seems clear that there are both advantages and disadvantages about nuclear power. ___5___ Without a doubt, the debate over nuclear energy will surely continue.

(A) To begin with, nuclear power does not produce large amount of greenhouse gases.

(B) This can damage the environment.

(C) And any accidents involving uranium can be deadly for humans and environment.

(D) It is also clear that many people around the world have strong feelings about this energy, with some in favor of it and others against it.

(E) It then becomes expensive and even dangerous to manage and dispose of this radioactive nuclear waste.

(F) Uranium is an unstable element, so we should be careful while using it as.

1. _____ 2. _____ 3. _____ 4. _____ 5. _____

Reading Trouble

Reading is a unique ability of mankind that allows new generations to learn from the heritage of their ancestors. It is also the entire foundation of education. ___1___ Yet, many parents encounter problems teaching children to read well.

Many parents believe that the earlier their children start recognizing letters, the better. But, in fact, this is not necessarily true. ___2___ Reading is a complex process, and it is not easy for a young child to identify words in print. But parents may start to force their children to read. ___3___ This keeps some children from becoming fluent readers.

One method that parents can use to help children become good readers is to read to them every day from an early age. ___4___ By reading books with their parents, kids come to understand the purposes and pleasures of reading.

However, there are times when, despite parents' positive efforts, children may still have difficulty in reading. One reason is that they may suffer from dyslexia. ___5___ In this case, parents must seek professional help and be prepared to do everything they can to support their children.

(A) Once children are forced to read, it stops being pleasurable to them.

(B) That is why it is so important for a child to succeed in learning how to read.

(C) That is a specific disorder which causes problems with reading, writing, and spelling.

(D) Studies have shown that it's parents who can help the children most when it comes to developing reading ability.

(E) For example, a child may know the alphabet, but he or she may not make out the word that a group of letters represents.

(F) The ideal time to begin sharing books with children is during babyhood.

1. _____ 2. _____ 3. _____ 4. _____ 5. _____

Songkran

If you visit Thailand near the middle of April, you will see some unusual sights. Along country roads, children throw water at anyone who passes by. ___1___ All over the country, pick-up trucks full of passengers drive around, and when two trucks pass, they stop, and the passengers soak one another with water.

All these people are celebrating "Songkran", the traditional Thai New Year, which falls on April 13. This is the middle of summer in Thailand, when the temperature often climbs as high as 40 degrees Celsius, so getting wet helps people cool down. ___2___

In the past, however, the holiday was celebrated far more peacefully. ___3___ At that time, the younger relatives gently poured small bowls of perfumed water over their older relatives' hands and wished them happiness and good health in the year ahead. It was believed that the water would wash away anything bad from the old year. ___4___

Some families still take part in that kind of quiet ceremony but only briefly; over the years, throwing water has become the principal way to celebrate Songkran. In fact, to acknowledge the custom's popularity, the government has extended the official holiday from one day to three. ___5___ Not only has Thailand's most festive holiday become wetter, but it is growing longer as well.

(A) The custom was that younger people visited their older relatives to pay their respects at the beginning of a new year.

(B) In the northern province of Chiang Mai, the annual celebration now even lasts a full week.

(C) Older relatives responded by patting the younger ones' heads, wishing them luck, and sometimes giving them money.

(D) It is a wild celebration, with lots of crowds, water guns, and wet streets.

(E) If you happen to visit Thailand during Songkran, don't miss the opportunity to take part in it.

(F) In cities, pedestrians throw water at people on buses.

1. _____ 2. _____ 3. _____ 4. _____ 5. _____

Warning: 7% of the Earth Disappearing!

Covering an area of about 7 percent of the earth's surface, tropical rainforests are found mainly near the Equator. ___1___ These are areas that are warm and wet year round. Average rainfall in rainforest areas ranges from about 80 inches to an almost incredible 400 inches a year and the average temperature hovers around 24 to 27 degrees Celsius.

Rainforests contribute to the planet's well-being in many ways. First of all, they recycle the world's oxygen, nitrogen, and carbon; in doing so, they help influence the temperature of the planet. ___2___ In fact, fifty percent of the plant and animal species on the planet live in the rainforests. ___3___ Rainforests also provide us with wood, wicker, latex, turpentine, cork, gums, dyes, oils, foods, medicines, and resins.

Unfortunately, increasing demand for these treasures is the cause of a major problem: the rainforests are shrinking fast. ___4___ An astonishing twenty-seven acres of rainforest are destroyed every minute, and one hundred thirty-seven species of its plants and animals become extinct every day. ___5___ If this is true, shouldn't we, as caretakers of the future, do everything possible to make sure it won't happen?

(A) Some of these species could not survive anyplace else.
(B) They cover a large portion of the northern part of South America and are also found in Central America, Africa, and Southeast Asia.
(C) Experts say that a large portion of the world's rainforests will be gone in less than 50 years.
(D) Other causes include the widespread clearing of the rainforest for farming use.
(E) Rainforests can also cut down on the proportion of greenhouse gases.
(F) They provide shelter for many humans and animals.

1. _____ 2. _____ 3. _____ 4. _____ 5. _____

Euthanasia

Euthanasia is the practice of deliberately ending the life of a person who is hopelessly ill. ___1___ People who oppose euthanasia argue that life under any circumstances is better than death and that no one, not even a doctor or a relative, has the right to end the life of another person. Nevertheless, in recent years, there has been an increase in the number of people who support euthanasia. ___2___ For example, in 1996, United States federal courts lifted bans on doctor-assisted suicides in many states.

___3___ Supporters of euthanasia say that these patients should have the right to choose how and when to die. ___4___ Additionally, according to proponents of doctor-assisted suicide, keeping unconscious or dying patients alive on life-support systems is not only senseless and cruel, but also wastes valuable medical resources.

Euthanasia is clearly a topic about which people have strong views. Opponents say that life is so important that not even governments have the right to decide how it is ended. ___5___ It seems that the jury is still out: the argument will continue.

(A) On the other hand, supporters see it as a matter to be decided by patients along with their families and doctors.

(B) The main argument in favor of euthanasia is that it brings relief to those who are suffering unbearable pain or who are terminally ill.

(C) We can also call it doctor-assisted suicide.

(D) This would allow them the opportunity to die with dignity rather than continue to live in a miserably hopeless state.

(E) Several countries have introduced legislation to permit voluntary euthanasia.

(F) According to some estimates, more than sixty percent of Americans are in favor of euthanasia.

1. _____ 2. _____ 3. _____ 4. _____ 5. _____

Mars, Mankind's Next Home

Late in August 2003, when Mars was at its closest distance to Earth in 60,000 years, the red planet was the focus of the world's attention. Astronomers once believed that intelligent civilizations existed on Mars. ___1___ On the other hand, a deeper understanding of Mars has encouraged us to consider another issue: might it be possible for human beings to live on Mars someday in the future?

Scientists look to Mars because it is more similar to Earth than any other planet. ___2___ What's more, Mars also has an atmosphere, although it is not as thick and warm as that of Earth. Judging from the appearance of the planet, many people believe that much of it was covered by water in the ancient past. ___3___ Despite this, not a few scientists think Mars once had a biosphere: an environment in which life could thrive.

Scientists are thinking about the possibility of making Mars suitable for life again. They will have to thicken and warm its atmosphere by releasing gases into it. ___4___ The higher temperature would cause the melting of the polar ice caps, then water comes. Where there is water, life can exist and plants will begin to grow. ___5___ Some scientists argue that by the year 3000, mankind's dream of moving to Mars will come true, while others doubt it.

(A) Scientists have been trying to figure out a way for humans to build a colony on Mars in the future.

(B) Now that scientists have come to know Mars better, they have concluded that the rocky and cold planet is apparently lifeless.

(C) If all of this happens, Mars will finally become habitable.

(D) For example, both have seasonal weather patterns and a Martian day is only a little bit longer than ours.

(E) This could produce a greenhouse effect and trap the sun's heat.

(F) Somehow water has disappeared from its surface except for great volumes of ice at its poles.

1. _____ 2. _____ 3. _____ 4. _____ 5. _____

Ramadan: A Holy Time for Muslims

Although there are many different religions around the world, most of them seem to have special holy days or important periods of time. ___1___ This month is called Ramadan, and it is the holiest of holidays for Muslims.

There is no fixed starting date for Ramadan, since it is part of the lunar calendar. ___2___ One thing that stays the same each year, however, is the length of Ramadan. It usually lasts for a full thirty days.

What do Muslims do during Ramadan? They do several things, but the biggest one is fasting, especially for healthy adults. This means not eating or drinking anything from dawn to dusk. ___3___ Then, at night, the fast is broken with a meal called iftar. Oftentimes, guests, or the poor and the needy, are invited to these meals, and nightly prayers may then be held afterwards at mosques.

During Ramadan, Muslims also try to avoid becoming angry, and many take this opportunity to pray, read the Quran, and help others. ___4___ In fact, fasting is one of the five most important parts of Islam.

___5___ Of course, fasting is a very important part of it, but for many Muslims, Ramadan provides them with the chance to reflect on their lives and try to become even closer to God.

(A) Some of Muslims think that they would know how much their God once suffered by doing this.

(B) This means that it is celebrated at different times every year.

(C) Without a doubt, Ramadan is a very important religious holiday for Muslims.

(D) It is believed that Ramadan should be a time of worship, and acts like fasting are thought to teach patience and compassion for others.

(E) This is especially true of Islam, which actually has an entire holy month.

(F) During Ramadan, most Muslims eat a meal before dawn that is called suhoor.

1. _____ 2. _____ 3. _____ 4. _____ 5. _____

Hip Hop

Do you like hip hop? Many people today do, but it might be surprising to know that few people know much about its birth and history.

By all accounts, hip hop was born in some of the poorest areas of New York City in the 1970s. ____1____ Some began to play records as DJs at discos and block parties. ____2____ Eventually, some people began to rap over the DJ's beats, and they became known as "MC's" or "rappers."

Hip-hop music's first hit was "Rapper's Delight" in 1979, and for many Americans, this was the first time they had ever heard rapping. ____3____ In the years that followed, hip-hop music would spread across America, first to California and the West Coast, where Ice T and NWA found success. ____4____

Today, hip hop is popular all over the world, including Taiwan. ____5____ An MC from Taiwan, for example, may rap in Taiwanese about the challenges he or she may face.

Although hip hop began in America, it now definitely belongs to the world.

(A) Hip hop continued to grow in popularity in the 1980s, but it remained centered on New York City and America's East Coast.

(B) It later would take hold in the South, with groups like Outkast, and the Midwest, with Eminem and Kanye West.

(C) In many countries, young people have taken the basic structure of hip hop and adapted it to their own lives and cultures.

(D) At that time, African-American and Latino teenagers wanted to develop something that was unique to their lives.

(E) Hip-hop music has become a kind of culture and rappers like to write the lyrics to reflect the society.

(F) These DJ's used two turntables to "mix" two records and keep the beat going without any pause.

1. _____ 2. _____ 3. _____ 4. _____ 5. _____

Bias in the News Media

Do we get a balanced view of current affairs from the news media? A lot of news media, such as TV companies and radio stations, are businesses.　1　These facts tend to encourage audience-drawing biases in news presentations.

"Bad news travels fast," but it's also great for attracting audiences. Why do you think the news often begins with "shock horror" type headlines about terrorist bombs, fires, floods and so on?　2

"Have you heard the latest news?" We all want to hear something new. This is time bias.　3　"Stay with us," they say, and in the meantime we receive a minute or so of prime time commercials.

News such as celebrity lawsuits and sex scandals can be blown up into dramatic stories, perfect for serial, audience-grabbing headlines.　4　Will the president who had an affair lose his job? Did the rock star commit a sex crime? Guilty or not guilty? Wait for the next episode!

"No news is good news," goes another old saying, but this is not true for the news media.　5　This means that what we actually get from the news is a selective image, rather than a mirror, of what is happening.

(A) This is bad news bias and it boosts ratings and commercial income.

(B) People are often unaware of these news biases and thus easily influenced by them.

(C) To survive, they need income from advertisers, and advertisers want big audiences.

(D) They have to make news all the time and have strong motives to present the world in a certain way.

(E) The words "Breaking News," splashed across our TVs, keep us rooted to our seats.

(F) This is narrative bias, giving the news a soap opera feel.

1.　　　　　2.　　　　　3.　　　　　4.　　　　　5.

閱讀測驗
理論篇

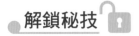

大考閱讀測驗的文章字數經常高達三百多字，但是卻只考四題，因此在做閱讀測驗的題目時，並不需要將文章中的每一個字都看懂，運用一些閱讀技巧與作答技巧，即使對全文沒有百分之百的瞭解，仍可以達到百分之百的正確性。善用本單元所提供的閱讀策略便可輕鬆過關斬將。

閱讀測驗之策略分析 ▶▶

◎ 策略一：用英文模式思考 (think in English)

閱讀時，盡量以英文思考、理解文章內容，切勿逐字將文章翻譯成中文，因翻譯過程中難免產生誤差，阻礙我們對文句與字義的理解；更糟的是，這會大幅降低閱讀速度，因此建議閱讀時直接以英文的方式思考、理解。

◎ 策略二：增加詞彙量 (expand your vocabulary)

⑴ 平日多培養閱讀英文的習慣，從上下文中認識新的詞彙、片語以及它們的搭配用法；豐富的詞彙量是閱讀理解的關鍵。

⑵ 閱讀時遇到生字或難字時切勿驚慌，通常文章作者會以較簡單的文字來解釋或定義；若無，則大多數的情況下，我們可以透過前後文意來推測字義。

◎ 策略三：練習略讀與瀏覽 (practice skimming and scanning)

擅用略讀 (skimming)，可迅速找到段落大意，透過閱讀文章的主題句 (topic sentence)，跳過段落中的細節，以最快的方式找到文章主旨。而另一技巧為瀏覽 (scanning)，如掃瞄器般快速掃視整段文章，以獲得相關細節。以閱讀報紙為例，當我們只想知道某則新聞的大意時，便使用略讀 (skimming)，只看標題或文章的前幾句；而當我們欲找到時間或地點等細節時，便使用瀏覽 (scanning) 快速掃視整篇新聞。擅用此兩種閱讀技巧，應付閱讀測驗便能事半功倍。

◉ 策略四：加快閱讀速度 (speed up your reading)

像是 It-is-well-known-that-color-can-affect-people's-mood 這樣逐字閱讀，不僅速度慢，對理解也沒有幫助；相反地，在閱讀時應快速地將句子分解成一組一組的字詞，像是 It is well known that-color-can affect-people's mood，將句子分為四個部分，閱讀起來不但快，也更容易理解。

◉ 策略五：瞭解句型與句構 (understand sentence structures)

掌握句子的結構才能完整地理解句意，而不會被很長或結構複雜的句型影響理解過程。若能快速分析句子的組成，以及找出長句中的主要子句，便能快速理解作者所欲傳達的意思。

EXAMPLE

Controlled remotely by humans, drones even launch missiles that kill human targets.
           S   V O

大解密 ?

1. 本句主詞為 drones，動詞為 launch，受詞則為 missiles。
2. 本句前方的分詞構句 Controlled remotely by humans，用來修飾 drones。後方的關係子句 that kill human targets 則修飾先行詞 missiles。

EXAMPLE

Some have called it a "lifestyle" disease, (since it is often caused by a bad diet, little
S V

exercise, and smoking or drinking), [whereas others have called it a disease of
              S   V

"prosperity" (because it often affects those in prosperous countries, especially
those who have adopted a Western diet.)]

大解密 ❓

1. 本句由主要連接詞 whereas，連接兩組副詞子句，第一組為 some have called it a "lifestyle" disease, since it is often caused by a bad diet, little exercise, and smoking or drinking，第二組為 others have called it a disease of "prosperity" because it often affects those in prosperous countries, especially those who have adopted a Western diet.

2. 第一組副詞子句中的主要子句為 some have called it a "lifestyle" disease，而從屬子句為 since it is often caused by a bad diet, little exercise, and smoking or drinking。第二組副詞子句中的主要子句則為 others have called it a disease of "prosperity"，從屬子句為 because it often affects those in prosperous countries, especially those who have adopted a Western diet，此兩組子句為平行結構。

3. 最後一句的關係子句 who have adopted a Western diet，來修飾先行詞 those。

◈ 策略六：瞭解文章脈絡及轉折詞
   (understand the flow of content and transitional words)
   若是可以掌握此一閱讀策略，閱讀文章時便能預測作者接下來要講的話，快速抓住文章重點；若能對轉折詞的用法更加熟悉，也能更快理解作者的邏輯。

閱讀測驗── 攻略 ▶▶

◈ Step 1：略讀文章 (skim the passage)
   有些題目只測驗文章的主旨或大意，不需知道文章的細節，因此只需使用略讀 (skimming) 即可。

◈ Step 2：閱讀題目 (go over the questions)
   快速瀏覽題目，辨別題目的性質與類別。

◈ Step 3：找到答案 (find answers)
   閱讀完題目後，回到文章尋找答案，不同類別的題目以不同的技巧作答。
   ⑴ 找到主題句　⑵ 找到關鍵字詞　⑶ 推理

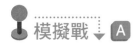

模擬戰 A

Taiwan's northern regions have a lot splendid natural sights and attractions to offer the curious traveler. The bustling cities of Taipei, Tamshui, and Keelung have scenic mountains, waterfalls, beaches, and paddy fields. Numerous billboards along the 60-kilometer Coastal Highway from Tamshui to Keelung advertise a number of popular scenic spots, such as Baishawan, Shimen Cave, Jin San, Yehliu, and Green Bay.

Located near the mouth of the Tamshui River, the town of Tamshui was once a major port, but now is mostly a tourist attraction with cozy little cafes, the lovely Fishing Wharf and a large number of shopping alleys. It has become a weekend get-away spot from the crowded Taipei. There are several historically significant buildings in Tamshui. The most famous is Fort San Domingo, which was built in 1629.

Another wonderful scenic area on the northern coast is Yehilu. Yehilu park is formed by a peninsula that stretches almost two kilometers into the sea and contains an incredible variety of rock formations. There are thousands of strange shaped rocks, fossils, and veins of colored minerals that fascinate even the most fastidious tourist. Another natural wonder, located near the northernmost point of the island, is the cave of Shihmen, which is in fact a stone arch formed by erosion. It stands overlooking the coast, and offers a magnificent view of the sea.

In addition, you can also explore the area of Yangmingshan, discover the spiritual heritage of Taiwan at 18 Kings Temple, or relax in the hot springs at Peitou. You can wander among Ju Ming's amazing sculptures, try paragliding at Green Bay, or just lie lazily on Baishway, watching clouds roll by. If you get tired, just stop at one of the little restaurants and try northern Taiwan's famous snacks.

Taiwan's north coast is truly a traveler's paradise and a unique recreational spot where one can find a large variety of historical, cultural and scenic attractions within an hour drive distance.

1. Where is the passage mostly to be taken from?

    (A) a weather forecast.　　　　　　(B) a magazine on tourism.

    (C) a book about travel insurance.　　(D) a brochure for interior design.

2. Which of the following is **NOT** mentioned by the author that people can enjoy along the area of Yangmingshan?

    (A) Hot springs.　　(B) Beach.　　(C) Sculptures.　　(D) Cave.

3. This passage is written mainly to _____.

    (A) list the attractions

    (B) compare the ways of travelling

    (C) warn about danger

    (D) invite readers to share their experience

⚠ 戰略分析

1. **B**

根據全文第一句和最後一句，可快速得知作者介紹的是臺灣北海岸的美景和旅遊景點，故本題答案為 (B) 觀光旅遊雜誌。

2. **D**

文中第二、三、四段，作者使用了 another 和 in addition 等轉折詞，可看出文章的脈絡為逐項列出北臺灣的景點主要有三：Tamshui、Yehilu/Shihmen 和 Yangmingshan area，再至第四段找出作者提到的景點，可知 Cave 並未被提及，故答案選 (D)。

3. **A**

同上題，作者主要列舉北臺灣的旅遊景點，並分別在二、三、四段一一說明，故答案選 (A)，若可清楚掌握文章脈絡，便可迅速找到答案。

Unit 2 題目類別
Types of Questions

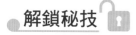
解鎖秘技 🔓

此單元為近年來大考閱讀測驗題型分析,不同的題型會有不同的應答方式。本單元分為七個不同關卡,針對常見的大考題型加以說明,並提供同學們突破每個關卡的致勝攻略,並附上實戰例子。若同學能依照攻略練功,便能對閱讀測驗更加得心應手。

⚠️ 戰略分析

1. 大意 (main idea)、主題 (topic)、最佳標題 (best title)
2. 文章出處 (source)
3. 目的 (purpose)
4. 細節 (detail)
5. 字義 (word in context)
6. 代名詞 (pronoun)
7. 推論與暗示 (inference or implication)

閱讀測驗─題型關卡 ▶▶
◉ 關卡一:大意、主題、最佳標題

此一類型的題目主要測驗讀者是否能掌握文章大意和作者主要傳達的想法,切勿在過多細節或無關緊要的句子上花費太多時間,只要能快速找到文章或段落中的主題句,便可輕鬆知道大意。需注意主題句最常出現於段落的第一句,但也可能出現在任何其它地方。

🔫 技巧:先找出主題句

1. 當文章只有一段時,主題句通常會出現於前兩、三句話。
2. 當文章有兩段以上時,可綜合每段的主題句來決定主旨或標題;有時全文的主旨也會出現於第一段最後一句。
3. 可使用略讀,跳過不重要的細節快速找到全文主旨。
4. 有時先閱讀題目也能幫助我們推測文章大意或相關內容。

Sometimes, success often involves struggling. By the time he was ready to graduate from Cambridge, Stephen Hawking's health had started to fail. A terrible disease called ALS was mounting an attack on his ability to control his body. Confined to a wheelchair since then, Hawking's life has been anything but easy. But while the disease may have crippled his body, it couldn't erase his formidable intelligence. The scientist's message is this: "However difficult life may seem, there is always something you can do and succeed at."

1. What is the main idea of this passage?

   (A) ALS is a frightening disease that has left Stephen Hawking paralysed.

   (B) Sometimes, challenges and difficulties are a part of great accomplishments.

   (C) Stephen Hawking's encouraging words can help people succeed.

   (D) Stephen Hawking's intelligence was not influenced by his disease.

大解密

本段的第一句 Sometimes, success often involves struggling. 為主題句，點出本段大意，成功並不容易，常常經過了許多奮鬥與掙扎；本段以 Stephen Hawking 為例，提到他並未因 ALS 疾病抹去他過人的智慧，以佐證說明克服困難與挑戰才能成功。選項 (A)、(C) 和 (D) 只提到段落中的細節，並非主旨，故答案為 (B)。

Few things seem quite as all-American as football. On holidays football games play an important role to many families. Almost every high school in the U.S. has a football team and most colleges too. Professional football is watched on TV by millions of people. Removing football from America would leave a big hole in the culture. Though football has evolved as a uniquely American sport, it has its roots in England.

Football developed from the British games of soccer and rugby. In the Middle Ages in England, soccer became a popular game. The objective was to get a ball into the opposing team's goal only by moving with one's feet and kicking the ball. In the 1800s, rugby was created when an English soccer player decided to pick up the ball and run with it rather than kicking it. At that time, American college students played soccer, but liked the rules of rugby as well. In 1874, Americans created rules for a new game that borrowed from both soccer and rugby and became known as "football".

Football maintained the same objective of getting the ball into the other team's goal, but they did it with a combination of kicking, running with the ball, and passing the ball to teammates. Initially, football was an extremely rough contact sport. In 1905 alone, eighteen players were killed and 158 were seriously injured when playing the game. President Roosevelt wanted to make football illegal to prevent deaths and injuries, but a committee changed the rules to make the game safer.

Today, football is more than just a game. True, there are simple neighborhood football matches, but for the most part, football has become as much entertainment as sport. Many games, from junior high school to professional games are started off with a marching band. Cheerleaders, with carefully orchestrated dance steps perform before and during the game. The fans often have noise makers and signs and cheer loudly. If it is a really important game, there are even parties before the game to encourage the players and parties for the winners after.

If you want to watch a simple sport, try tennis or golf. If you want to witness a unique cultural event, there is nothing like an American football game.

1. What of the following is the best title for this article?
   (A) The Differences of Football and Soccer
   (B) The History and Significance of Football
   (C) Violence in Football Games
   (D) The Rules of American Football

大解密 ?

從文章第一段引言加上其它段落的主題句與結論，可看出本篇文章主要介紹美式足球的歷史以及此運動對美國人的重要性。作者於第二和第三段提到了美式足球的起源和演進，第一和最後兩段則提到了美式足球對美國人的重要性，故答案選 (B)，而不是選項 (A) 比較美式足球和足球的不同，也不是選項 (C) 美式足球的暴力和選項 (D) 美式足球的規則。

◎ 關卡二：文章出處

此一類型的題目考文章出自何處，常見的選項類別有：各種領域的期刊、雜誌、書籍或報紙等。

🔫 技巧：透過主題句和關鍵字來了解文章屬性，藉此可幫助我們判斷文章出處。

EXAMPLE

For moviegoers around the world, 2007 will be a summer of sequels, and *Pirates of the Caribbean: At World's End* already looks to be an early favorite. This film is the third in the popular Disney series, and it earned over US$142 million in the United States during its weekend debut.

At World's End begins where Dead Man's Chest, the second film of the trilogy, left off—with Captain Jack Sparrow trapped in Davy Jones' Locker. Sparrow, played by Johnny Depp, is rescued by his old friends, Will Turner (Orlando Bloom) and Elizabeth Swann (Keira Knightley), and they begin an adventure that takes them, as the film's title suggests, to the end of the world.

The movie also brings back some notorious characters, such as Captain Barbossa and Davy Jones, and introduces some new colorful ones, such as Captain Sao Feng. Sao Feng is known as the pirate lord of Singapore, and he is played by the famous Hong Kong actor Chow Yun-Fat.

Although *At World's End* is the final film of the Pirates trilogy, Depp, who was nominated for an Academy Award for his portrayal of Captain Jack, left open the possibility of a fourth film. "I'd consider another Pirates," he said during an interview at the film's premiere.

For the most part, *At World's End* has received mixed reviews from film critics. Some have called it a fun and exciting tale of swashbucklers, but others have stated that it was too long. A few have even mentioned that this movie was hard to follow, especially for viewers who may not have seen the first two films.

Moviegoers, however, had the final say about this sequel, which earned more than US$600 million worldwide. So, while *Pirates of the Caribbean: At World's End* might not be considered a critical success, it can definitely already be called a commercial one.

1. Where is this passage most likely to be taken from?
   (A) A research paper
   (B) A movie magazine
   (C) A travel brochure
   (D) A fashion magazine

大解密 ？

本文內容主要圍繞在 2007 年夏天推出的某一部電影的介紹，第一段點出這一年的電影多數為電影續集 (sequal)，接下來各段則對 World's End 這部電影進一步說明，並於最後一段提出這部電影的票房很高。因此我們可以推斷答案為 (B) 電影雜誌，而不是選項 (A) 研究論文、(C) 旅遊手冊、(D) 時尚雜誌。

◎ 關卡三：目的

此類型的題目考作者寫文章的目的為何。通常需要徹底理解全文，才能正確地判斷答案。

技巧：先仔細閱讀選項內容，並於閱讀文章時，從主題句和轉折詞來找到作者撰文的目的。而某些應用文，會在文章最後一段才會出現作者真正的目的，如：書評、邀請讀者響應某個活動等。

EXAMPLE

An Australian national icon, koalas are much loved all around the world. Unfortunately, ever since 2012, koalas have been considered "vulnerable" under the Environmental Protection and Biodiversity Conservation Act. Despite this, no laws protect these beautiful animals from becoming endangered and they possibly become extinct soon.

It is estimated that a mere 80,000 koalas are living wild in the forests of eastern and southern Australia. A stark contrast compared to the millions that lived and were hunted in the early 20th century. Habitat loss and disruption are the biggest reason for the decline in koala numbers. Ever since Europeans settled the continent, 80% of the koala's native habitat, eucalypt forest, has been cleared and the remaining 20% is still not protected. As you read this, eucalypt forest is constantly being cleared to make way for farmland, roads and housing, leaving more and more koalas homeless.

This is why the Koala Foundation needs your help. Funds donated directly to the foundation will go towards lobbying for the passing of the Koala protection act, koala research and conservation, rescuing displaced koalas, and maintaining our 40-acre koala sanctuary. Additionally, you can subscribe to our koala foster program or fund the planting of your own eucalypt trees. We also appreciate any and all volunteers that can spare whatever time they have participating in the Koala Foundation various endeavors.

Koalas really need your help if they are going to survive in the wild. Whatever support you are willing offer will bring us closer to securing the future for the koala.

1. What is the author's purpose of writing this passage?

(A) To emphasize the fact the koalas are an endangered species.

(B) To ask people to be actively involved in animal conservation.

(C) To raise money for the Koala Foundation.

(D) To urge the government to pass the laws to protect koalas.

大解密 ?

雖本文前面介紹無尾熊以及說明無尾熊需要受到保護的事實，但若仔細閱讀完文章，可以在倒數第二段發現作者真正的目的是替 the Koala Foundation 募款和招募志工，

本段第一、二句便點出募得資金的用途為「This is why the Koala Foundation needs your help. Funds donated directly to the foundation will go towards lobbying for the passing of the Koala protection act ...」，最後一段作者也提到 Whatever support you are willing offer will bring us closer to securing the future for the koala.，表示這些基金會得到的幫助都將用來幫助無尾熊，故答案選 (C)。

◈ 關卡四：細節

此一類型的題目考文章中的一處或多處細節，是閱讀測驗常見題型。

🔫 技巧：憑著略讀 (skimming) 時的印象，快速找到細節的位置或利用瀏覽 (scanning)，掃過整篇文章，尋找文章中關鍵字，需注意有時候題目會改變用字遣詞。

EXAMPLE

However convenient "convenience stores" may be, you still need to go there to buy what you want. There is always internet shopping, of course, but then you have to wait till the postman stops by your house and delivers what you ordered. But what if it didn't have to be that way? A new technology may be about to change everything.

Amazon is one of the world's best-known digital stores and internet brands, selling goods ranging from books to clothes and electronics. The company continues to be a pioneer of new technology, and its latest venture may revolutionize shopping as we know it: drones.

Drones are small unpiloted aircraft. We have become familiar with their use on spying missions in various conflicts around the world. Controlled remotely by humans, they even launch missiles that kill human targets. But drones aren't just used in war. As the technology improves and becomes cheaper, peaceful, civilian applications for it are also being found.

For example, Amazon is now exploring the possibility of using drones to deliver products to its customers. The company is already talking about flying small items to the door of your house within 30 minutes when receiving your order.

It remains to be seen, however, whether this bold vision can become reality. Unlike military drones, delivery drones are piloted automatically, not remotely controlled by a human being. Due to the high accident risk, drones are still illegal in many countries.

If the legal and technological obstacles can be overcome, you may soon enjoy the ultimate convenience of having your purchases fly to you around the clock.

1. According to the passage, what does Amazon plan to use drones for?
   (A) Picking out products from the warehouse.
   (B) Sending products to people who purchase them.
   (C) Researching possible locations for new shops.
   (D) Packing and wrapping goods for delivery.

大解密 ?

此為考單一細節的題目，關於 drones 的細節出現在第三段，而答案就出現在下一段的第一句，「 . . . to deliver products to its customers」，且再下一句表示 Amazon 已經計劃著要將貨品在三十分鐘內遞送到顧客家門口，故答案選 (B)，選項有稍改用字，但不影響作答。

2. According to the passage, which of the following statement is true?
   (A) Amazon does not sell electronic products.
   (B) Drones are known as spying tools by most people.
   (C) Drones are legalized in most countries in the world.
   (D) Drones are always operated remotely by humans.

大解密 ?

此題為考多個細節的題目，回答的重點為抓住每個選項的關鍵字，如此一來就能快速找到答案。選項 (A) 的關鍵字是 electronic，出現在第二段第一句，但內文提及 Amazon 有賣電子產品，故此選項錯誤。選項 (B) 的關鍵字為 spying tools，出現在第三段第二句，作者提到無人機通常是用在 spying missions，故此選項是正確答案。選

項 (C) 的關鍵字是 legalized。本題題目用字與選項中的 legalized 不同，故需要格外留意，以免判斷錯誤。相關線索出現在第五段最後一句：無人機在大部分國家仍不合法，故 (C) 選項錯誤。選項 (D) 的關鍵字為 always operated remotely by humans，需注意此選項的用字遣詞與內文稍微不同，以挑戰讀者的閱讀能力。第三段中間提到軍隊使用的無人機是由人類遠端搖控，但在第五段中間提到 delivery drones are piloted automatically，operated 被換成 piloted，by humans 變成 automatically，由此可知 (D) 選項錯誤。

EXAMPLE

In the universe, nothing lasts forever. Just like humans, stars have a lifespan of their own. Scientists believe that stars form when large clouds of gas come together. The force of gravity pulls hydrogen atoms to the center of the cloud, which heats the gas. After millions of years, the hydrogen ignites, which causes a chain of nuclear reactions. It is in this process that the star is composed. For millions of years, the star will continue to shine and give off light.

Yet eventually, the star will run out of hydrogen to use as fuel. When this happens, the star starts to expand and becomes a red giant. Millions of years later, the star will collapse in on itself and become a white dwarf as it is dying. Stars that are substantially larger than our sun, however, end their lives suddenly.

When they run out of hydrogen fuel, these large stars blow up in a huge explosion called a supernova. For a short time, the supernova shines brighter than any other star in the galaxy. After that, it rapidly fade away and a black hole is left in its place.

To this day, black holes are still one of the biggest mysteries in astronomy. Black holes pull in every stray atom and particle that is close to them. When anything enters a black hole, it can never escape. This has led scientists to come up with some bizarre theories about what black holes truly are.

Some researchers claim that black holes are like a permanent detention hall for matter. Since gravity in the black hole is so powerful, it's believed that a person would be crushed to become flatter than their own shadow. However, other scientists believe that black holes could be the gateway to another dimension.

Perhaps one day scientists will solve the riddle of black holes, but it probably won't be any time soon.

1. When do stars become white dwarves?

    (A) After they bump into other stars.

    (B) After they blow up in a huge explosion.

    (C) After they are swallowed by black holes.

    (D) After they fall in on themselves.

大解密 ?

本題關鍵字為 white dwarves，可在第二段第三句找到答案，而選項 (D) 將文章的 collapse in on themselves 換句話說，寫成 fall in on themselves。

2. Which of the following statements is **NOT** true?

    (A) Stars are born after a series of nuclear reactions.

    (B) Large stars die more slowly than stars of smaller or normal sizes.

    (C) Supernova can be brighter than all the other stars in the galaxy briefly.

    (D) The author compare black holes to permanent detention halls for matter.

大解密 ?

此題為測驗多個細節的題型，回答重點為抓住每個選項的關鍵字，如此一來就能快速找到答案。選項 (A) 的關鍵字為 born 和 nuclear reactions，出現在文章第一段第五句，故此敘述正確。選項 (B) 的關鍵字為 large stars die more slowly，講到體積較大的恆星死亡的速度，而線索在文章第二段最後一句：Stars that are substantially larger than our sun, however, end their lives suddenly，由此可判斷此敘述錯誤，故答案選 (B)。選項 (C) 的關鍵字為 supernova 和 brighter，在文章第三段第二句有提到。選項 (D) 的關鍵字為 permanent detention halls for matter，在文章最後一段第一句有提到，故此敘述正確。

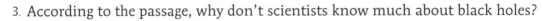

3. According to the passage, why don't scientists know much about black holes?

   (A) Because they are too dark.

   (B) Because nothing can come out of them.

   (C) Because no instruments can measure them.

   (D) Because they are too far away from us.

大解密

本題關鍵字為 don't know much about 和第四段的 mysteries 是換句話說，線索就在第四段後方 it never escapes，表示物體被黑洞吸進去就逃不出來，導致缺乏可研究的資訊，所以科學家對黑洞內部的情況所知不多，故答案選 (B)。

◉ 關卡五：字義

有些題型為考字義或詞義，並在文章中以粗體出現，通常透過對上下文的理解，可以推敲出這些字詞的意義。

⚔ 技巧一：在上下文或在同一句話找到相近字義。

EXAMPLE

Speaking of basketball, we cannot help but talking about NBA, the National Basketball Association. The NBA game is becoming more and more admired around the world, competing for popularity with spectacular sports like soccer. The NBA star-players are **doted on** by teenagers, and often the matches draw thousands of fans to stadiums and millions to their TVs. There were times when basketball was little known outside the U.S.; now side by side with the NBA, it is taking over the world.

1. Which of the following words is closest in meaning to **doted on** from the passage?

   (A) doubted   (B) adored   (C) dreaded   (D) controlled

大解密

本句的後半提到 often the matches draw thousands of fans to stadiums and millions to their TVs，由此可知 NBA 比賽很受歡迎，並推論 doted by 是正面的意思，表示這些球星相當受青少年喜愛，故選 (B) adored，而非選項 (A) 懷疑、(B) 害怕或 (D) 控制。

技巧二：在前後句找到字義。

EXAMPLE

Without a doubt, Lionel Messi is one of the best soccer players of all time. Though the Argentinean now plays for Barcelona, he is famous in many other countries. In fact, it seems that he may be one of the most well-known soccer players in the world. This certainly was proven to be true recently when a photo of a young Messi fan in Afghanistan was posted online and quickly **went viral**.

The famous photo showed a young Afghani boy playing soccer in the snow in the Afghan countryside. The thing that caused so many people to take notice of the photo was the boy's jersey. It seemed that the boy had has his heart set on wearing a Messi jersey, so he had made a home-made version of Messi's soccer jersey using a blue-striped plastic bag. On the back, he had even written Messi's last name and his number, 10.

After the picture of the young Messi fan was posted on Facebook, it quickly began to appear on other sites all over the Internet. Soon, a search for the boy in the photo had begun, although most didn't hold out much hope for finding him. At first, people assumed the boy was from Iraq and some even speculated that he was an orphan. However, later, the boy's uncle, an Afghani living in Australia, identified the boy.

"Messi's biggest fan" turned out to be Murtaza Ahmadi, a five-year-old boy from the isolated eastern Ghazni province of Afghanistan. After that Ahmadi received an authentic soccer jersey from Messi, which the star player even signed himself. For his part, Ahmadi was overjoyed, saying, "I love Messi, and my shirt says Messi loves me."

So, thanks to the power of Internet, a young soccer fan in the countryside of Afghanistan quickly became an international sensation. In addition, this young boy was able to receive a splendid gift from his idol Lionel Messi and wear a real soccer jersey while he played soccer, instead of a plastic bag.

1. Which of the following is closest in meaning to the phrase "**went viral**" in the first paragraph?

(A) Causing a lot of controversy and was immediately removed.

(B) Infecting a lot of people and became a contagious disease.

(C) Proving to be a fake photo and attracted lots of criticism.

(D) Becoming famous and popular on the Internet very quickly.

大解密 ?

同句話點出這張照片被貼到網路 (posted online)，並且接下來敘述這張照片吸引許多人注意並造成轟動 (appear on other sites all over the Internet 和 became an international sensation)，故可推知答案為 (D)，表示刊出照片後受到大眾矚目的速度就像病毒般迅速蔓延。

技巧三：利用標點符號或轉折詞來判斷。

出題的字詞，其後若有破折號 (─)、冒號 (:)、或括弧 ( ) 等標點符號，或是轉折詞如：or (或者說)、in other words (換句話說)、that is (也就是說)；亦或者是舉例用的字詞：for example/instance (舉例說)、such as (例說)、like (像是) 等，出現在它們後方的文字，通常是進一步地解釋、定義或舉例說明前面的字詞。它們可以幫助我們找到答案和瞭解文意。若能掌握此關鍵，對於文章的理解力將會大增。

EXAMPLE (在括弧的裡的解釋)

Scientists believe that a phenomenon known as **UHI** (urban heat island) is responsible for cities being up to 3 degrees centigrade hotter than nearby areas.

大解密 [?]

(urban heat island) 就是對 UHI 的解釋。

EXAMPLE (在 or 的後面解釋)

Apart from criticizing religion, Nietzsche also developed the concept of an "Übermensch," or superman who could face the harsh realities of life and excel in various fields.

大解密 [?]

superman who could face the harsh realities of life and excel in various fields 是對 Übermensch 的解釋。需注意的地方是，or 在做進一步解釋前方字詞用法時，前面通常有逗點。

EXAMPLE (在破折號中間的解釋)

The coral reefs—the "rainforests of the sea"—are equally important.

大解密 [?]

the "rainforests of the sea" 是對 the coral reefs 進一步的解釋。

◉ 關卡六：代名詞

此類題目是要讀者找到文章中粗體標示的代名詞所指稱的名詞為何。在篇章結構的部分，已經很詳盡地說明代名詞的概念，有此基礎後，遇到此一類型的題目，就可迎刃而解。

技巧：往前找答案。代名詞通常指涉前方的名詞，可以把前面提及的名詞都代換，然後找出最符合上下文義的名詞。有時候，像是 this、that、it 的代名詞，也可能指前方的某個句子，而非名詞。

EXAMPLE

Sometimes, we face difficult situations that we cannot control. The important thing at such times is to remain positive. Attitude counts, and this truly inspirational story will show you why.

Helen Keller was born on 27 June 1880 with full vision and hearing. However, when at nineteen months, a mysterious brain fever left her blind and deaf, life became difficult. Helen was constantly smashing things, screaming, and throwing tantrums out of frustration. Unable to cope with this situation, her family found her a teacher, Anne Sullivan.

Anne started with teaching Helen by spelling things out on her hand. **She** also taught her table manners and tasks like combing her hair. Helen often behaved violently, but Anne would punish her by stopping her tutoring. Slowly, Helen learned to do small tasks. When people spoke, she would hold her hand to their mouths and try to copy the sounds. This was one of the hardest times of her life, but Helen did not give up. Through continued effort, she learned Braille and was able to read, write, and type in it.

In 1900, Helen became the first deaf-blind person to attend college and later, the first to earn a Bachelor of Arts degree. Throughout her life, she wrote several essays and made many public appearances. She was also involved in fundraising activities for the American Foundation of the Blind. Today, Helen Keller Worldwide, which she helped establish, works for blind people across the world through eye health and awareness programs. A child's struggle to deal with a disability has grown to a global resource for the disabled.

Helen Keller's story shows the importance of never giving up. It was Helen's positive attitude that helped her overcome her difficulties and has now brought help to millions.

1. What does **she** in paragraph 3 refer to?
   (A) Helen Keller
   (B) Anne Sullivan
   (C) Braille
   (D) Helen Keller's mother

大解密 ❓

本句前方有兩個名詞 Helen Keller 和 Anne Sullivan，因此將這兩個名詞都代入。本句是 「she also taught her . . .」，從情境可看出 she 是指老師，而所有格 her 則是指 Helen Keller，故答案選 (B) Anne Sullivan。

EXAMPLE

Some have called it a "lifestyle" disease, since it is often caused by a bad diet, little exercise, and smoking or drinking, whereas others have called it a disease of "prosperity" because it often affects those in prosperous countries, especially those who have adopted a Western diet. **This** can be seen in particular in China, Russia, and Brazil, where an unprecedented number of cases of colorectal cancer (大腸癌) have occurred as these countries have developed economically.

2. What does the pronoun **this** in the paragraph refers to?

   (A) The fact modern ways of living need changing.
   (B) The fact the global economy is taking off.
   (C) That fact more people are diagnosed with colorectal cancer.
   (D) That fact people eat and live following the Western ways.

大解密 ❓

本句的代名詞指涉的是前方的句子 ： in prosperous countries, especially those who have adopted a Western diet，雖選項 (D) 稍微改了原來的用字，但意思是一樣的，故選 (D)。

◉ 關卡七：推論或暗示

此類型的題目要求讀者推敲字裡行間作者沒有明講的內容 ， 通常無法直接找到答案，但可以經由邏輯或常理做出合理的推測。題幹中常有 infer 或 imply。

🔫 技巧 ：仔細閱讀四個選項 ， 並在文章中找出相關且能佐證的字 、 詞或句子，或使用消去法，刪掉不正確或找不到證據的答案。

On May 5, 2003 thousands of Americans in the Midwest greeted the new day with sorrow. Around them they found buildings destroyed, trees uprooted and, most sadly, neighbors dead and injured. In fact, 40 people died and there was over a billion dollars of damage. What could cause such destruction? For those living in Tornado Alley, the answer is not surprising. Powerful storms of rotating winds, known as tornadoes, are frequent visitors to this area. Tornado Alley, covering parts of the Midwest and southern regions of the United States, experiences more tornadoes than any other place, killing an average of fifty-five people per year.

Scientists have been researching tornadoes for decades in the hopes that the information they gain will save lives. They have a basic understanding of the mechanics of these storms. First, warm humid air gets trapped under a layer of colder, drier air. If there is a disturbance in the cap of cold air, then the warm air rushes upward and begins to rotate, causing a thunderstorm. If conditions are just right, the thunderstorm begins rotating more rapidly and a tornado forms below it. However, the exact circumstances that cause a thunderstorm to become a tornado are still unknown. This makes tornado prediction extremely difficult.

Though scientists still cannot predict tornadoes with great accuracy, early warning systems are saving lives. Education programs that teach people what to do during a tornado have also contributed to dropping death rates over the past few decades.

1. What can we infer from the last sentence in the passage?
   (A) Education programs are able to predict when tornadoes are going to strike.
   (B) The government is funding education programs to lower the death tolls caused by tornadoes.
   (C) Education programs have helped reduce the number of people when tornadoes lash.
   (D) Education programs need to hire more experts to teach people to take proper precaution against tornadoes.

大解密 ?

從本段最後一句就可以直接找到本題的答案 「... have also contributed to dropping death rates ...」可知死亡率已經由教育改善，故選 (C)。

EXAMPLE

The television show CSI: Crime Scene Investigation followed a team of forensic scientists working together to solve crimes for the Las Vegas police department. Unlike normal detectives, the team relied on science to decipher clues and catch criminals.

When it first appeared in 2000, CSI immediately became a hit. The show used a lot of crime scene images, sometimes showing gunshot wounds and other violent injuries, accompanied by explanations spoken by the characters. Details of the crime were thoroughly investigated in the team's lab, and the scientists used technology that produced almost instant results, which would be impossible to do in real life. CSI was one of the most-watched shows on American television, with close to 30 million viewers each week.

CSI's popularity had inspired fans to create thousands of websites based on the series. Many of these websites published stories about the show's characters that fans wrote themselves In addition, the original CSI's success led to the creation of CSI: Miami and CSI: New York, two show that followed similar teams of scientists in other cities. Neither was as popular as the original, but each had a unique style based on the city in which it takes place. Other countries also have their own versions of CSI, such as Silent Witness in the UK and Forensic Heroes in Hong Kong. Although critics of CSI claimed that it was unrealistic, people continued to watch the show because of its fascinating stories and interesting characters. CSI presents a different side of police work, reminding viewers that science is very important in solving crimes.

1. What can be inferred from the passage about CSI's popularity?

   (A) It inspired a craze for similar shows both in the US and the world.

   (B) It brought about the creation of more popular shows, such as CSI: New York.

(C) It sparked heated debates among fans about the authenticity of the show.

(D) It led to a revolution in how the police use science to solve crime.

大解密 ❓

關於本題的詳細線索於第三段，說明 CSI 的熱門所導致的影響。文中提到 CSI 大受歡迎，所以在美國和其它國家都有推出續集或類似的影集，在美國的續集叫做 CSI: Miami 和 CSI: New York；在英國則是 Silent Witness；在香港的影集為 Forensic Heroes，故 (A) 為正確答案。關於 (B) 選項，文中雖提到 CSI: New York 為接續推出的姊妹作，但作者也提到該作品沒有原來的 CSI 受歡迎，故此敘述不正確。另外文中提到因為 CSI 大受歡迎，所以影迷們創建很多的粉絲網站，分享同人作品，而非熱烈地討論影集的真實性，故 (C) 選項不正確。而最後一句點出影集提醒了觀眾科學辦案的重要，但並沒有說警方因此有改變辦案方法，故 (D) 選項為非。

EXAMPLE

Dear Readers,

Today's column is a special treat. I've decided to share some of my successful advice stories with you. A few weeks after giving fifteen-year-old, tidy Linda advice about sharing her room with a messy nine-year-old, I received the following letter:

Dear Dulcie,

I talked to my mother and she agreed to help me teach my sister to be neater. At first, nothing worked. But then I got a calendar with the days of the week on it. Whenever my sister put her things away neatly, she got a gold star for the day. Every time she got 5 gold stars, I let her try on my clothes to play dress up. My sister loves this new "game" and I actually like playing dress up with her too! Now we have lots of fun playing dress up together. Thanks for helping us!

Sincerely,

Linda

Linda took my advice to heart and used a smart trick to help her sister be tidy. Great job, Linda! Here's a follow-up letter from Adam, who needed advice about his parents, who were always making him study.

Dear Dulcie,

At first I put off talking to my parents because I was afraid they would get mad. When I finally got up my nerve, I told them I understood how important school work was, but that I needed to have some free time as well. Then, I could rest my mind and study even better. Well, guess what? My parents weren't mad at all! They were proud of me for knowing what I needed to make myself a better student. Now, my parents don't push me to study so much and they even tell me to go outdoors to play with my friends! Thanks!

Sincerely,

Adam

There you have it, Readers! My advice does work, but only if you use it! Until next time, keep on reading and asking me for advice!

Sincerely,

Dulcie

1. What can be inferred from the passage about Dulcie's occupation?

(A) Dulcie may be a columnist that gives advice.

(B) Dulcie probably is a post office employee that delivers letters.

(C) Dulcie might be an agent that replies fan mail.

(D) Dulcie is a full-time journalist that writes stories.

大解密 ❓

仔細從文章裡尋找線索可推論出 Dulcie 的工作。由 column 和 advice，再加上文中讀者的感謝信，可推測出 Dulcie 應是報紙的專欄作家，專門提供讀者意見，故答案為 (A)。

閱讀測驗
題目篇

Round 1

How Pets Can Help People

From the moment animals become pets, they really stop being animals and turn into something else. They suddenly become Douglas the dog, Catherine the cat, Raffy the rabbit and Sandra the snake. By naming our pets, they instantly can be our companions, playmates and friends. In short, they are almost like humans.

It is well known how much pets give to their owners. Douglas the dog is more than just a pal for a child: he can teach his young owner responsibility. When the child gives Douglas a bath or a meal, he's learning that others can depend on **him**. Of course, pets offer a lot to older owners too. For senior citizens, pets break down the walls of isolation. It is even said that pets can make the aged physically fit. The daily walks they take with their dogs or cats do wonders for their health.

Considering all the things pets do for us, it's no surprise we return the favor. We do so most obviously and especially when we treat them like people. Take Noriko Uchiyama, for example. This Japanese lady goes to a spa every month. Why? Because of Pon-chan. Pon-chan is nervous about going with her but he absolutely has to go because his fur is falling out. According to Noriko, Pon-chan's skin problems which cause his loss of fur can be cured by a relaxing time at the spa.

Noriko Uchiyama is no unusual pet owner. Owners worldwide are "humanizing" their beloved animals. They give Raffy the rabbit clothes to wear during winter time. They dress up Catherine, the cat, as a hot dog during Halloween. Some dogs even have cosmetic surgery to have their ears stick out straight. Other pets travel with their owners using their own passports. No wonder pet owners now object to the word "owner"—they'd rather be called pet "guardians."

(　　) 1. What is the main idea of this passage?

(A) Pets are treated as human companions by a lot of people.

(B) Pets require a lot of money and time to look after.

(C) Pets offer more than love and companionship to their owners.

(D) Pets are given many different and creative names.

(　　) 2. What does "**him**" in the second paragraph refer to?

(A) Douglas. (B) The child.

(C) Noriko Uchiyama. (D) Raffy.

(　　) 3. According to the passage, what can pets give to the elderly besides companionship?

(A) A sense of purpose. (B) Responsibility.

(C) A sense of belonging. (D) Wellness.

(　　) 4. Which of the following is true about Pon-chan?

(A) He goes to a spa every month.

(B) He enjoys going to spas.

(C) He suffers from the loss of teeth.

(D) His skin problems are solved.

?

It is midnight. You are on Bourbon Street in the French Quarter of New Orleans; crowds of people are all around you. They are dancing, singing, and drinking. In fact, most of them are already drunk. Bands parade by, playing their music. People in crazy, colorful costumes toss candies, plastic beads, and coins to you from their floats. Welcome to the lively but decadent scene. That is the greatest free show on earth: Mardi Gras.

New Orleans is the biggest city in the American State of Louisiana. It was founded in 1718 by French colonists, who brought the Mardi Gras tradition with them. The festival's origins can be traced back to ancient times; when people celebrated the end of winter and the beginning of spring. Spring was a time of rebirth; animals came out of hibernation, plants sprouted new growth, and trees put on new leaves. Christians preserved and adapted the festival, giving it a religious character. Mardi Gras means "Fat Tuesday" in French, and is the last day before the start of Lent in the Christian religion. Lent lasts for forty days before Easter, and is a period of fast, prayer and religious contemplation. This is why the Louisiana French **live it up** the week before Lent starts; they eat, drink, and party to excess, knowing that at midnight on "Fat Tuesday" all the fun must stop.

What started out as a purely regional celebration among the French in Louisiana is today a world-famous event. Improvements in transportation and communication make it possible for everyone to enjoy Mardi Gras. Mardi Gras' fame and popularity stem from its uniqueness. In no other place in America can you experience such a spectacle.

(   ) 1. How does the author start talking about the festival?

        (A) By talking about the history of the festival.

        (B) By mentioning the meaning of the festival.

        (C) By explaining why the festival is unique.

        (D) By describing a specific scene of the festival.

(   ) 2. What is the best title for this passage?

        (A) The History of New Orleans.   (B) Fat Tuesday.

        (C) Mardi Gras in New Orleans.   (D) Mardi Gras and its Variations.

(   ) 3. The phrase **live it up** is closest in meaning to _____.

        (A) make the most of it.   (B) put an end to it.

        (C) come up with it.   (D) cut down on it.

(   ) 4. What can we infer from the conclusion of the passage?

        (A) The best place to enjoy the event in the US is probably in New Orleans.

        (B) People celebrating the event today are mainly devoted Christians.

        (C) The government does not really encourage the celebration of the event.

        (D) The festival is famous and popular because of the celebrities involved.

Music and Learning

Do you like to listen to music? Many people enjoy listening to music for pleasure. But did you know that music might actually be able to improve your ability to learn, as well?

According to several recent reports, music can be very powerful when it comes to learning. A study done at Stanford University showed that listening to music can help listeners increase their focus. In a highly focused state, it is easier for people to take in new information. Another study at Johns Hopkins University also indicated the same result. This is particularly true if the information is paired with a special rhythm or rhyme. And an author named Chris Brewer believes that music can make students more willing to learn. For example, upbeat music can motivate students to learn new things while classical music can help them to concentrate on reading or writing.

What's more, learning how to play a musical instrument can have an even bigger effect on overall learning. In fact, a Northwestern University study has found that musical training can improve speech, attention span, and even foreign language skills. According to the study, when the brain is exposed to music, it can adapt and change more quickly and easily. In addition, the study found that students who had received musical training could read better and had a larger vocabulary than students who had not received any musical training. These students were also better at using new sound patterns when learning a different language.

So, if you really want to improve your ability to learn, consider listening to music or even learning how to play a musical instrument. It seems clear that music can be a very powerful tool.

(　　) 1. What is the author's attitude toward music's role in assisting learning?
(A) Positive.　　(B) Negative.　　(C) Neutral.　　(D) Conservative.

(　　) 2. According to the passage, what two aspects of music can help students learn better?
(A) Listening to music and reading musical theories.
(B) Reading musical theories and composing music.
(C) Listening to music and learning to play an instrument.
(D) Learning to play an instrument and composing music.

(　　) 3. What has the study done by Northwestern University found?
(A) Music that is inappropriate may have a negative effect on students' learning.
(B) Music soothes and calms down students when they are agitated.
(C) Music allows students to concentrate better in a noisy environment.
(D) Music helps students learn languages other than their mother tongue.

(　　) 4. Which of the following statements is true?
(A) A study done at Stanford University found music improves memory.
(B) A study done at Johns Hopkins University found that music helps students concentrate.
(C) Chris Brewer found that music increases students' willingness to learn.
(D) Chris Brewer found that upbeat music actually distracts students.

A Closer Look at Stress

Have you ever felt worried or tense because of some challenge or difficulty that you had to face? If so, you have experienced stress. And while this may have been uncomfortable, recent studies have shown that long-term stress can also be dangerous, since it can have a very bad effect on a person's health.

Stress began as an automatic response that enabled the first humans to protect themselves from life-or-death threats, such as facing predators. Increasing the body's heart rate and boosting the body's energy enabled people to deal with such deadly situations. Some have called this the "fight-or-flight" response.

These days, however, we rarely face the same problems that our ancestors did. Yet, our bodies still continue to react in the same way. As a result, we experience stress because of the challenges that we face in the modern world, such as passing a test, paying bills, or dealing with others at school or work.

In the short term, stress is usually unpleasant. In the long run, though, stress can be very bad for our health. When stress continues for a long period of time, it is called "chronic stress", and it can lead to fatigue, headaches, and even certain diseases, such as Alzheimer's disease. It also has been linked with obesity and depression.

Fortunately, there are some steps we can take to deal with stress. The first is to simply take a deep breath, since this can help you to calm down quickly. You can also focus on the present moment, instead of thinking about the past or future, and keep your problems in perspective by trying to remember all that you are grateful for.

After all, stress lives in our lives, so we should do our best to make sure that stress does not negatively affect our health.

(　　) 1. Where is this passage most likely to be taken from?
    (A) A health magazine.   (B) A dietary guide.
    (C) An ad for a personal trainer.   (D) An encyclopedia.

(　　) 2. According to the passage, what is a fight-or-flight response?
    (A) Short-term and long-term stress.
    (B) Chronic stress that leads to serious illness.
    (C) How our body reacts to a life-threatening situation.
    (D) One of the steps we can take to deal with stress.

(　　) 3. Which of the following is **NOT** mentioned as a possible effect of long-term stress?
    (A) Tiredness.   (B) Overweight.
    (C) Pain in the head.   (D) Sleep deprivation.

(　　) 4. What is the author's purpose of writing this passage?
    (A) To explain the many different aspects of stress.
    (B) To list recent studies that are related to stress.
    (C) To persuade readers that stress is a double-edged sword.
    (D) To promote a healthier way of life free from stress.

Round 5

Athletes on Drugs

For amateur athletes, the chance to compete in the Olympics is a thrill. If they are fast enough, or strong enough, they may even win a medal and bring much glory and attention to their country.

But in some cases, that pride and glory turn to shame and embarrassment when it is discovered that the winning athlete used drugs in the competition. When that happens, the medals are taken away, and the athletes are **banned** from competing for a period of time, possibly forever.

Sometimes, drug use in sports is an accident. For example, a runner might take a pill for a headache or a cold. That pill could contain a substance that is illegal under the rules of the Olympics. However, in some circumstances, some athletes take the drug anyway even theyknow that it is not allowed.

One famous case involving drug use at the Olympics happened in 1988 in South Korea. A Canadian athlete, Ben Johnson broke the world record in the 100 meters race and won the gold medal. After a test showed that Johnson had used drugs, his medal was taken away and he quickly became a disgrace to Canada. The government of Canada held an investigation into the case, which helped lead to tougher rules and tests regarding drugs in sports.

Why do athletes use drugs and risk getting caught? There is a lot of pressure on athletes to win, and they may not satisfy with their own performance. They may also imagine that their competitors are using drugs, and believe that doing the same is something they have to do.

Taking drugs to increase the chances of winning is not only wrong but also dangerous. It can harm athletes' health. While most know that drug use is not worth the risk to their career and health, some still continue to cheat.

(   ) 1. What is the main idea of this passage?

      (A) Some athletes risk taking drugs in order to win a competition.

      (B) The Olympic Games are so competitive that winning a medal is hard.

      (C) Drug addiction is a serious problem in modern society.

      (D) Cheating in sports competition is a common phenomenon.

(   ) 2. What does the word **banned** in the second paragraph probably mean?

      (A) Not invited. (B) Not allowed. (C) Encouraged. (D) Replaced.

(   ) 3. Which of the following statements about Ben Johnson is true?

      (A) He won a gold medal in the 1988 Olympics and kept the medal.

      (B) He represented the United States to participate in the 1988 Olympics.

      (C) His involvement in drug use cost him his gold medal in the 1988 Olympics.

      (D) He was proved innocent after an investigation was conducted into his case.

(   ) 4. What can be inferred from the passage?

      (A) Due to tougher rules and tests, cheating is a thing of the past.

      (B) Despite risks involved, some athletes will still attempt drug use.

      (C) Athletes resort to drug use because they're unaware of the danger involved.

      (D) Governments in the world should work together to stop cheating in games.

?

Because Ireland is a country that has seen centuries of violent political struggles, you might be surprised that its culture is known for its joyful music, dancing, and fine literature, and that its people have a reputation for being optimistic and friendly.

The island of Ireland has been settled for about nine thousand years, but its biggest cultural influence came a little more than two thousand years ago when the Celts invaded. They united the island under a common language (Irish, or Gaelic). Although most people speak English, Irish is still an official language of Ireland. In the fifth century, Saint Patrick brought the Christian religion to the island. Today, about 95% of the population is Roman Catholic, and Saint Patrick's Day is the most important national holiday. In more recent centuries, Ireland has had a long and bitter struggle with the British. England took control of Ireland in the seventeenth century and there was an on-again, off-again struggle for independence until separation of the island into north and south in 1921.

The political struggle continues in the north despite a peace agreement in 1998; nevertheless, when most people think of the Irish they think of music, dancing, storytelling, literature, and pubs. Every city and village has at least one pub where locals gather to listen to music and meet with their neighbors. The music is Celtic folk and usually features instruments like violins, tin whistles, drums, and pipes. Irish storytelling also has ancient roots and features fairies and little people called leprechauns. The literary tradition has grown over the years and Ireland is now known for some of the finest writers in the history of English literature; William Butler Yates, James Joyce, and Oscar Wilde are just three of them.

Beyond the political drama, Ireland is a land of rich culture that will entertain and welcome you.

(　　) 1. What is the best title for this passage?
- (A) Music and Literature of Ireland. (B) Conflicts in Ireland.
- (C) Irish Culture. 　　　　　　　 (D) Saint Patrick's Day.

(　　) 2. Which of the following is **NOT** mentioned as having influenced Irish culture?
- (A) Roman Catholic. 　　　　　 (B) The British.
- (C) The Celts. 　　　　　　　　(D) The Vikings.

(　　) 3. Which of the following statements is true about Ireland?
- (A) Ireland's culture didn't come into being until the 5th century.
- (B) England has been in control of Ireland since the 17th century.
- (C) Ireland has been peaceful due to a peace agreement since 1998.
- (D) Most Irish people nowadays speak English and believe in Christianity.

(　　) 4. What is the third paragraph mainly about?
- (A) The music and literary traditions of Ireland.
- (B) Leprechauns.
- (C) The political struggle in Ireland in recent days.
- (D) Finest writers in Ireland.

Get!

詳解請參閱解析本 p. 32–

The Trojan War

To understand a country or a culture, one must know something of its history. To understand Western civilization, one must have some knowledge about a war which occurred some thirty-two centuries ago. Why? Because the ten-year Trojan War greatly influenced the development of Western history and literature. Understanding the past, even when the historic record is legendary, is vital to understanding the present.

In the 12th century B.C., in the eastern Mediterranean, flourished the city-state of Troy. King Priam and his sons, Paris and Hector, ruled it wisely. Their major competitors were the Greeks, who were developing their own great city-states. This much is a historical fact. **Legends, however, often mix fact with fiction.** The Greeks believed in a world divided between man and gods; however, these gods could and often did interfere in the affairs of man. According to Homer, the greatest writer of ancient Greece, a goddess promised Paris that he could have the most beautiful woman in the world. That woman happened to be Helen, and she happened to be married to a Greek. With the aid of the goddess, Paris went to Greece, kidnapped Helen, and took her back to Troy. Both romantics and historians can guess what happened next: the Greeks began an invasion of Troy to recapture Helen.

For ten years, neither side could win. Finally, the Greeks came up with a plan. They built an enormous, empty wooden horse, filled it with soldiers, left it at Troy's gates, and pretended to depart. The Trojans believed the horse was a gift and took it inside the city. That night, the Greek soldiers crept out of the horse, opened the city gates, and let their waiting comrades in to destroy the city. With this victory, the Greeks became the undisputed masters of the Mediterranean.

Homer wrote about the Trojan War in the Iliad and the Odyssey, two early works of Western literature. Greek culture later strongly influenced the Romans and later the Europeans and Americans. This is why understanding the cultural roots of the West requires a basic familiarity with the events, both fact and legend, of the Trojan War.

(　　) 1. Why does the author talk about the Trojan War?

(A) Because it is essential to understanding Western civilization.

(B) Because it is an important war that defined the border of Greece.

(C) Because it is one of the longest wars in the history of mankind.

(D) Because it represented a new way of how wars could be fought.

(　　) 2. According to the passage, what triggered the Trojan War in Homer's writing?

(A) The fact that the Greeks wanted the land of Troy.

(B) The fact that Paris went to Greece to kidnap Helen.

(C) A feud that had existed between the Greeks and the Trojans.

(D) The differences in religious beliefs between the Greeks and the Trojans.

(　　) 3. What is the author implying by saying "**Legends, however, often mix fact with fiction**"?

(A) We are unable to determine whether the Trojan War actually existed.

(B) Homer is a historian who recorded history very faithfully.

(C) The story of the Trojan War is basically a made-up myth.

(D) The story of the Trojan War is not without its historical background.

(　　) 4. According to the passage, what was the plan the Greeks came up with?

(A) They gave every soldier a horse and had them charge at Troy.

(B) They hid soldiers in a gift wooden horse and gave it to the Trojans.

(C) They prayed to Zeus for help and Zeus gave them a large army.

(D) They built a wooden fortress and shot fire arrows at the Trojans.

Get!

詳解請參閱解析本 p. 33~

Marc Jacobs: A Fashion Icon

When it comes to the world of fashion, there are some big names, such as Calvin Klein, Karl Lagerfeld, and Vera Wang. However, one of the most important names on the fashion scene for the past twenty-five years has been Marc Jacobs.

Jacobs was born in New York City in 1963. Sadly, at the age of seven, Jacobs' father passed away, and the young boy went through a rough time as his mother dated and remarried. Fortunately, Jacobs ended up living with his grandmother, and he found a stable home with her. His grandmother always encouraged Jacobs to be creative and try new things, and at the age of fifteen, he already had a job in a clothing store. He even convinced the store to let him design sweaters for them.

These designs helped Jacobs get into the prestigious Parsons School of Design. There, he won several awards, and after graduating in 1984, he quickly went on to design his first fashion line. Jacobs soon became the head fashion designer at Perry Ellis, which was quite an honor at such a young age. Although he won several awards and critical acclaim at Perry Ellis, Jacobs eventually left the brand to start his own fashion line.

The Marc Jacobs label was a success, but in 1997, Jacobs decided also to go to work for Louis Vuitton as the brand's creative director. In the years that followed, Jacobs would win a number of honors for his work, including Menswear Designer of the Year and Accessories Designer of the Year. Today, Jacobs not only has his own stores but his own perfumes and accessories, as well.

Clearly, in the world of fashion, Marc Jacobs is one of the most important designers working today, and he will likely have a strong influence on fashion for many years to come.

(　　) 1. What is this passage mainly about?

    (A) Designer brands.

    (B) Marc Jacobs' childhood.

    (C) Marc Jacobs' life and success.

    (D) Marc Jacobs' talent as a designer.

(　　) 2. Which of the following statements is true about Marc Jacobs' early life?

    (A) His mother died when he was 7 years old.

    (B) His father left him when he was 10 years old.

    (C) His grandmother raised him and inspired his creativity.

    (D) He started working in a clothing shop when he was 16.

(　　) 3. What's the correct order of places that Marc Jacobs has worked for?

    (A) Perry Ellis → Marc Jacobs → Louis Vuitton

    (B) Marc Jacobs → Louis Vuitton → Perry Ellis

    (C) Perry Ellis → Louis Vuitton → Marc Jacobs

    (D) Louis Vuitton → Perry Ellis → Marc Jacobs

(　　) 4. What is the author's attitude toward Marc Jacobs?

    (A) Approving.　　(B) Disapproving.(C) Indifferent.　　(D) Neutral.

詳解請參閱解析本 p. 34-

The Disappearing Rainforests

It goes without saying that the earth's rainforests are important. These large natural areas can be found around the world, particularly in South America, Africa, and Asia, and they are said to be home to more than 50 percent of the world's species. Rainforests are also a major source of many of our important modern drugs and medicines, and they play a key role when it comes to climate change and global warming. Unfortunately, it has recently been reported that the world's rainforests are now disappearing at an alarming rate.

Believe it or not, experts say that around 80,000 acres of rainforest are being destroyed every day. As a result, around 135 species of plants, animals, and insects are lost each day. Some experts say that around 50,000 species in total disappear every year because of the rapid destruction of the world's rainforests.

Simply put, the rainforests are often in the poorer, developing areas of the world, and the people in these areas are pushing to expand into new places. In addition, commercial activities, such as logging, farming, ranching, and mining, continue to grow in these areas. Sadly, this often means that large areas of rainforest are now being cleared away to make room for these people and activities.

Still, some scientists have hope for the future. They point out that some areas of rainforest are now under protection and will likely remain until at 2030, at least. Other scientists, however, are not so hopeful. They point out that at the current rate of destruction, all of the world's rainforests will disappear in about 100 years. This, quite obviously, would be a disaster for our planet.

Clearly, the world's rainforests are important, and they are disappearing. So, it seems clear that we should do something about this—soon!

(　　) 1. What is the main idea of this passage?

    (A) Rainforests are disappearing and need protection.

    (B) Rainforests are home to more than half of the world species.

    (C) Climate change is destroying the earth we live in.

    (D) Economic growth comes at the expense of rainforests.

(　　) 2. According to the passage, how many species are estimated to die out in rainforests every year?

    (A) 50.   (B) 135.   (C) 50,000.   (D) 80,000.

(　　) 3. According to the passage, why are large areas of rainforests disappearing?

    (A) Because extreme weather phenomena make it hard to for them to survive.

    (B) Because the ecosystem of rainforests is imbalanced.

    (C) Because humans are clearing out rainforests for development.

    (D) Because the lack of rainfall is causing droughts.

(　　) 4. What can be inferred from the passage?

    (A) Rainforests are important but not necessary for human survival.

    (B) Scientists haven't reached a conclusion about what the future of rainforests will be like.

    (C) Governments in the world are doing their best to make sure no more rainforests will be cleared out.

    (D) Rainforests will disappear from the planet earth within a hundred years.

A Closer Look at Wildfires

When we think of the world's forests, we usually think of calm, peaceful places full of tall trees and green plants. However, every year, the world's forests become home to something violent and dangerous—forest fires. In fact, forest fires, which are sometimes also called wildfires or wildland fires, occur thousands of times each year and destroy millions of acres of natural land.

Wildfires can be started in several different ways. Many are caused by lightning, especially if the area is dry, without much rain. Perhaps this shouldn't be surprising, since reports say that lightning strikes our planet more than three billion times every year. What's more, these lightning strikes are often in remote places, which means the wildfires in these areas are more difficult to put out.

Unfortunately, many other wildfires are caused by human beings. Campers and hikers often accidentally start wildfires, usually when they forget to put out their campfires or do so improperly. Some wildfires are also started by people who burn garbage. In a few cases, wildfires are even set deliberately by criminals called "arsonists."

Wildfires often spread very quickly, especially in dry, windy areas. **This** means that responding to wildfires as quickly as possible is very important. Firefighters often use large amounts of water to try to put out wildfires, but sometimes they must use other methods, including creating firebreaks by removing trees and plants.

Although wildfires can be very destructive to both forests and humans, they do serve an important purpose. By destroying old or even dead plants and trees, they allow new plants and trees to grow in their place. They also enable vital nutrients to be put back into the ground.

Clearly, wildfires will continue to play an important role in nature, so we should do our best to understand them.

(   ) 1. What is the best title for this passage?

        (A) A Closer Look at Wildfires.

        (B) The Dos and Don'ts in a Wildfire.

        (C) Arsonists and Wildfires.

        (D) How to Put out a Wildfire.

(   ) 2. What does "**this**" in the fourth paragraph refer to?

        (A) The fact that wildfires can become out of control very quickly.

        (B) The fact the wildfires are sometimes started by people.

        (C) The fact that firefighters should respond to wildfires very quickly.

        (D) The fact that wildfires are destructive to both forests and humans.

(   ) 3. According to the passage, what good can wildfires do?

        (A) They stop lightning from striking the same place twice.

        (B) They create firebreaks by getting rid of trees and plants.

        (C) They help humans develop areas covered with trees.

        (D) They allow important nutrients to be placed in the ground.

(   ) 4. Which of the following is **NOT** mentioned as one of the ways that wildfires can be started?

        (A) Lightning strikes.   (B) Unattended campfires.

        (C) Cigarettes.   (D) Garbage burning.

?

Where do most people find out new information? In the past, the media—television, radio, and magazines—were usually the most important sources of information for many people, especially when it came to breaking news and world events. In many countries, particularly in democracies, it has often been assumed that the media should present fair and unbiased news, since people often vote for their leaders based on this information. Unfortunately, and despite the best efforts of many in the media, a phenomenon called "media bias" has appeared.

Generally speaking, media reporters are supposed to do their best to present a fair and balanced news report. However, this does not always happen, and media bias can occur in several different ways. For example, a reporter might leave out one side of a story or ignore certain facts. This is called "bias by omission." A reporter might also use "experts" or "observers" that all tend to agree with a certain point of view. This is called "bias by selection of sources," and it often occurs when reporters try to find people who will supply them with quotes that will fit a particular story. When only certain stories are reported, and others are left out, this is called "bias by story selection." In a similar way, when certain stories are given more emphasis and receive a large headline or appear at the top of a newspaper or news report, this is called "bias by placement." And if there is only one interpretation of a news event or government policy, without any other opinions or viewpoints, this can become "bias by spin."

Of course, it is the job of the media to present clear, unbiased stories to the public. When they fail to do so, however, it is up to the public to identify—and publicize—this media bias.

(   ) 1. What is the best title for this passage?

        (A) Media Bias.   (B) Freedom of the Press.

        (C) Unbiased Reports.   (D) Fact or Fiction.

(   ) 2. What is the passage mainly about?

        (A) To talk about how modern media can be very biased.

        (B) To list the different types of media bias.

        (C) To educate the public about how not to be misled.

        (D) To compare the media now and in the past.

(   ) 3. When news reports only mention how good a government policy is without talking about other different viewpoints, it's called _____.

        (A) bias by selection of sources   (B) bias by story selection

        (C) bias by placement   (D) bias by spin

(   ) 4. According to the passage, why should the media be fair and unbiased especially in democratic countries?

        (A) Because with more freedom comes more responsibilities.

        (B) Because democratic governments do not control their media as much.

        (C) Because the media generate money that can influence elections.

        (D) Because people choose their leaders using the information from the media.

詳解請參閱解析本 p. 37

Lifestyle Diseases

Modern medicine has accomplished remarkable things. For example, many infectious diseases have been **eliminated** or brought under control so that they are no longer spread from one person to another. However, there is a whole other class of diseases that are on the rise. These are called lifestyle diseases, and are suffered by people in developed countries as a result of unhealthy lifestyles.

The major lifestyle diseases are heart disease, strokes, some types of cancer, Type 2 diabetes, and lung disease. These diseases are caused by such things as having a poor diet, being overweight, not exercising, and smoking. In developed countries, having a poor diet generally means that one consumes too much fat and not enough fruits, vegetables, and grains. It is estimated that about one-third of all cancers could be prevented with a healthier diet. Most of the other diseases are tied to the combination of poor diet and lack of exercise. Eating more calories than your body uses results in being very overweight, or obese, which in turn can lead to heart disease, stroke, and Type 2 diabetes. Finally, cigarette smoking causes lung disease, heart disease, and stroke. Other lifestyle factors that contribute to lifestyle diseases include alcohol and drug use, and stress.

These diseases are a great burden on the world's healthcare systems and the situation is predicted to get worse. In 2003, four million people die from smoking related illnesses and it is estimated that this figure will rise by 3 million per year. The World Health Organization says that three million deaths per year are related to being overweight, and they expect this to shoot up to five million deaths by 2020.

Lifestyle diseases are killers and **we cannot wait for science to cure them.** However, the good news is that we can prevent them by simply choosing a healthier lifestyle.

(　　) 1. What is the main idea of this passage?

    (A) Lifestyle diseases are a real problem in modern society.

    (B) Lifestyle diseases are a nuisance that we can hardly tackle with.

    (C) A healthy diet can prevent people from developing many lifestyle diseases.

    (D) Being overweight is the combination of eating too much and not exercising.

(　　) 2. Which of the following is **NOT** mentioned as one of the lifestyle diseases?

    (A) Cancer.   (B) Stroke.

    (C) Heart disease.   (D) High blood pressure.

(　　) 3. What can we infer from the sentence "**we cannot wait for science to cure them**"?

    (A) We need to devote a lot of money and effort to finding cures for them.

    (B) We need to take prompt action to stop things from getting worse.

    (C) We should have more patience to wait for cures to be invented.

    (D) Better healthcare systems should be in place to help people.

(　　) 4. The word "**eliminated**" can be best replaced by _____ .

    (A) wiped out   (B) spread out   (C) opened up   (D) wound up

Round 13

Devil Dancing in Sri Lanka

Sri Lanka is an island just south of India, primarily Buddhist in religion. Many folk customs and non-Buddhist religious practices are still followed there. Devil dancing is one such example. Basically, this dance is performed in order to get rid of an evil spirit, disease, or even bad luck.

The dance is performed by several dancers and drum players, all from a socially low-ranking group of people that specialize in this. First, though, three tiny temples are constructed in front of the victim's residence. These palm-leaf structures are dedicated to demons, gods, and evil spirits. The dancers then attempt to draw these creatures out of their newly-built homes and into the performance area. As the drummers beat frantically, the male dancers perform a series of energetic and strenuous dance routines to excite these beings. This can go on for quite some time, so occasionally, breaks are taken, during **which** other performers may perform magic tricks or other entertainment for the gathering crowds.

At the high point of the performance, the dancers put on masks and become possessed by the evil thing or things causing the victim's disease or trouble. From within their borrowed bodies, the spirits then introduce themselves to the audience and tell them their reason for coming. At that point, the head priest starts to question and threaten them. Sometimes, he may even offer them money or other gifts and ask them to leave the victim alone.

This custom probably predates Buddhism, but it still continues to be followed in rural Sri Lanka. Like other mainstream religions, Buddhism has adopted and adapted elements of local practice and belief in order to strengthen its bond with the local people. This, though, makes Sri Lankan Buddhism quite different from Tibetan Buddhism, or Thai Buddhism, or Chinese or Japanese Buddhism. Regardless of what this means for the unity of the global Buddhism community, rituals such as Sri Lanka's devil dances certainly are colorful and fascinating.

(　　) 1. What is the subject matter of this passage?

    (A) Buddhism in Sri Lanka.

    (B) The differences Buddhism around the world.

    (C) Devil dancing in Sri Lanka.

    (D) Evil spirits in Sri Lanka.

(　　) 2. What does the word "**which**" in the second paragraph refer to?

    (A) Dance routines.　　　　(B) Drumming.

    (C) Magic tricks.　　　　　(D) Breaks.

(　　) 3. What happens when the performance reaches the climax?

    (A) The evil spirits take dancers' bodies and start engaging in conversation.

    (B) Drummers beat their drums really fast and hard to excite the beings.

    (C) Small structures are erected in front of the victims' houses.

    (D) Head priests start driving out the evil spirits chanting spells.

(　　) 4. What is suggested in the last paragraph about Buddhism?

    (A) Buddhism hasn't changed much with its spreading to other countries.

    (B) Buddhism blended with local cultures and is different in each region.

    (C) Buddhism is rarely the major religion in these areas.

    (D) Buddhist beliefs contradict with local practices and customs and are banned.

Thin Film Solar

Solar panels are becoming increasingly popular, both in industrial and residential settings. This is helping reduce electric energy use, reduce pollution, and further our understanding of what is possible with solar technology. One of the newest developments in this field is the use of "thin film" solar panels.

These materials are extremely thin and flexible and therefore can be curved, lending themselves to interesting and elaborate new architectural designs. Thin film solar sheets can be applied to almost any surface, including metal, plastic, paper, or roofing materials. In terms of design, no other solar material is as versatile as this one. **They** have been in development for a long time, but it has taken about twenty years to move from research to manufacturing. Currently, there are three types of thin film panels: amorphous silicon (used in pocket calculators); cadmium telluride (cheap, but telluride availability is limited and cadmium is toxic); and copper indium Gallium diSelenide (CIGS). Of these, CIGS companies have attracted a lot of investor funds. The material is efficient, and despite being hard to work with is predicted to become dominant by 2020. Energy developers today continually try to reduce the cost per watt of energy, and to be successful these must be comparable to fossil fuels. No matter how advanced the technology, it will not be widely adopted unless it is affordable.

In the race to develop low cost, high efficiency solar materials, thin film solar panels are a solution to watch. Many are making huge financial investments into their development and China is a leader in this area. They enjoy growing acceptance in residential and commercial building design, suggesting a positive trend for future growth. Certainly there is strong market demand, from industrial builders as well as those who want efficient green energy for their own dwellings. Hopefully we will see them become more readily available soon.

(   ) 1. Where is this passage most likely to be taken from?

        (A) Scientific magazine.   (B) Interior design magazine.

        (C) Pamphlet on recycling.   (D) Medical journal.

(   ) 2. What does "**they**" in the second paragraph refer to?

        (A) Thin film solar sheets.

        (B) Traditional solar panel materials.

        (C) Roofing materials.

        (D) Solar panel companies.

(   ) 3. What is projected to be the main kind of thin film panels in the near future?

        (A) Amorphous silicon.   (B) Cadmium telluride.

        (C) CIGS.   (D) fossil fuels.

(   ) 4. According to the passage, what is true about the future of thin film solar panels?

        (A) They are the answer to the affordability of solar panels.

        (B) The United States is the leading country in the industry.

        (C) Widespread commercial usage of them doesn't seem plausible anytime soon.

        (D) They generate more pollution than traditional solar panels.

Songs of the Sea

Mariners of days gone by described hearing the ghosts of drowned sailors: loud groaning, growling, screaming, and shrieking noises that arose from the sea. Today's sailors still hear these sounds and know they are listening to the songs of whales. Several species of whales sing, but the most complex and beautiful songs are sung by the humpback whale. These are highly structured collections of notes of high, low, and intermediate pitch, which typically last from 20 to 40 minutes. The tunes are repeated over and over, with the singing often lasting for hours. Are these love songs? Many researchers think so.

Only male humpbacks sing, possibly to attract a female or to warn off other males. It seems that the songs may be performed to demonstrate fitness as a mate. A humpback may be showing how long or how loud he can sing, or how long he can hold his breath. Male humpbacks begin singing their songs in autumn as they migrate from cold waters to warmer areas where they will breed and spend the winter. Their singing sessions become longer and more frequent as the breeding season nears, and lessen when it ends.

Humpbacks in different areas of the world sing different songs, but within a social group, or school, all males sing the same song. The song changes slightly but constantly as the season progresses, perhaps with new details added or a long deep moan left out. When the song changes, all of the whales in the school begin singing the new version. Amazingly, even humpbacks that travel far from the rest of their group will sing the revised song. Scientists tracked one humpback that left his group in Hawaii to swim to Japan, all the while singing his own population's song, complete with **variations** that had occurred after he left Hawaiian waters.

Biologists are continuing to study the songs of the humpback whale in hopes of solving the mystery of their purpose and learning more about the life of this enchanting singer.

(　　) 1. What is this passage mainly about?

   (A) The mating season of humpbacks.

   (B) The singing of male humpbacks.

   (C) Mariners' stories of the sea.

   (D) Songs sung by different species of whales.

(　　) 2. What does the word "**variations**" in the third paragraph probably mean?

   (A) Accidents.　　(B) Pauses.　　(C) Changes.　　(D) Mysteries.

(　　) 3. How does a humpback demonstrate fitness by singing?

   (A) The humpback that can swim the fastest while singing is the fittest.

   (B) The humpback with the most beautiful and pleasing voice is the fittest.

   (C) The number of female humpbacks attracted shows the male's fitness.

   (D) It shows how long a humpback can hold its breath.

(　　) 4. Which of the following statements is true?

   (A) Humpbacks sing random notes by improvising most of the notes.

   (B) A humpback can sing the same new version even if it's away from its school.

   (C) The songs that humpbacks sing are war songs to scare off enemies.

   (D) Biologists have solved the mystery of how and why humpbacks sing.

Get!

詳解請參閱解析本 p. 41~

Cosmic Dust Comes from Exploding Stars

Every star gleaming in the night sky has a lifespan. And it just so happens that after growing for millions of years, when it finally comes time for stars to die, they go out with a bang. Here's what happens. When a star gets too large and has built-up more energy than can be released, the star's center, known as the core, starts to collapse. When the core finally reaches its densest and heaviest point, the collapse can go no further and the dying star's energy is released in an explosion. In the process, massive heat and light which even brighter than our sun can be observed. Astronomers refer to this as a star going supernova.

When it goes supernova, the massive explosion marking a star's destruction sends a huge volume of dust streaming out into space. This "cosmic dust" is composed of atoms of the elements that made up the star, like oxygen and carbon. Once they've cooled down, the stray atoms join together. Each particle of cosmic dust measures only around a thousandth of a centimeter across, but the cloud the dust forms will keep expanding as it moves outward from the explosion. While larger chunks of matter are permanently destroyed in a supernova explosion, evidence has emerged that cosmic dust can survive the powerful shock waves.

To learn more about the universe, scientists using advanced equipment have been studying cosmic dust in the shadow of a black hole with a powerful gravitational pull. It has been reported that one particular dust cloud created when a star went supernova 10,000 years ago contains more than enough material to make 7,000 planets the size of Earth. And in fact, it is now known for sure that the cosmic dust which comes from exploding stars is actually the source that new stars and planets are made of.

(　　) 1. What is this passage mainly about?
      (A) Supernova.   (B) Cosmic dust.
      (C) Black holes.   (D) Exploding stars.

(　　) 2. According to the passage, when does a star's life end?
      (A) When a star runs out of energy.
      (B) When a star has more energy than it can handle.
      (C) When a star collides into another star.
      (D) When a black hole swallows a star.

(　　) 3. How long is each particle of cosmic dust across?
      (A) 1000 centimeters.   (B) 1/7000 centimeter.
      (C) 1/1000 centimeter.   (D) 1/10000 centimeter.

(　　) 4. What can be inferred from the last sentence of the paragraph?
      (A) The death of a star is actually the beginning of new stars and planets.
      (B) Cosmic dust causes stars' lifespan to end in a big explosion.
      (C) The universe is too big for scientists to measure and observe with current technology.
      (D) New stars and planets won't end up exploding as they are generally smaller.

Genetically Engineered Foods: Are You Afraid?

For thousands of years, food crops have been selectively bred to produce faster-growing, high-yielding, better-tasting, and more-resistant foods. This has been a lengthy and inexact process. Today, though, scientists are able to speed this process up dramatically through genetic engineering(G.E.). They are able to select specific traits that they wish, whether they are from a different plant or even animal, and transplant the gene responsible for that trait into the target plant. By doing this, scientists have already been able to create rice with extra vitamin A, faster-growing and tastier vegetables, and even potatoes that are even able to produce their own insecticides. It looks like science is creating a better tomorrow, but sometimes **looks can be deceiving**.

There are still potential risks and dangers associated with the creation and use of G.E. foods. Short term consequences to the environment and human health may not be apparent. However, modified plants may spread into the wild and become "super weeds." Others may squeeze the original plants out of existence. Some foods may cause allergic reactions in certain people. Tests done recently on rats found that G.E. potatoes weakened their immune systems and shrank their internal organs. Would the same thing happen to humans?

Although some aspects of G.E. food development look promising, the risks and unknowns surrounding it are disturbing. At the very least, these new foods should be extensively tested for any short to long-term effects on the environment and on the health of the humans and the animals that eat them. Genetic engineering puts the power of God into Man's hands, but perhaps, this power, along with the responsibility that goes with it, is something which the level of technology today is not yet ready to handle.

(　　) 1. Which of the following risks is **NOT** mentioned in the passage?
　　(A) Genetically engineered plants may become super weeds.
　　(B) Genetically engineered plants may completely replace the original plants.
　　(C) Genetically engineered foods may weaken our immune systems.
　　(D) Genetically engineered foods may cause cancer in people.

(　　) 2. What does the word **they** in the first paragraph refer to?
　　(A) Plants.　　(B) Animals.　　(C) Traits.　　(D) G.E. foods.

(　　) 3. What does "**looks can be deceiving**" mean?
　　(A) The truth may not be as it appears to be.
　　(B) Most people are not very good at lying to others' faces.
　　(C) The truth is hidden somewhere within lies.
　　(D) Facts are sometimes disguised as lies.

(　　) 4. What is the author's attitude toward G.E. food?
　　(A) Concerned.　(B) Optimistic.　(C) Neutral.　　(D) Indifferent.

Round 18

詳解請參閱解析本 p. 44

?

When it comes to the future, it's impossible for anyone to predict exactly what it will be. However, most experts agree that artificial intelligence will definitely be a big part of it.

Artificial intelligence is often called "AI" for short. Basically speaking, it is a kind of machine intelligence. In other words, with AI, machines are able to think for themselves and take steps on their own to accomplish certain tasks. Some examples of AI include machines that can understand human speech or interpret large amounts of complex data. Self-driving cars are another example.

However, some have warned of the dangers of AI. Famous scientists like Stephen Hawking have said that we must be very careful with the development of AI and military weapons. After all, once machines have learned how to use these weapons themselves, humans might not be able to control them. Although this may sound like something from *The Terminator*, some worry that it may become a reality.

Others fear AI for another reason: it will almost certainly change the world of work. To put it bluntly, AI will enable machines to take over many of the jobs that humans do today. In fact, some predict that within ten years, more than half of today's jobs will be done by machines. This is especially true of jobs that involve repetitive tasks or data analysis.

Yet, others believe that humans will be able to adapt to AI and learn how to collaborate with these machines. To prepare for the future, leaders like Bill Gates have said that people should concentrate on Science, Technology, Engineering, and Mathematics (STEM) and look for the opportunities that AI will bring about.

Of course, no one knows what the future will bring, but it's safe to say that AI will be a part of it.

(　　) 1. What is the best title for this passage?

      (A) AI and Unemployment.   (B) AI and the Future.

      (C) STEM.   (D) The Danger of AI.

(　　) 2. What could *The Terminator* possibly refer to?

      (A) A scientific theory.   (B) A science fiction novel or movie.

      (C) A weapon of mass destruction. (D) An AI laboratory.

(　　) 3. What of the following is an example of an AI machine given in the passage?

      (A) A computer system that teaches STEM at school.

      (B) A robot pet that interacts with people.

      (C) A car that can drive itself.

      (D) A robot that can play chess.

(　　) 4. According to the passage, what kind of jobs will mostly likely to be replaced by AI in the future?

      (A) Jobs that require accuracy.

      (B) Jobs that involve repetitive tasks.

      (C) Jobs that demand a lot of strength.

      (D) Jobs that require a lot of reasoning.

Are Mobile Phones a Health Risk?

With billions of mobile phone users worldwide, media attention has focused on the possible health risks associated with these electronic devices. At the moment, there is a debate on the impact of the RF (Radio Frequency) waves that mobile phones use when making calls.

Some researchers believe that these RF waves could cause cancer. They make the atoms and molecules in the body vibrate. They claim this causes extra heat which could damage body tissue. This could increase the possibility of unusual cell growth and cancers. Others, however, believe this is nonsense because the RF waves are not the dangerous type of waves such as those from x-rays.

Nevertheless, the World Health Organization (WHO) is worried, and in 2011 issued a statement which said there is a possible increased risk of cancer from high mobile phone usage. Yet, there are not enough statistics and data for proof either way, because diseases like cancer can take decades to develop.

However, there are two areas in which mobile phones have already been proven to be health dangers. The first is road safety. Studies have demonstrated that using a mobile phone while driving greatly increases the risks of road accidents, especially if people take their hands off the steering wheel to use the phone. The second is the spread of germs. People take their phones everywhere, including the bathroom. The surface of their phones may become covered in germs which can enter the body through the skin when they touch their phones.

People currently need to consider the evidence about the health risks of RF waves and make up their own minds about how they use their mobile phones. They can take precautions by keeping their phones away from their bodies when switched on. They can make shorter calls and use traditional landline phones more often. In the case of driving and mobile phone usage, the decision has been made for them because many countries have made laws banning their use when driving. In addition, everyone should be careful to keep their mobile phones clean by wiping them frequently.

(　　) 1. What is the main idea of this passage?

    (A) Mobile phones pose a threat to our health.

    (B) WHO is worried about the overuse of mobile phones.

    (C) The danger of RF waves to our bodies needs more proof.

    (D) The use of mobile phones should be banned.

(　　) 2. What is true about RF waves?

    (A) They are short for radio frequency waves.

    (B) They are the same as waves from x-rays.

    (C) It's confirmed that they cause cancers.

    (D) All phones use them when making calls.

(　　) 3. According to the passage, why is the surface of mobile phones covered in germs?

    (A) People do not clean the surface of their mobile phones as much as possible.

    (B) The materials used to make the surface harbor germs more easily.

    (C) People use their mobile phones everywhere, including in toilets.

    (D) People allow others to use their mobile phones too much.

(　　) 4. What is the last paragraph mainly about?

    (A) The controversy over whether mobile phones cause cancer.

    (B) Steps that can be taken to prevent health risks caused by mobile phones.

    (C) The indispensable role mobile phones play in our daily life.

    (D) The many dangers of using a mobile phone too much.

Google

Today, the World Wide Web is most people's preferred source of information. With its rich collection of information and easy access, a lot of hard-to-find information is brought to our computer screen with only a tap of our finger. This is made possible by the magic of modern search engines, the most popular of which is Google. However, life online has not always been this easy.

In the early days of the web, there was simply no way one could search. In an effort to keep track of information, Yahoo created a web directory and offered it to the web. Using this directory, people could for the first time search the web. So important was this development that many still by mistake consider Yahoo a search engine!

As falling computer hardware prices and easier web access began to encourage more and more people to use the Internet, the need to find information quickly and efficiently became more and more apparent. This led to Lycos, the first true search engine to hit the web. Since then, the launch of many improved search engines has made searching the web enjoyable.

As the popularity of search engines grew, many of them began offering services like e-mail, news, weather forecasts, and chatrooms. But in doing so, they were neglecting the need to improve their search technology. It was during this period, in September 1999, that a new search engine called Google was launched.

The founders of Google, Larry Page and Sergey Brin, first worked together on a search engine project at Stanford University. Out of this grew today's best known search engine. The main reason behind Google's success is its emphasis on quality search results. While most search engine developers were content with results of 80% accuracy, Google's founders not only understood the importance of quality, but strove to better their already powerful technologies and services.

Google has since grown from strength to strength by hiring only the best. Googleplex, its headquarters in California, boasts a piano, a gym, a videogame arcade, and 3 full-time chefs! The employees at Google are not only proving good at their mission to organize every bit of information they **lay their hands on**, but are doing it in style!

(　　) 1. What is this passage mainly about?
(A) The history of search engines.
(B) How Google became successful.
(C) Yahoo and Google.
(D) A myth about the beginning of search engines.

(　　) 2. According to the passage, which of the following is the first true search engine that hit the web?
(A) Google.　　(B) Yahoo.　　(C) Lycos.　　(D) Googleplex.

(　　) 3. Which of the following statements is true about Google?
(A) It was founded solely by Larry Page.
(B) It originated from a search engine project in NASA.
(C) It has an 80% accuracy of search results.
(D) It hires the most brilliant minds in the industry.

(　　) 4. What does "**lay their hands on**" in the last paragraph mean?
(A) Obtain.　　(B) Harm.　　(C) Control.　　(D) Monitor.

英文指考致勝：考前衝刺100天

王靖賢、曲成彬、周彩蓉、蘇文賢／編著

★ 超詳盡應考策略：
針對指考七大題型，從準備考試的複習方式，到實際應考時的答題技巧，極其詳盡，應有盡有！

★ 超精選單字片語：
收錄指考必備單字1,000及片語200，並補充生字、介系詞及重點句型，讓您一書在手，完美複習！

★ 超豐富模擬試題：
20回考前模擬試題，題題切中核心，打通英文任督二脈，保證讓您越寫越有自信，大考高分So Easy！

★ 超完美作文解析：
含近十年歷屆指考試題的作文練習，附有優秀範文與詳實解析，讓您溫故知新，百戰百勝！

英語 Make Me High 系列

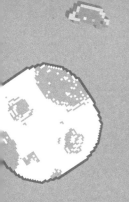

指考篇章 閱測秘技

解析本

王靖賢、蘇文賢　編著

三民書局

篇章結構－題目篇

Round 1

翻譯

　　十九世紀末期，許多移民從歐洲航向美國。他們生活貧困且別無出路，來到美國是為了尋找更美好的生活。但並不是每個人都有能夠尋得工作的專業技能，自然而然地，其中有些人就會利用他們唯一的專長，開餐廳，來服務與他們一同前來的移民。一九〇四年，有位德國移民在聖路易開了一家小餐館，他供應的其中一道菜是法蘭克福香腸。為了給顧客更好的服務，他提供每位客人一雙手套，這樣一來，客人在吃熱騰騰的香腸時就不會燙到手了。但店主人不久就發現到，許多客人離開時會將手套帶走，而清洗這些手套也要花上一大筆錢。他日思夜想，希望找出解決之道。有沒有可以不必使用手套又能保護客人免於燙傷的方法呢？最後，他想到了一個妙方。他烘烤長型麵包，再把當時暱稱為「法蘭克福」的這種香腸擺在中間。客人也都很滿意這個新點子，而這就是著名的「熱狗」的由來。

1. F

　　邏輯 在第一句中提到許多移民從歐洲航行到美國，第二句則提到這些移民既貧困又絕望。而 (F) 選項中提到 look for a better life (尋找更好的生活)，可見第二句和 (F) 選項之間存在著因果關係，因此可以確認 (F) 為正確答案。

　　同義詞 在第一句當中所提到的 the U.S.，和在 (F) 選項中的 America 為同義字。

　　代名詞 在第一句中的 many immigrants、和第二句的 They、以及第三句的代名詞 them 都是重要線索。不論是 they 或 them，所指涉的對象都是第一句的 many immigrants (移民)。作者利用這些代名詞來串連這幾句，而 (F) 選項中的 they 正是答題關鍵。

2. C

　　邏輯 在第一段的結尾處提到，由於移民缺乏找到工作的必要技能，為了謀生，有些人開設餐廳。我們可以從此訊息判斷作者接下來可能會提出與開餐廳有關的例子，而在 (C) 選項中就提到了 opened a small restaurant in St. Louis，呼應第一段最後一句的內容，也提出了具體例子，故為正確答案。

　　代名詞 再下一句中的代名詞 he 是重要線索，這代表前面一定提過某個特定的人，因此我們可以確認，

此處的 he 所指涉的對象正是在 (C) 選項的 a German immigrant，而下一句的 Frankfurt sausage (法蘭克福香腸) 也提供了相關線索：其一，Frankfurt 是德國的城市，呼應了 (C) 選項中的 German；其二則是 sausage，呼應了 (C) 選項中的 a small restaurant，因此可以確定 (C) 為正確答案。

3. E

　　邏輯 前一句提到該餐廳主人提供手套給顧客，而空格後一句則提到顧客在離開餐廳時會將手套拿走，前後兩句都重複提到 gloves，可見本題應與 gloves 有關。但在所有選項中皆沒有直接提到 gloves 這個字，因此我們必須思考餐廳主人提供手套給顧客的原因，如此一來就可以發現，(E) 選項中提到 their hands would not be burned，正是說明了手套的作用，因此可知為正確答案。

　　轉折詞 在 (E) 選項中的 in this way 也是重要線索，這個轉折詞常用來解釋前一句裡所做的某件事而後想達到的目的或是結果，因此可以確認 (E) 選項的內容是在說明手套的作用。

4. A

　　邏輯 前兩句提到，顧客在離開時會拿走手套，除此之外，清洗這些手套的成本也很高，而這暗示我們要找出這個問題的解決之道。在 (A) 選項中就提到了 the problem，所指涉的對象就是前面兩句所提到的問題，因此我們可以判斷 (A) 選項在邏輯上承接了前兩句的語意。

　　換句話說 在 (A) 選項中，除了 the problem 是以換句話說的方式來指涉前兩句所提出的問題外，其中提到的 solution，也是以換句話說的方式意指下一句的 any way to ... (任何…的方法)。

5. D

　　邏輯 作者的邏輯次序安排為：現象→問題→解決之道。前面兩段的內容分別提出了現象與問題，從邏輯上來看，最後一段應會提出關於解決之道的說明，而 (D) 選項裡提到了 a marvelous idea (一個很棒的點子)，正是暗示了解決之道。

　　換句話說 在 (D) 選項中的 a marvelous idea，就是指下一句的整個內容，因此在語意上可以達到連貫的效果。

　　轉折詞 在 (D) 選項中的 finally 是一個常常用於結論句或是事件最後發展的轉折詞，暗示了 (D) 選項可能是最後一段的主題句。

　　在本題中只有 (B) 選項不是正確答案，以 (B) 選項的內容來判斷，該選項的主題是指餐廳裡的 sausage 大

受歡迎，在邏輯上而言，應是屬於第二段的內容，然而，就第 2 題來說，因為下一句才提到餐廳主人提供了 sausage，所以在時間次序上不恰當，不能當作第 2 題的答案，而在第 3 題的敘述，文章的焦點轉移到 gloves，而不是 sausage，故也不適合。至於第 4 題，文章的焦點已經從 gloves 轉移到了由 gloves 所衍生出來的問題，亦不是在討論 sausage，故也不適合。因此，(B) 選項，無法當作任何一題的正確答案。

 Round 2

翻譯

　　平溪放天燈的活動逐漸變成中國傳統元宵節最有名的民俗活動之一。天燈又叫孔明燈，可以追溯到三國時代，當時軍隊把天燈當成發出信號的裝置。不過平溪人到了這個節慶時，為什麼要放天燈而不懸掛普通的燈籠呢？

　　清朝時，屯墾的先民從福建省來到平溪。在那個年代他們的生活極為艱困，每年過年期間，土匪會來村裡打家劫舍。此時，平溪的老弱婦孺就會帶著值錢物品到山上躲避。到了元宵節結束時，保衛家園的男丁會把燈籠放到空中，通知他們村子安然無恙的消息。一看到這樣的信號，村民就會開始返家，放天燈的習俗就是這樣來的。不過現在天燈卻是來將人們的願望傳達給上天。看著天燈一個接著一個地在夜晚的天空飄動，各自帶著小小的願望，豈不令人讚嘆？明年元宵節期間，何不親自到平溪看看這獨特且迷人的民俗活動呢？

1. F

　　邏　輯　在前一句當中提到，天燈又稱 Kong Ming lanterns (孔明燈)，可追溯到 Three Kingdoms era (三國時代)，且「孔明燈」這個名稱，可聯想到天燈應該是由孔明所發明的，加上三國時代是戰亂的時代，因此可以推測孔明燈應該和戰爭或軍隊有關係。在 (F) 選項中提到，軍隊會用天燈來當作發送信號的裝置，與此處的敘述邏輯相符，故為正確答案。

　　用　字　前一句提到的 Three Kingdoms era，與 (F) 選項中的 in those times (在那時) 都是指古代，可視為重要線索。而在三國時代，自然會聯想到與戰爭相關的事物，在 (F) 選項中的 armies (軍隊) 也與此意象相符。

2. E

　　邏　輯　前兩句提到，清朝時期來自福建的移民到平溪定居，當時的生活非常困苦。而下一句又說，到每年特定的時期，平溪地區的女人、兒童、老人會到山區躲藏，並隨身帶著貴重物品。(E) 選項中提到，每年新年，有成群的強盜到村莊裡搶劫。由這兩句的描述可以看出，(E) 選項和下一句之間有明顯的因果關係，而這就是為什麼女人、兒童和老人要帶著貴重物品躲到山上去。因此 (E) 選項為正確答案。

　　用　字　在下一句的 go to the mountains to hide，以及 carrying valuables with them 等，都在暗示這些人是為了躲避劫掠，與 (E) 選項中的 bandit gangs 以及 rob people 有密切的相關性。

3. C

　　邏　輯　本題前兩句提到，平溪的村民為了躲避強盜的劫掠，會在新年期間帶著貴重物品逃到山上。(C) 選項中提到，新年結束時，留守家園的男性會放天燈以表示一切安全。而下一句則提到，看到這樣的訊息，人們就會開始回家。由此可以看出，(C) 選項和前兩句之間是依照時間的描述，且 (C) 選項與前一句之間也有因果關係，因此符合此處的邏輯次序。

　　用　字　(C) 選項中提到發送信號的方式是 send lanterns skyward，這樣的訊息是用「看」的，而下一句則提到 seeing this message，使兩者之間的用字完全吻合。

　　同義詞　在本題當中，最重要的關鍵線索就是在本題下一句中提到的 message。這個字與 (C) 選項中的 signal 雖然詞性不同，但都是指同樣的事，因此可以視為同義字，故 (C) 為正確答案。

4. A

　　邏　輯　在第一段的最後，作者提出了一個問題，也就是為什麼住在平溪的人們要在新年期間放天燈，而不是像一般人那樣掛上傳統的燈籠呢？而在第二段就說明了此種習俗的由來，故到了第二段的最後一句，就會做個總結。(A) 選項中提到了「由此衍生出放天燈的習俗」，正好呼應本段的內容並提出結論，故為最適合的答案。

　　用　字　在 (A) 選項提到的 the custom of launching sky lanterns 是關鍵線索，因為這正是第二段的主旨，讓我們確認 (A) 是此處的正確答案。

5. D

　　邏　輯　前一句提到，天燈現在是人們的把願望傳達給上天的方式，而在 (D) 選項中也提到了一盞接著一盞承載著人們小小願望的天燈升向夜空的景象，可見

兩者所描述的是同一件事，因此可以推論 (D) 選項為正確答案。

用字 前一句提到了 Heaven，而在 (D) 選項中則提到了 the night sky，這兩者之間具有密切關係，且也相互呼應。

重複 在前一句以及 (D) 選項中都重複提到了 wish 這個字，暗示這兩句之間具有關聯性。

> 在本篇題目中唯一沒有使用的選項是 (B)。在 (B) 選項中提到了 Kong Ming lanterns，而這個說法在文章中曾經出現過的地方，就在第 1 題前面，因此乍看之下 (B) 選項似乎也可以是第 1 題的答案。然而，(B) 選項敘述孔明燈是用來警告人們某個地區是危險的，但是在第二段則說明，天燈的作用是告訴人們一切平安，可見 (B) 選項為非。

Round 3

翻譯

　　用音樂來增進健康已經有相當久遠的歷史了，但是用音樂來幫助學習能力卻是最近幾十年的事。比利時有位身兼精神科醫師和教育學家的喬吉·羅札諾夫醫生注意到，有許多前來求診的病人受到一種常見但不知名的疾病所困擾。他的研究發現了一項驚人的結論：這些人的疾病是由不良的教學方法所引起。因此，羅札諾夫開始實驗不同的方法來改善學習經驗，其中一個方法就是聽音樂。據羅札諾夫醫生推論，如果音樂能降低手術的痛苦，當然也能降低學習的痛苦。他先教學生怎麼放鬆，然後一邊放著古典樂作為背景音樂，一邊唸唸資訊給他們聽。然而，不是所有的古典樂都適合，只有一被稱為巴洛克的音樂類型才有效。雖然可以適用於所有學科，但羅札諾夫醫生的方法對語言學習特別有效。據報導，有些使用他這種方法的班級一天能學會四百個新字，也難怪羅札諾夫醫生的方法在西方又稱為「超級學習法」。

1. C

邏輯 本文的邏輯次序安排為現象→問題→解決之道。前一句提到了 Dr. Georgi Lozanov 注意到的一個現象，而下一句則提到他開始實驗一些解決問題的方法，因此可推論此處應為討論前一句現象背後的問題，而 (C) 選項當中提到「the disease was caused by ...」，正是暗示了「問題」的存在，故選 (C)。

代名詞 在前一句裡的主詞是 Dr. Georgi Lozanov，而 (C) 選項中的代名詞 He 可合理推測對象正是 Dr. Georgi Lozanov，故為重要的答題線索。此外，在 (C) 的 their，經由判斷可知所指涉的對象為前一句的 many patients。故在 (C) 選項中的兩個代名詞分別指涉了前一句裡兩個重要的名詞，因此可以推論 (C) 為正確答案。

重複 在前一句以及 (C) 選項中都提到了 disease，因此可以判斷作者利用重複這個關鍵字，來達到語意上的連貫。

2. E

邏輯 前一句提到 Lozanov 實驗了各種不同的方法來改善學習經驗，這就是在尋找「解決之道」。作者接下來依循著「廣泛籠統→具體明確」的邏輯次序來說明後續發展，因此 (E) 選項中的 listening to music 就符合此種具體明確的要求。

代名詞 在 (E) 選項中的 these 所指涉的對象就是前一句裡的 various techniques，可視為重要的答題線索。

重複 在 (E) 選項和下一句當中都提到了 music 這個字，因此可以得知這兩句在語意的邏輯上是連貫的，由此推論 (E) 選項為正確答案。

3. D

邏輯 前一句裡提到了 take the pain out of learning，下一句則提及 classical music plays in the background。而在 (D) 選項中的 how to relax 與上述的兩個概念相呼應，故在語意邏輯方面是連貫的。

代名詞 由句意來判斷，(D) 選項中的 students 為下一句當中的代名詞 them 所指涉的對象，因此可以推論 (D) 為承接前後兩句的正確答案。

4. F

邏輯 在前一句當中出現了一個很重要的轉折詞 however，表示語意有所轉變。前面文章裡提到用古典音樂來提升學習的成效，而在這裡語氣轉變，作者提到 not all forms of classical music are suitable，因此可以合理推論「只有」某些或某一種才適合。在 (F) 選項中一開始就提到「only a special type ...」，呼應了前一句的語氣轉變，故為正確答案。

重複 在前一句提到了 classical music，而在 (F) 選項中則提到 Baroque music (巴洛克音樂)，這兩句都與音樂有關，而且 Baroque music 正是古典音樂的其中一種，因此可知作者利用 classical music 一詞達成語意上的連貫。

5. B

邏輯 前一句提到了 Dr. Lozanov 的方法在 language learning 方面特別有效。作者接下來會提出一些證據來支持這個說法。(B) 選項中的 learn 400 words in a day 正是一個可以用來支持上述說法的論點，故為正確答案。

同義詞 在前一句中提到的 Dr. Lozanov's technique，與 (B) 選項中的 his method 和下一句的 Dr. Lozanov's method 為同義詞，也是貫穿這三句的關鍵線索，所以可推論 (B) 為正確答案。

代名詞 在 (B) 選項中的代名詞所有格 his 是重要的線索，可以看出指涉對象正是前一句的 Dr. Lozanov's 以及下一句的 Dr. Lozanov's，故 (B) 為銜接前後兩句的句子。

> 在本篇題目中 (A) 選項非答案。從內容來看，(A) 選項提到了 His techniques 以及 proven successful (被證實是成功的) 等關鍵字，可以判斷這句話在說明 Dr. Lozanov 所提出的方法的結果。如果這一句話是文章中的一部分，那麼應該會出現在文章中後段，也就是可能作為第 4 題或第 5 題的答案。但在第 4 題的前一句語氣出現轉折，與 (A) 選項的語氣不符。而在第 5 題討論的主題是 language learning，與 (A) 選項中所提到的 how to solve problems by themselves 亦不符，因此 (A) 選項不能當作這兩題的答案。

 Round 4

翻譯

導盲犬協助盲人或是視力受損者四處走動。不過不是每一種狗都能被訓練來執行這項任務，大部分的導盲犬學校訓練的是黃金獵犬、拉不拉多和德國牧羊犬。這三種品種的狗聰明、聽話、友善而且精力旺盛。

最早的導盲犬是一隻叫做「巴弟」的德國牧羊犬，巴弟的飼主是住在瑞士的桃樂希‧尤斯特絲女士，原本訓練德國牧羊犬是為了協助警務工作。後來於一九二七年，尤斯特絲女士在報紙上寫了一篇文章，內容是有關德國訓練狗來協助失明的退伍軍人。有位美國年輕人墨里斯‧法蘭克因為聽說了這篇文章，就寫了一封信給她。他寫道：「有很多像我一樣的盲人都討厭依賴別人，請幫助我，我也會幫

助他們，訓練我，然後我會把我的狗帶回來告訴這裡的人，盲人是能夠完完全全獨立的。」那封信讓法蘭克在瑞士待了五個禮拜的時間，學習讓巴弟來引導他。

法蘭克和巴弟回到家鄉後，他們行遍全國，推廣導盲犬的訓練及使用。一九二九年，尤斯特絲女士前往美國，在法蘭克與巴弟的協助之下，她於田納西州那什維爾市成立第一座導盲犬學校「The Seeing Eye」，這間學校帶給學員重拾獨立自主的希望。而今「The Seeing Eye」仍於紐澤西州的墨里斯城持續運作。

1. C

邏輯 空格前一句提到了導盲犬的任務，而 (C) 選項提到並不是所有種類的狗都能夠執行這項任務，空格後一句則提到大多數受訓的導盲犬的種類，因此可以看出空格後一句的內容是進一步詳細說明 (C) 選項，兩者之間具有密切的關係，因此 (C) 選項為此處的正確答案。

用字 在 (C) 選項中的 the task 所指的就是前一句的 help blind or visually impaired people get around。

重複 在前一句、(C) 選項、以及下一句當中都重複提到 dog 這個字，暗示 dog 是這三個句子的共同主題。

2. E

邏輯 上一句提到了有哪些種類的狗會被訓練為導盲犬，而 (E) 選項則提到這三個品種的狗比其他狗更為 intelligent、obedient、friendly，以及 energetic，由此可以得知，(E) 選項的內容與上一句有明顯的因果關係。其邏輯次序的安排為「提出現象或結果→說明原因」，因此可知 (E) 選項為正確答案。

用字 在前一句裡提到了通常被訓練成為導盲犬的三種不同品種的狗，而 (E) 選項中也提到了 three breeds (三個品種)，與上一句互相呼應。

3. F

邏輯 本文的第二段和第三段的安排方式依循著時間順序，在時間上的安排是由「先到後」的順敘法。以本題來說，在前一句先提到了 Mrs. Eustis 這個人，而在 (F) 選項中用了 then 來表示時間順序的重要轉折詞，暗示 (F) 選項的時間順序。在 (F) 選項中提到 Mrs. Eustis 寫了一篇文章，而在下一句裡則提到 Morris Frank 聽到關於這篇文章的消息。因此可以看出，(F) 選項所敘述的內容，符合時間順序的要求。

代名詞 在下一句當中所提到的代名詞 her，其指涉的對象就是 (F) 選項中的 Mrs. Eustis。

重複 在前一句以及 (F) 選項中都提到了 Mrs. Eustis，作者正是利用重複同樣的人物，使這兩句之間產生連貫性。除此之外，在 (F) 選項中以及下一句裡面，也都重複使用了 article 這個字，因此也可以用來確認 (F) 選項確實為兩個句子之間的重要銜接句。

4. D

邏輯 本段同樣採順敘法：Mrs. Eustis 訓練出第一隻導盲犬 Buddy→她在報紙上寫了一篇文章→Morris Frank 聽說了這篇文章並寫信給 Mrs. Eustis→Morris Frank 到瑞士接受與導盲犬合作的訓練。因此可以看出 (D) 選項為正確答案。

因果關係 從前段文字裡可以得知，Frank 寫了一封信給 Mrs. Eustis，而在 (D) 選項裡則提到正是那封信使得 Frank 留在 Switzerland 五個星期，由此可知 (D) 選項的內容正是前面事件所造成的結果。

重複 在第 3 題的下一句提到了 letter 這個字，而 (D) 選項中也重複此字，為重要答題線索。除此之外，在本段第二句以及 (D) 選項中也都重複提到了 Switzerland 而在本段第一句和 (D) 選項中也重複提到了 Buddy 這隻導盲犬，因此可以看出 (D) 選項與本段內容關係密切。

5. B

邏輯 本段為順敘法：Frank 和導盲犬 Buddy 從瑞士返回美國，並到處宣揚導盲犬的益處→ Mrs. Eustis 也來到美國，成立了第一所導盲犬學校。由此可知，(B) 選項正好符合此處的時間發展次序。

代名詞 在 (B) 選項中的代名詞 she，所指涉的對象正是上一句裡的 Mrs. Eustis。

重複 在 (B) 選項中提到了 the first guide dog school，而在下一句也提到了 school。school 一字接連在兩句中重複出現，為重要的線索。除此之外，在本段第一句，以及在 (B) 選項中也重複提到了 Buddy 和 Frank，可看出 (B) 選項與本段關係密切。

本篇題目中唯一沒有使用的選項為 (A)。(A) 選項提到，Eustis 與 Frank 成立了一個基金會。由於本文是依時間順序來撰寫的文章，而 Eustis 與 Frank 兩人認識的經過是發生在第二段的最後一句，也就是 Frank 到瑞士去接受訓練時，因此以時間順序來判斷，(A) 選項的敘述內容應該會出現在最後一段裡，如此一來在時間順序才比較合理。然而，由最後一段的倒數第二句得知，Eustis 女士所成立的是

school，不是 foundation，因此 (A) 並不能成為第 5 題的正確答案。

 Round 5

翻譯

雖然一八六五年的內戰 (南北戰爭) 解放了南方的奴隸，但當時的有色人種仍被當成次等公民，直到將近一世紀後，他們才開始要求身為美國公民的權利。一九五五年，馬丁‧路德‧金恩博士帶領五十萬人抗議市政府的公車搭乘制度。他們拒搭公車，直到業者更改非裔美國人必須坐在公車後半部的政策。這項聯合抵制的行動持續了約一年，直到最高法院最終裁定公車上的種族隔離是違法的。和平抗爭最後終於獲得成功。

在抗爭成功之後，金恩博士決定要運用非暴力的思想，致力於改變其他歧視的法律。他四處演講，宣揚他的非暴力抵制觀點，他鼓勵黑人同胞使用非暴力的靜坐、遊行和示威來爭取充分的自由與平等。他因為打破歧視性的法律條文而遭到逮捕，進出監獄數十次。他鼓舞了全球以和平手段抗議不公平的法律。金恩博士於一九六四年獲頒諾貝爾和平獎，這是對他成就的高度肯定。然而在四年後，悲劇發生了，這位熱愛和平自由的鬥士在出席田納西州孟斐斯市的人權大會時遭到暗殺，離開了愛他與崇敬他的群眾。

1. C

邏輯 在前一句裡提到，美國內戰於 1865 年結束後，雖然黑奴被解放了，但是有色人種 continued to be treated as inferiors (持續被當作低賤的人民)。此處的邏輯與 (C) 選項中所提到的敘述相呼應。因為不被當作平等的人民來對待，所以才必須去要求應得的權利。除此之外，在前一句提到了 1865 年，下一句提到了 1955 年，兩者相差近 100 年，剛好就是 (C) 選項最後面提到的 almost a century later。在時間順序的邏輯上是正確的，故 (C) 為正確答案。

代名詞 在 (C) 選項中的代名詞 They 所指涉的對象，就是前一句裡的 people of color，作者利用代名詞使兩個句子連貫。

2. B

邏輯 從本段第三句開始，文章主要開始敘述 Dr. King 所領導的一場抗議活動。在敘述事件時，常常

會依時間順序來敘述，較能使讀者瞭解事情的先後次序。在空格的前兩句敘述了事件一開始的情況，而在 (B) 選項中則提到該起事件持續一年，並且後半段提到了 finally 這個字，以說明整起事件最後的發展，完整交待了整個事件。再者，下一句裡的 succeeded 也呼應了 (B) 選項後半段的美國最高法院之判決。因此，不論在時間順序或語意連貫性方面，(B) 都是正確的答案。

用 字 在前兩句與下一句裡提到了 protest (抗議)、refused (拒絕) 等字，這兩個字與 (B) 選項中的 boycott (聯合抵制) 具有高度的相關性，可聯想在一起。在前一句中所提到的拒絕搭乘公車的行動，其實正是 (B) 選項中 boycott 的具體內容，因此得知 (B) 選項為合理答案。

3. **E**

邏 輯 本篇文章在邏輯次序方面主要是依照時間來安排，因此在 (E) 選項中提到的 After this success，很清楚地暗示了這個句子所要提到的事情正是上一段抗議成功之後發生的事，在時間次序上完全吻合整篇文章的安排。

同義詞 在 (E) 選項中的 nonviolent tactics (非暴力的思想) 與下一句的 philosophy of nonviolent resistance (非暴力抵抗的哲學)，雖然說法並不完全相同，但是被視為是同義詞。

代名詞 經由句意判斷，可知在下一句裡的代名詞 He 所指涉的對象就是 (E) 選項中的 Dr. King，據此得知 (E) 選項為此處的正確答案。

重 複 上一段的最後一句裡提到了 succeed 這個字，而在 (E) 選項中也提到了 success，這兩個字為同義，雖不同詞性，也可視為是同一個字的重複，其目的在於使文章產生連貫性。在 (E) 選項與下一句裡面也都重複使用了 nonviolent (非暴力的) 這個字，故可知這兩句之間具有密切的關聯性。

4. **A**

邏 輯 前一句提到 Dr. King 到處演講以宣揚他的非暴力抵抗思想，而 (A) 選項中則提到他鼓勵黑人採取一些非暴力的措施以取得自由平等。因此可以看出，(A) 選項正是在說明前一句裡 Dr. King 四處演講的目的，在邏輯發展上相當合理。

用 字 在前一句的 preach (宣揚) 一字通常帶有「鼓勵」人們去做某事的意味，此種涵意正好與 (A) 選項中的 urge (力勸、鼓勵) 相似，因此可推論出 (A) 選項為正確答案。

重 複 在本段的前兩句 (包括第 3 題的答案)、以及 (A) 選項中都重複使用了 nonviolent 這個字，因此

可以看出作者以該字把這些句子連結在一起。

5. **D**

邏 輯 本段一開始就以 Dr. King 為了黑人民權所做的努力作為敘述主題，並且依時間次序來敘述。本題的前一句更是提到他已經成為全世界人民的 inspiration，因此可以推論出 Dr. King 已獲得全世界的推崇與認可，而在 (D) 選項中的 the Nobel Peace Prize 以及 in recognition of his achievements (認同他的成就) 等，在邏輯上為合理的發展結果，故可推知 (D) 為正確答案。

換句話說 在下一句中的 his achievements，則是指 (D) 選項中的 protest against unjust laws (抗議不公正的法律)，因此可以得知前一句與 (D) 選項的句子是相呼應的。

重 複 在前一句裡提到了 peacefully，與 (D) 選項中的 Peace 正是作者刻意重複的關鍵字，可作為答題線索。

在本篇題目中，只有 (F) 選項沒有被選到。以其內容來判斷，句子前半段提到 After receiving the prize，而在整篇文章中唯一提到 prize 的地方，為第 5 題答案 (D) 的敘述裡所提到的 Nobel Peace Prize。然而，(F) 選項的開頭是 After，表示該選項所描述的事情發生在得獎之後，而 (D) 為是第 5 題的答案，所以 (F) 選項所描述的事情當然不可能有對應的題目。

Round 6

翻譯

　　想到大象的時候，你可能會想到牠的長鼻子、大耳朵、象牙或是龐大的體積。除了有長長的鼻子和尖銳的長牙，牠的行為更是令人驚訝。舉例來說，某隻大象死亡後，其他大象會圍過來，站在死掉的大象旁邊，用象鼻的前端撫摸牠的身體。有時候，牠們還會在某隻大象死後一段時間，用鼻子捲起死去大象的骨頭或象牙，在象群中傳遞。這些古怪的行為在一天內可以進行四小時之久，並且持續五到六天。沒有人知道這些儀式真正的原因，但這讓我們知道，大象想必帶有情緒和感情。

　　象群的家族結構井然有序。公象年紀達到十四、五歲左右時，他們便準備要交配並且離開家族團體。而母象則終其一生守著團體。帶領象群的是年紀最長的母象，她也主導了象群的行動，危險來臨時她

會向其他的大象示警，這種呼叫通知象群，讓牠們聚集在幼小成員的四周，加以保護。

如你所見，大象是很有趣的動物，不過大象的數量正快速減少當中，主要是人類為了掠取象牙而殺害許多大象。除此之外，大象生存繁衍的地區逐漸被改建為城市、住家和農地之用。除非儘速採取行動，否則有一天大象或許會絕種，步上恐龍的後塵，想到便讓人覺得難過啊！

1. D

邏輯 前一句提到的內容如 trunk、ears、tusk、huge sizes 等，均屬於大象外觀，而下一句的描述卻偏向於行為。由此可以看出論述的方向與重點發生改變，因此本題必定得發揮承接上句、開啟新方向的功能，而 (D) 選項能使這三句在邏輯上整個連貫。

轉折詞 在 (D) 選項中所使用的轉折詞 besides (除了…之外) 亦是一個明顯的提示。在使用 besides 時，通常會先把前面提過的事物稍微重複，接著提出其它的論點。此處則是重複提及前一句的 trunk 與 tusk，因此可以判斷 (D) 選項為正確答案。

重複 在前一句當中提到了大象的 trunk (象鼻)、tusk (象牙) 這兩項特徵，而在 (D) 選項中亦重複出現，暗示這兩句之間具有連貫性。

2. A

邏輯 本題已經是第一段的最後一句，通常作者會在這裡針對該段的主題或內容作簡單的總結。而在第一段裡，大部分的內容都在描述大象特別的行為，像是在大象死亡後，其他大象會圍繞在遺體旁邊，並且用象鼻尖端去碰觸屍體。此種行為會讓人聯想到某種儀式，因此正好呼應 (A) 選項中的 these rituals。除此之外，(A) 選項還用了 emotions 和 feelings 這兩個字，與前面句子所描述的情景相符合。因此可以推知 (A) 為本題的正確答案。

3. B

邏輯 本段的主題句相當明確，旨在討論象群的家庭結構，而且牠們的家庭結構是有條理的。從 family structure 一詞可以想到，所有動物的家庭基本上都是由雄性和雌性所組成，不難推斷接下來應該會針對不同性別來作說明。在本題的下一句裡提到了 females，更用了轉折詞 however，表示此處所要提出的論述和前面的事物相反。根據以上線索，可以反推得知本題的討論對象為 males，故答案為敘述中有提到 the males 的選項 (B)。

重複 在前一句和 (B) 選項中都提到了 group

一字，可視為關鍵字詞的重複，亦是答題的重要線索。

4. F

邏輯 在前一句中的 warn、danger 等字，與 (F) 選項中的 protect 具有關聯性，因為遇上「危險」時，通常要去「保護」族群中較為弱小的成員，因此 (F) 選項在邏輯上是針對前一句的合理延伸。

重複 本題最重要的線索，就是前一句中的 calling 和 (F) 選項中的 this call，這兩個字雖然詞性不同，但字義相同。重複使用關鍵字，將這兩句聯結在一起，以完整表達象群遇到危險時的反應。

5. E

邏輯 在最後一段裡，從第二句開始就提到象群的數量 decreasing fast。第三句提到象群的棲息地被人類破壞並改為城市或農田等。順著這個邏輯，可以合理推測若這種情況一直持續下去，象群可能會因此而滅絕，(E) 選項的敘述正好符合此種因果關係中的「結果」，故為正確答案。

用字 在前兩句裡提到的 decreasing 以及 killed 等字，都和 (E) 選項中的 extinct 有緊密的關聯性。在 (E) 選項中甚至提到了已經滅絕的 dinosaur 來作為類比，加以突顯大象所面臨的危機。在下一句中連用了兩個 sad，也呼應了 (E) 選項的主題，讓人聯想到大象的處境堪憂。

本篇題目當中，只有 (C) 選項沒有被選到。以其敘述的內容來判斷，裡面提到母象主要負責的工作是照顧幼象，因此可以推測其主題應該與第二段裡的 family structure 相符合。換句話說，(C) 可能是第 3 題或第 4 題的答案。在第 3 題中，似乎可以把 (C) 當作合理的答案，但是在下一句裡的轉折詞 however 則強烈暗示，第 3 題的句子必須與該句所討論的主題不同。由於 (C) 選項和下一句的討論對象都是 female elephants，明顯不符合 however 所表達的轉折語氣，因此無法成為第 3 題的答案。第 4 題則是承接上一句的句意，主要是說明象群遇到危險時的應變方法，與 (C) 的內容不符，所以亦不能當作正確答案。

 Round 7

翻譯
歷來大部分學生高中畢業後會直接進到學院或大學就讀。但有些學生決定走不同的路。他們先過

一年的「空檔年」，然後再接受高等教育。

簡單來講，空檔年是高中和大學中間的一段休息時間，也可以是學院和研究所間的空檔。空檔年通常長達一年，有時也叫「休假年」。

空檔年的目的是給學生探索的時間。大多數人利用這個機會去世界各地旅遊。有些人在各國當背包客，有些人會在某地找工作並工作幾個月。

普遍認為，空檔年開始於英國。不過，空檔年現在已受各國學生歡迎，包括加拿大、澳洲，甚至台灣。

空檔年已受歡迎到有人會過不只一次的空檔年！舉例來說，現在有些年輕人換工作時也會休息一陣子和旅遊，直到下一個工作開始。人們開始稱呼這段時間為「生涯休息」，這也正漸漸被業界接受。

如果你打算過一段空檔年，在開始之前你必須先做幾件事。首先，做好調查並嘗試和有空檔年經驗的人交流。接著，務必在事前做好規劃，包括預算規畫——確定好你有足夠的錢過這一年。最後，玩得開心！畢竟，空檔年是一段探索和學習的時間，離開校園、走入世界！

1. F

轉折詞 在 (F) 選項中的轉折詞 however 扮演一個關鍵角色，表示 (F) 選項中所提到的事，和前一句是不同的、相反的。而 (F) 選項中的 a different path 正好相互呼應，接著由下一句來說明內容，因此在語意上 (F) 選項和下一句是具有連貫性。

換句話說 在 (F) 選項中提到，有些學生決定走一條不同的路，這件事所指的就是下一句裡提到的 They are taking a "gap year" first (他們先過一個「空檔年」)。若能迅速判斷出這兩個說法其實是指同一件事，答案即呼之欲出。

代名詞 下一句裡的代名詞 they，指涉的對象就是 (F) 選項中的 some students，故答案為 (F)。

重複 在前一句和 (F) 選項中都重複提到 students，而作者正是以這個方式來產生兩句之間的連貫性，因此我們可以得知此為重要的答題線索。

2. C

邏輯 作者在第一段裡提出 gap year 的概念，第二段就會開始針對這個概念進行深入的說明。本段第一句提到 gap year 通常是指在高中和大學之間的一段空窗期，而 (C) 選項則舉例，它也可以指在大學和研究所之間的短暫休息時期。由此可以看出這兩句在邏輯上

有銜接性，也就是「高中→大學→研究所」的次序。故 (C) 選項為正確答案。

同義詞 在前一句裡提到的 a period of time off (一段空檔的時間)，其涵意與 (C) 選項中的 break 相同，因此可以確認這兩句所談論的主題一致，而且有密切關係。

代名詞 在 (C) 選項中的代名詞 It 所指涉的對象，就是本段第一句裡的 gap year (空檔年)，是重要的答題線索。

3. E

換句話說 在前一句裡提到的 explore，即 (E) 選項中的 travel to other parts of the world，也就是說，(E) 選項的內容正是在更進一步解釋前一句所提出的 explore 概念。同樣地，在 (E) 選項中的 other parts of the world，其實和下一句的 different countries 也相互呼應，因而使這三句環環相扣，產生了意義上的連貫。

代名詞 在 (E) 選項中的代名詞 most，所指涉的對象為前一句中的 students，因而使得兩句之間產生密切的關聯性。

4. A

邏輯 由前一句可以得知，原本的 gap year 是指學生在求學過程中暫停學業一年，去世界各地壯遊或工作。進入職場後，許多人也想效法此種方式，在換工作的空檔時去旅遊充電一下。由於時間點是在進入職場工作之後，因此在邏輯上以 (A) 選項中所提到的 a career gap 是最適合的。

同義詞 在前一句提到的 job 一字，與 (A) 選項中所提到的 career 可以視為同義字，都是指「工作」或是「職業」，因此可以幫助我們判斷這兩句之間具有密切的關係。

代名詞 在 (A) 選項中的代名詞 This，所指涉的就是前一句後半段所提到的「... they may also take some time off to travel ...」這件事。

5. B

邏輯 作者在本段的主題句中提到「..., there are a few things you can do ...」，這裡的 a few things 是重要的關鍵線索，因為通常當作者這麼說，就代表接下來會針對這些 things 進行說明。一般來說都會用 for example 的說法來破題，並用條列的方式來舉例。而 (B) 選項提到「首先，你要先做研究以及…」。祈使句的語氣表示作者是直接對讀者溝通，這也和本段主題句的口吻一致，故可得知 (B) 選項為正確答案。

轉折詞 作者在 (B) 選項中用了 First 這個轉折詞，且在下一句用了 Next，在倒數第二句用了 Finally，

這些都是重要的線索，作者以條列的方式進行說明。只要看出這些轉折詞之間的關係，即可簡單地找到正確答案。

> 在本篇題目中唯一沒有使用的選項是 (D)。在 (D) 選項中提到「空檔年能幫助人們發現真實的自己」，由敘述內容來判斷，其主題是在談論 gap year 的影響或是目的。然而，在本篇文章中，第一段先提出 gap year 這個概念，第二段討論何為 gap year，第三段討論 gap year 的起源以及目前受歡迎的狀況，第四段討論 gap year 變成 career gap 的情況，最後一段則是討論如何好好利用 gap year。換句話說，在這些段落當中都沒有主題與 gap year 的影響或目的有關，因此 (D) 選項的描述與內文不符。

 Round 8

翻譯

　　你怕體重過重嗎？你想要看起來更迷人嗎？對很多人來說，這兩個答案都是肯定的，不過他們也常發現要減輕多餘的脂肪不是那麼簡單。吃少一點是一種方法，不過飢餓感是難以忍受，更糟的是，你可能得到厭食症，這是一種不肯足量進食而變得極度消瘦的疾病。一般人考慮的另一個方法是抽脂，這是一種從身體特定部位移除脂肪的手術，不過這項選擇費用高且可能不安全，因為所有的手術治療都帶有一定的風險。

　　運動可能是保持苗條的最佳方法，這個方法健康、無痛且保證不貴，應該適合所有的人。的確，只要從事最普遍的有氧運動，像是健走和跑步，每個人都能減重。像舉重這類的運動也很不錯。

　　運動對每個人都有益處，即使體重沒有過重的人也一樣。剛開始運動時你可能覺得筋疲力盡，但時間一久，你一定會習以為常，進而發覺規律運動的好處，你不只會覺得身體更強壯了，連心態上也會更快樂、更有自信。這些改變絕對會進一步激勵你繼續往正確的方向走下去，何不馬上開始，發現自己驚人的「正向運動循環」呢？

1. B

　　邏　輯　在前一句中，句尾提到飢餓的感覺可能會相當地難以忍受的，而在 (B) 選項的開頭使用 even worse (更糟的是)，接著描述 anorexia (厭食症) 的症狀，表示如果不進食的話，可能到後來會罹患厭食症。

在邏輯上來說，這是一種漸進式的次序，先提比較不嚴重的狀況，再進一步提到比較嚴重的情形。

　　重　複　在前一句和 (B) 選項中都提到了 eat 這個字，因此可以得知兩句主題都和「吃」有關，作者利用這個字使句子產生語意的連貫性，eat 這個字重複出現的情況，正是重要的答題線索。

2. D

　　邏　輯　作者在本段中提出了兩種人們常用來減重的方法：吃少一點以及局部抽脂手術。作者在提出少吃一點之後，則警告讀者這麼做可能會導致厭食症。而本題接在抽脂手術的後面，就邏輯上，作者勢必會對抽脂手術這個方法提出警告，或是進一步描述其缺點。而 (D) 選項中提到了這個手術昂貴且有時不安全，正好符合答題邏輯，故為正確答案。

　　換句話說　在 (D) 選項中提到的 this option，所指的正是前一句提到的 liposuction (抽脂手術)，這也是我們能夠加以利用的答題線索。

　　同義詞　在前一句中提到了 surgery (外科手術) 這個字，而在 (D) 選項中也提到了 surgical treatments (外科療法)，這兩者雖然用字有點差異，但其實都是指同一件事物，因此可以確認這兩句的主題一致。

3. A

　　邏　輯　作者在前兩段先提出兩種比較不好的減重方式，其目的是要當作對比，以襯托出本段所提出的方法和好處。作者在本段就先以 taking exercise 是最好的方法來開頭，在 (A) 選項中更把此種方式描述為 healthy, pain-free and definitely inexpensive，以突顯出本段方法的優點與好處。因此 (A) 選項在邏輯上符合此處的需要，故為正確答案。

　　用　字　前一句的 the best way，與 (A) 選項中的 suitable for all people，這兩者說法雖然不盡相同，卻有異曲同工之處。一般而言，最好的方法通常都能夠適合所有人，所以這兩種說法在邏輯上是相符合的。除此之外，在 (A) 選項中的 this solution，所指的就是前一句裡的 taking exercise 這件事，這兩句也因而產生連貫性。

4. F

　　邏　輯　本段所談論的主題為「運動所帶來的益處」，例如使人們身體變得更健康，心情也更快樂、更有自信，而 (F) 選項也提到運動會為人們帶來許多好處，與本段主題相符，故適合當作主題句。除此之外，作者在本段中大量使用 you 這個代名詞，其目的就是要讓讀者覺得作者給予自己建議，使作者的論點更具有說服力。而在 (F) 選項中亦採取相同方法，故 (F) 選項為正確答案。

同義詞 在 (F) 選項中的 taking exercise 與下一句最後的 working out，廣泛來說都可以指「運動」一詞，因此可視為同義詞，使前後兩句產生連貫性。

重複 不論是在 (F) 選項、或是在該段的其他句子，作者都不斷地重複使用 you 這個代名詞，其目的就是要使敘述語氣一致，故可視為重要的線索。除此之外，在 (F) 選項中以及下一句的後半段，也都有提到運動所帶來的 benefits (益處)，因此也為解題的關鍵線索之一。

5. C

邏輯 在本段的最後一句，作者以問句反問讀者為何不開始運動。表面上是問句，事實上是一種呼籲，即「鼓勵」讀者開始培養運動的習慣，此種立場與 (C) 選項中所提到的 encourage you to go on in the right direction 一致，因此兩者在邏輯上吻合。

用字 在 (C) 選項中提到的 these changes，就是指前一句裡的 physically stronger、mentally happier and more confident。除此之外，在 (C) 選項中的 right direction，與 positive exercise cycle 也具有密切的相關性，而這些用字都是重要的答題線索。

> 在本篇題目中唯一沒有使用的選項是 (E)。在 (E) 選項中提到「現在有愈來愈多的人們傾向於進行整形手術，使他們自己看起來更漂亮」。就語意內容來判斷，因為作者在第一段中曾經提到 Do you want to look more attractive?，而 more attractive 和 prettier 幾乎可視為同義，因此，(E) 選項適合出現在第一段。然而，在第一段其它的內容裡，都是在提減重的兩種常見方式，也就是少吃及抽脂 (liposuction)，這兩者與整形手術 (plastic surgery) 並無絕對的關係，因此 (E) 選項並不適合當作第 1 題或第 2 題的答案。

Round 9

翻譯

現今社會中，壓力已經成為影響各年齡層的廣泛問題，我們都曾經歷過壓力，也許來自於學校、職場、家庭方面的問題，或甚至在城市的車水馬龍中開車也可能是壓力的來源。有時候適度的壓力能讓我們在生活中完成更多的事情，但是過多的壓力其實可能讓一個人身體產生疾病，甚至造成死亡。

一項經過設計的研究，目的是要找出壓力如何導致疾病。他們找來了一群體內都有一種常見病毒的人來進行這項研究。這一群人被分為兩個小組，其中一組是常處在壓力狀態之下而活得不快樂的人，另一組則是經常能保持愉快的人。結果如何呢？第一組的人逐漸產生疾病，不過第二組的人卻常保健康！而另一項研究也找到了進一步的證據，發現人在摯愛死去後產生的壓力對於我們的身體的確有所影響。人的免疫系統靠的是白血球，在抵抗體內疾病時少不了它們，而這些人的免疫系統無法正常運作，若情況持續很長一段時間，這些人比較容易生病，或因此而早死。

所以，我們該怎麼做才能避開壓力、保持健康呢？在壓力管理領域方面的專家建議我們，「關鍵就在於維持正向積極的態度」。我們可以選擇不同的方式來面對事情，以減輕日常生活中的壓力，也要訓練自己成為正向思考的人！另一個要素就是生活習慣，只要飲食正常，運動充足，就能確保更為長久快樂且沒有壓力的人生。

1. C

邏輯 本篇文章為討論壓力的說明文，此類文章會先針對探討的主題簡略說明，接著引入要具體說明的面向，其邏輯次序是「廣泛籠統→具體明確」。以本文而言，廣泛主題是「壓力」，而具體的面向是壓力所造成的「影響」。從第一段的結構可明顯看出，前兩句簡單說明壓力是所有人都會面臨的問題，而且有多種可能來源。最後一句則提到過多壓力可能會使人身心俱疲，甚至是死亡。顯然，這是從廣泛轉變到具體的論述，且因為有個重要的轉折詞 However，因此可以推論第 1 題內容應該是要討論壓力的「正面」影響。在所有選項中，只有 (C) 選項提到 pressure can help us get more done，符合此處邏輯，故為正確答案。

同義詞 (C) 選項中的 pressure 與前後兩句中的 stress 是同義字，可視為將這些句子連貫起來的線索。

用字 在下一句中的轉折詞 However 暗示了本題答案應和下一句的立場或論述相反。在 (C) 選項中的 get more done，與下一句的 physically weak、cause death 等詞在論述方面為相反的，故為正確答案。

2. F

邏輯 第一段的結論句已經指出了壓力所造成的害處，因此本段將會針對這個論點提出更多的說明。第二句中提到把一群人分成兩個次群組，接著比較其結果，這是一種進行「研究」的程序，也是重要的線索。在所有選項當中，只有 (F) 選項中提到了 study，符合

本段主題，故為正確答案。

用 字 下一句所提到的 The group，與在 (F) 選項中的 a number of people，所指涉的是同一群人，故為重要的線索。尤其是選項中的 study 一字，更是直接點出本段前半部的核心主題，故 (F) 選項的敘述得以成為本段的主題句。

3. B

邏 輯 (B) 選項所提到的情況為「因」，而下一句後半段所提到的情況為「果」，有明顯的因果關係。因此可以確認 (B) 選項為正確答案。

換句話說 在下一句當中的 this situation，指的就是 (B) 選項裡所提到的 Their immune systems did not work properly 這件事。因此可以得知這兩個句子具有密切的關聯性。

代名詞 (B) 選項中的代名詞所有格 their，所指涉的對象是在前一句裡面提到的 people whose loved ones had died，以及下一句裡的 these people。

4. D

邏 輯 本段的第一句話就提出了一個問題，通常使用此種提問法時，接下來就會針對這個問題提出解決之道，而所使用的詞彙包括 answer、solution、method、way、key 等字，以明確地提示讀者答案為何。在 (D) 選項中的 key (關鍵) 正是針對前一句的問題而提出的解決方案。

用 字 前一句中的 avoid stress (避免壓力)，與 (D) 選項中的 stress management (壓力管理) 具有高度的相關性，而前一句中的 stay healthy (保持健康) 則與 (D) 選項中的 stay positive (保持正向樂觀) 有因果關係，因此可以確認 (D) 選項正是前一句所提出之問題的解答。

5. A

邏 輯 這一題是第三段的最後一句，通常會針對第三段的內容提出結論。作者在本段中提出了兩個關鍵：stay positive 以及 lifestyle。在 (A) 選項中的 eat properly 和 get enough exercise，正是呼應了前一句的 lifestyle。而 (A) 選項中後半段提到的 a longer and happier stress-free life，也呼應了本段第一句提到的 avoid stress and stay healthy，因此可知 (A) 為本段的結論句。

在本篇題目當中，只有 (E) 選項沒有被選到。在該選項中提到了 make us feel blue or depressed，因此可以判斷所討論的主題是壓力所產生的負面影響。而由該選項一開始提到的 As is known to everyone

(眾所皆知) 來判斷，該選項的論述應該是偏向比較廣泛的層面。由於第二段在討論關於壓力的研究結果，而第三段則是提出避免壓力的方法，都與 (E) 選項的主題不符，因此該選項比較有可能出現在第一段。但是因為第一題下一句一開始就用了重要的轉折詞 However，而且該句的內容是關於壓力的負面影響，因此，第 1 題所敘述的內容勢必要與原本的論點相反，因此可以得知 (E) 選項並不適合當作第 1 題的答案。

Round 10

翻譯

每年，成千上萬名外國遊客造訪希臘。有些人因料理或購物而來，其他許多人則是因其歷史和文化，特別是因為希臘的古老神廟，它們幾乎在每位遊客的口袋清單。然而，造訪希臘的旅客若知道這些神廟可能是在好久以前因某個神秘的原因而被建造，可能會十分驚訝。

多年來，人們認為希臘神廟是為了收藏古希臘眾神的雕像而建。神廟不像某些人誤以為的是聚會場所，因為人們通常在神廟外聚會、舉行儀式。更確切地說，它們的主要目的是為了存放、保護神像和供品。

然而，最近有人提出了一個新理論。有些人認為古希臘神廟其實是為了與天上的行星相應而建。他們注意到一件有趣的事，許多重要的希臘古廟從地圖上檢視，會形成精準的等腰三角形。這可能意味著古希臘人有超乎我們以往認為的天文知識。有趣的是，大部分神廟都指向慶祝其供奉的神明的節日當天太陽升起的方向而建。

雖然有些人認為要證實這個理論需要更多證據，但有件事是肯定的：如果你去希臘旅遊，你一定得去參觀古神廟。無論它們的建造理由為何，都值得一看。

1. B

邏 輯 本段前兩句提到每年都有許多外國遊客拜訪希臘，其中有些人是為了美食或購物，但是其他人則是為了歷史與文化。此處作者使用了連接詞 while (然而…) 以便在下一句提出真正要闡述的論點。因此，我們可以判斷作者真正關心的是 the history and culture。而在 (B) 選項中提到了希臘古代的神殿。毫無

疑問，神殿當然屬於歷史與文化的一部分，因此兩者在邏輯上相互關聯，故選 (B)。

同義詞 在本段第一句裡的 tourists、(B) 選項裡的 visitor、以及最後一句裡的 travelers 三個字雖然表面上意思不同，但都是指「遊客」或「旅客」，因此可視為同義字，亦是使這些句子產生連貫性的重要線索。

重複 在本段的第一句以及 (B) 選項裡都提到了 Greece (希臘)。而在 (B) 選項與下一句裡則是重複提及 temples (神殿) 這個字，表示這幾句的主題都和 Greece 以及 temple 有關，因此可視為使這兩個句子產生連貫性的重要線索。

2. D

邏輯 在 (D) 選項中提到，人們普遍相信希臘神廟被建造的目的，是為了放置古希臘諸神的雕像。而下一句則依選項中的敘述進一步解釋這些神殿並非集會場所，而是在神殿外面舉行儀式。因此可以確認 (D) 選項正是此處的正確答案。

代名詞 在下一句裡提到的代名詞 They，所指涉的對象正是在 (D) 選項中的 Greek temples (希臘神殿)。

重複 在下一句最後面所提到的 the temples，與 (D) 選項中的 Greek temples 是指同樣的事物，同一單字重複出現，亦是幫助我們找出正確答案的重要線索。

3. E

邏輯 在 (E) 選項中一開頭的 Rather 是一個重要的轉折詞，意指「更確切地說」，通常是針對前面所提過的某個論點進行更具體的說明，或者是換個說法來解釋前面提出的論點。就本題而言，前一句提到希臘神殿並不是聚會的場所，而 (E) 選項一開頭則用了 Rather 這個轉折詞，清楚地說明這些神殿的主要目的是存放與保護重要雕像和供品，符合此處的語意邏輯，故為正確答案。

代名詞 在 (E) 選項中所提到的代名詞 their，其指涉對象為前一句最後面的 the temples，並以此達到語意的連貫性。

4. A

邏輯 本段第一句提到，對於古希臘人建造神殿的目的，有人提出了新的理論。當作者在主題句裡提出這樣的陳述時，即可合理推測後續將會進一步說明這個理論。而 (A) 選項中所敘述的內容，正是在說明某些人所「相信」的想法，邏輯上符合「廣泛籠統→具體明確」的順序。

用字 在後兩句中提到的 astronomy (天文學)，和 (A) 選項中「...line up with the planets in the sky above」的說法有密切的關聯性。如果能夠辨識出這個重要的線索，就能很快地確認 (A) 選項為此處的正確答案。

重複 在 (A) 選項中以及後兩句都重複提到了 planets 這個字，因此可以確認 (A) 選與這些句子所探討的主題具有相關性。另外，在 (A) 選項中提到了「...the ancient Greek temples were actually built...」，而在後兩句裡也提到「...they may have built the temples...」，這些重複的字詞顯示出這些句子之間的密切關係。

5. F

邏輯 在前一句裡提到，古希臘人對於天文學的理解程度可能超過我們之前的認知，他們建造神殿的目的可能是為了要更加仔細地研究宇宙中的星球與恆星。在 (F) 選項中則提到，大多數的希臘神殿在舉行主神慶典的那一天，會指著太陽升起的方向。這可視為是古希臘人研究天文學和宇宙群星之後所得到的結果。因此在邏輯上 (F) 選項確實能夠承接上句。

用字 在前一句裡提到了 astronomy 以及 the universe's planets and stars，而在 (F) 選項中則提到了 the sun，這幾個詞彙都與天文相關，因此可以確認這兩句之間具有連貫性。

重複 在前一句以及 (F) 選項中都有重複提到 temples 和 built 這兩個字，因此可以看出這兩句之間有密切的關係。

> 在本篇題目中唯一沒有使用的選項是 (C)。在 (C) 選項中提到「希臘是西方文化的發源地」，而遊客都想一睹「神殿裡供奉的古希臘諸神的雕像」。從句意來判斷，(C) 選項內容所討論的主題是遊客到希臘觀光旅遊的「目的」，而這樣的敘述最可能出現在第一段裡。但由 (C) 選項中的描述可以得知，遊客想要看到的是「雕像」而不是「神殿」，然而整篇文章的主題都圍繞在「神殿」，與「雕像」沒有太大的關係，因此我們可以判斷 (C) 選項不能當作第 1 題的答案。

 Round 11

翻譯

　　街頭籃球是一項非常開放且較無限制的運動，讓人們有機會測試自己的創造力，並發揮體能的極限。它的規則簡單，而且各年齡層的人，從五歲到六十五歲，都可以參與，有些小孩甚至在幼稚園就

開始玩起這項運動。街頭籃球員的運動生涯可長達數十年，這和職業籃球不同，因為這項運動不需要太多的訓練和體力，它只是好玩而已。

　　這種籃球遊戲通常只會用到籃球的半場，也沒有明確的規則，參賽者可以一天打十場比賽，也可以十天打一場，每隊的參賽人數可以從防守球員和進攻球員兩個人(也就是一對一)，到完整的一隊五人制。

　　街頭籃球從一九四〇年代源於紐約市，至今已經發展了相當長一段時間，並普及到世界上數百個城市。它已經從一個遊戲，演變成一種有其擁護者的文化。而在一隊紐約球員開始遍遊全美，與各地球員一較高下的時候，更是引起一陣風潮。比賽經過錄影，一舉成為國際運動頻道 ESPN 的熱門節目。街頭籃球魅力強大的原因在於每個人都能參與，無論年齡大小、是男是女、或高或矮，從你步上球場的那一刻起，唯一重要的，就只有你對這場比賽的熱情而已。

1. C

邏　輯　由本段的主題句的內容可以得知，本段所探討的事物是 street basketball。而第二句提到了街頭籃球的優點。而 (C) 選項中提到這項運動的規則相當簡單，而且所有年齡的人都可以參與，剛好與下一句相呼應。下一句提到有些兒童甚至從幼稚園就開始這項運動。由上述內容可知，下一句是在強調「年齡」並不會成為打街頭籃球的限制，而這正好符合 (C) 選項中所提到的概念，故得知 (C) 選項為此處的正確答案。

代名詞　在 (C) 選項和前一句裡面所提到的代名詞 It，指涉的對象為本段第一句的主詞 street basketball。作者在此利用 It 這個代名詞來使這三個句子產生連貫性，表示這三句所談論的主題是一致的，因此若是我們能夠辨識出這個答題線索，就能很快地找出正確答案。

2. A

邏　輯　在 (A) 選項中使用了「That's because ...」的句型，意思是指「那是因為…」。當作者用到 That/This is because ... 的句型時，表示作者在前面先提出了一個現象或結果，然後再用這個句型說明其原因。換句話說，作者用此句型來明確地展現出前後兩句之間的因果關係，且次序為「結果或現象→形成的原因」。以本題而言，前一句提到了街頭籃球選手的生涯可長達數十年，而 (A) 選項則提到，那是因為這項運動不需要太多的訓練和體力。因此，我們可以看出 (A)

選項的內容正好在解釋或說明前一句的情況，兩者之間具有因果關係，故 (A) 選項為正確答案。

同義詞　在 (A) 選項中提到的 the game，就是指前面所提到的 street ball，因此可以確認這兩句所談論的主題是一致的。

3. F

邏　輯　從本段其他兩句的內容可知，本段所討論的是 street basketball 的比賽方式與特色，而 (F) 選項中提到「參加者可以在一天之內打十場比賽，也可以在十天內只打一場比賽」，這樣的內容正是談論比賽的方式，不但符合本段落的主題，且也呼應了前一句最後面提到的 there is no precise schedule，因此可以確認 (F) 選項是本題的正確答案。

重　複　在 (F) 選項和下一句當中，作者重複提到了 participants (參賽者) 這個字，表示這兩句所談論的內容具有連貫性，可視為是重要的答案線索。

4. B

邏　輯　由本段的主題句以及其他句子的內容可以看出，本段所談論的主題是 street basketball 的發展過程。主題句裡先提到了街頭籃球最初是於 1940 年代在美國紐約市出現，之後即迅速發展。而在 (B) 選項中提到，街頭籃球已經發展成為不只是一種運動比賽，而是一種「文化」。接著，在下一句提到街頭籃球讓人瘋狂的情況，這足以證明它不只是一種運動比賽。換句話說，接下來的兩句都在說明這項運動擁有大量支持者的盛況，因此在邏輯上符合此處的語意。

換句話說　在前一句裡提到了 has come a long way 這個動詞片語，意思是指「已經有了重大的進步或是發展」。而在 (B) 選項中則提到「... has grown from a game into a culture」，意指「已經從單純的運動比賽發展成為一種文化」，這兩種說法雖然在表面上不一樣，但是所表達的意思卻是相同的。

代名詞　在 (B) 選項以及下一句裡提到的代名詞 It，所指涉的對象都為本段第一句的主詞 street basketball。由於在 (B) 選項及下一句裡的代名詞 It 也都是主詞，可以確認這三句所談論的主題都是 street basketball。作者正是以此種方式使這三句產生語意上的連貫性，而這也是我們可以善加利用的答題線索。

5. D

邏　輯　在 (D) 選項中最後提到 everyone can play it，在下一句則提到了「Whether you are young or old, male or female, short or tall ...」，由此可知，這句話所指的正是 (D) 選項中的 everyone，因此可以看出這兩句之間在邏輯上具有密切關係，因此 (D) 選項為正確答案。

換句話說 在前一句裡提到了 a popular show，而在 (D) 選項中則提到了 street basketball is so powerful。這兩句裡所用的形容詞 popular 和 powerful 雖然表面上不同，但在此都是指街頭籃球極受歡迎並因而具有極大的影響力，因此可以視為以不同的方式來說明同一種情況。

在本篇題目中唯一沒有使用的選項是 (E)。在 (E) 選項中提到「許多 NBA 球員也喜歡打街頭籃球來與粉絲互動」，由本句敘述的內容來判斷，這一句話可能出現在介紹街頭籃球的第一段，或是討論街頭籃球發展為極受歡迎的運動的第三段。然而，在仔細看過這兩段之後，我們可以發現，在第一段裡主要是討論街頭籃球的特色，與 (E) 選項的內容沒有任何關聯性，因此 (E) 選項不適合當作第 1 題或第 2 題的答案。至於最後一段，其內容都是在討論街頭籃球的發展過程，而且裡面完全沒有提到街頭籃球與 NBA 之間的關係，因此 (E) 選項也無法當作第 4 題或第 5 題的答案。

Round 12

翻譯

近來，每個人似乎都在擔心全球暖化。因此，許多人想以替代能源，如風力和太陽能，來取代傳統的化石燃料。不過，有些人說核能早已給我們穩固的能量來源。

核能的確有其優點。首先，核能不會製造大量的溫室氣體。此外，它很可靠，尤其與風力和太陽能相比。而且，核電廠設立後的運作成本很小。最後，核電廠只需一點點燃料就能製造極大量的能量。

然而，核能雖有優點，它也有一些缺點。首先，核電廠需要鈾，鈾需要開採。這會損害環境。而且，鈾使用完會有放射性。管理及棄置放射性核廢料因此變得昂貴甚至危險。更糟的是，全球鈾礦有限，開採及運輸成本也很高。而且與鈾相關的意外對人類及環境來說都非常致命。最後，核電廠的設立需要數年和大量經費。

核能很明顯地是有利有弊。同樣明顯地是許多世界各地的人對這種能源有很強烈的意見，有些贊成有些反對。無庸置疑的是，核能議題會繼續爭論不休。

1. A

邏輯 在 (A) 選項中一開始所使用的 to begin with 這個轉折詞，是很明顯的答題線索。由於作者在前一句中提到核能確實有數個優點，因此我們可以合理推測作者接下來會針對這些優點進行說明。而在說明時，一開始最常使用的轉折詞通常是 to begin with 或是 first，以表示第一點。而由 (A) 選項後面的內容來判斷，這正是在說明核能的優點，正好呼應了主題句的論點，故可知 (A) 選項為此處的正確答案。

重複 在前一句和 (A) 選項當中不但都重複提到了 nuclear power 這個詞彙，而且也都是當作句子的主詞，因此我們可以確認這兩句在談論相同的主題。

2. B

邏輯 簡單瀏覽本篇文章，可以得知本文的結構相當清楚。本文總共分成四段，第一段是總論，提出「核能」的概念與主題。第二段探討核能的優點，第三段提出核能的缺點，而第四段則是提出結論。本題為第三段，從主題句中提到的「there are some disadvantages」可知本段要討論核能的缺點，因此本段中的第 2、3、4 題必定與核能的缺點有關。在本題的前一句提到了核電廠要能夠發電，就必須開採 uranium (鈾礦)，而 (B) 選項中則提到此元素會傷害環境，與前一句之間具有明確的因果關係，故為正確答案。

代名詞 在 (B) 選項中的代名詞 This，所指的就是前一句中提到的「開採鈾礦」這件事，因此 (B) 為正確答案。

3. E

邏輯 在前一句提到，一旦開始使用鈾後，鈾就具有放射性。在 (E) 選項中則提到，要管理與處理此種具放射性的核廢料是 expensive and even dangerous。由此可知這兩句之間符合邏輯上的時間次序，也就是「使用鈾礦→鈾礦變成核廢料→處理核廢料具有危險性」，因此可以確認 (E) 選項是此處的正確答案。

代名詞 在 (E) 選項的前一句的後半段都同樣用到代名詞 it，而這個代名詞所指涉的對象就是前一句所提到的 this uranium。因此，代名詞 it 使得前後兩個句子在語意上產生了連貫性。

重複 在前一句的最後，以及 (E) 選項的最後都重複提到了 radioactive (具有放射性的) 這個形容詞。這正是一個很重要的答題線索，暗示我們這兩句之間具有密切的關聯性。

4. C

邏輯 本段的主題是在討論使用核能發電的缺點，前一句提到了鈾礦的存量有限，而且開採與運輸鈾

礦的成本都相當高昂。而 (C) 選項中則提到任何與鈾礦有關的意外都會對人類和環境造成致命傷害，這樣的敘述內容不但和核能的缺點有關，而且在邏輯上與前一句的概念是吻合的，因此 (C) 選項為此處的正確答案。

重　複　在前一句和 (C) 選項裡都重複提到了 uranium 這個字，為作者用來使這兩句的語意產生連貫性的方式，為重要的答題線索。

5. D

邏　輯　在本篇文章中，作者把關於核能的正反意見與論述並陳，在結論的段落裡，作者並未直接提出本身到底是支持或反對核能，只是客觀地說明核能的優缺點，且此種爭議仍然會持續。(D) 選項的內容也正好符合作者在本段的客觀立場，故在邏輯上與本段一致，是判斷正確答案的關鍵。

用　字　在下一句裡提到了 the debate over nuclear energy，既然有 debate，就代表一定會有正反兩方的意見，而在本段第一句裡提到了 advantages and disadvantages，在 (D) 選項裡也提到了 some in favor of it and others against it，這都表示 debate 的存在，由此可知 (D) 選項的內容正符合下一句中的 debate，故答案選 (D)。

重　複　在前一句中提到了「it seems clear that ...」，而在 (D) 選項中也提到了「It is also clear that ...」，兩句都使用了 clear，且後面的 that 子句裡也都提到了關於核能的正反意見的存在，因此我們可以確認這兩句之間具有密切的關係。

> 本篇題目中唯一沒有使用的選項是 (F)。在 (F) 選項中提到，「鈾礦是不穩定的元素，因此當我們使用它時，應該要非常小心」。由此句意來判斷，此處的敘述比較偏向核能發電的「缺點」，而本篇文章的第三段也在討論核能的缺點，因此 (F) 選項最有可能出現在第三段。然而，在第三段裡的敘述內容，都以鈾礦本身的性質與可能對環境與人類造成的傷害為主，並未提到它是一種不穩定的元素，也未提到用它來發電時的問題，因此 (F) 選項並不能當作第三段裡的任何一題的答案。

 Round 13

翻譯

　　閱讀是人類特有的能力，使得新的世代能藉此學習祖先的遺產，而閱讀也是教育的一切基礎。因此，小孩學好閱讀就格外重要。不過許多家長在教導小孩順利閱讀時卻遇到了一些問題。

　　許多家長認為他們的小孩愈早開始學習認字愈好，但事實上這並不一定正確。舉例來說，小孩可能認識每個字母，但也許無法了解一串字母組成一個字後所代表的意思。閱讀是個複雜的過程，要讓幼童辨認印刷出來的字並不容易，但是家長們會開始強迫他們的小孩閱讀，而一旦小孩被迫閱讀，這對他們而言就不再是件快樂的事，而使部分的孩子無法順暢地閱讀。

　　父母親可以使用一種方法，來幫助小孩成為好的閱讀者，那就是從很小的時候就開始每天唸書給他們聽，嬰兒期是開始和小孩一起分享書籍的絕佳時機。藉由和家人一起讀書，小孩就能逐漸了解閱讀的目的與樂趣。

　　不過有些時候即使父母親用對了方法，孩子還是可能會有閱讀方面的困難，其中一個原因是孩子有閱讀障礙，這是一種特殊疾病，會造成閱讀、寫作和拼字上的問題。碰到這種情形，父母必須尋求專業的協助，並且要準備盡一切可能來支持他們的小孩。

1. B

邏　輯　由本段第一句的主題句可以看出，閱讀能力對於人類而言是獨特的能力。本題的前一句更指出閱讀是教育的基礎，(B) 選項中則提到了兒童成功學習如何閱讀是很重要的事，在邏輯上是一致且連貫的，故答案為 (B)。

轉折詞　(B) 選項中用了 That is why ... (那就是為什麼…的原因) 這個轉折詞的句型，本句型用來指出兩個事物之間的因果關係，其用法通常是前面先提出一個現象或事件，然後再用說明該現象或事件造成的結果。由於本題前一句指出了閱讀為教育的基礎，而 (B) 選項中提到兒童學習如何閱讀是很重要的，可看出前一句是原因、後一句是結果，形成緊密的因果關係。

用　字　在 (B) 選項中的 important 是個重要的線索，呼應了第一句中的 unique (獨特的)、以及前一句中的 foundation (基礎)。而在前一句中的代名詞 It，所指涉的對象除了是第一句的 reading 之外，也指涉了 (B) 選項中的 learning how to read，使得這三個句子環環相扣，完整論述了一個重要的概念。

2. E

邏　輯　作者在本段所採用的手法為，先提出一個普遍被大家所接受的觀念，然後用 this is not

necessarily true (這不必然為真) 的說法否定了此種觀念。通常為了進一步說明與論證自己的看法，作者就必須提出證據來支持自己的論點。而 (E) 選項中提到兒童在認得字母之後，並不一定知道整體字母所組成的單字之意義，是針對自己所提的新論點的證據。

轉折詞 在 (E) 選項中用了 for example 這個轉折詞，此為重要的線索，表示作者舉出實例來證明自己的論點，故可得知 (E) 選項為此處的答案。

同義詞 在 (E) 選項中前半句的 alphabet，其實就是本段第一句後面的 letters 的同義詞，且在 (E) 選項後面也重複提到了 letters 這個字，因此可以確認作者利用同義與重複的方式，使得這三句的語意產生連貫性。

3. A

邏輯 前一句提到家長可能會開始強迫孩子閱讀，(A) 選項提到如果孩子被迫閱讀，就會覺得閱讀不再有樂趣，而下一句則提到此種情況會讓孩子無法成為流利的閱讀者。此三句之間具有很明確而流暢的因果關係，前一句是造成 (A) 選項的原因，而 (A) 選項又是造成下一句的原因，因而產生很強的說服力。

換句話說 在前一句裡提到 force their children to read，而在 (A) 選項中則提到 children are forced to read，這兩句話雖然一句是主動語態、另一句是被動語態，但其實是同一件事的兩種不同說法，表達的意思是一樣的，因此可以確認 (A) 選項是正確答案。

重複 在前一句中提到了 force 這個字，此為重要的線索，而在 (A) 選項中也重複提到了 force 這個字。前一句中提到了 read，(A) 選項中也有提到 read，找出此種重複使用關鍵字詞的方式，我們就可以確認這兩句之間具有密切的關係。

4. F

邏輯 在前一句中提到，家長若要幫助孩子成為良好的閱讀者，理想的時間點是 from an early age。這是是一個很重要的語意邏輯線索，與在 (F) 選項中最後面提到的 during babyhood) 是相呼應的，因此可以確認這兩句在語意方面具有連貫性。

換句話說 在 (F) 選項中提到的 begin sharing books with children，與下一句裡的 reading books with their families，可視為是同一件事情的換句話說，因而可以確定 (F) 選項是前後兩句之間的重要橋樑，使這兩個句子流暢地銜接在一起。

同義詞 前一句中的 an early age 和 (F) 選項中的 babyhood 可視為意思相近的同義詞。

5. C

邏輯 由本段第一句可以看出，本段所討論的

主題是 have difficulty in reading，也就是在閱讀方面遇到困難，而在 (C) 選項中所討論的主題也是指在閱讀、寫作、拼字方面的問題，與本段邏輯完全相符，故為正確答案。

用字 在前一句中的 suffer from 是一個很重要的線索。因為 suffer 這個字暗示了承受像是疾病、痛苦、災難等等的負面事物，而這個涵意剛好與 (C) 選項中的 disorder、problems 相吻合。

同義詞 dyslexia 這個字比較困難，意思是指「讀寫障礙」，但是其實在文章中有線索可尋。最重要的線索就是前一句的 have difficulty in reading，這已經暗示了 dyslexia 的意義，而在 (C) 選項中的 a disorder which causes problems with reading, writing and spelling 則是更進一步地清楚說明 dyslexia 的字義，因此我們可以確認這三句所討論的是相同主題。

> 在本篇題目當中，只有 (D) 選項沒有被選到。由該選項的內容來判斷，應該是在討論家長對於培養兒童閱讀能力的重要性。就整篇文章而言，與這個主題比較相關的段落是第三段，因為在第三段的主題句中提到了「... help children become good readers ...」。再仔細分析的話，可以看出第三段的主要重點在於提出「具體的方法」，但是 (D) 選項的內容卻在討論「廣泛的概念」，與第三段的中心主旨是不符合的。除此之外，在第三段中只有一個題目，也就是第 4 題，從上下文來判斷，第 4 題是承接主題句的文意，因此要提出一個具體的論點，尤其是關於教導兒童閱讀的時間點，這也與 (D) 所敘述的內容不符，所以 (D) 選項不能當作此處的答案。

Round 14

翻譯

　　若你在四月中旬到泰國去，會看到一些特別的景象。鄉間路上，小孩會對騎機車或腳踏車路過的人潑水，在城市裡行人會向公車上的乘客潑水，而舉國上下都有滿載乘客的小貨車四處穿梭，兩輛貨車會車時就會停下來，乘客互相用水潑溼對方。

　　這些人全都在慶祝「潑水節」，也就是四月十三日泰國的傳統新年，時值泰國的盛夏，氣溫常高達攝氏四十度，所以弄溼後有助於降溫。這是個到處都是人潮、水槍和溼淋淋街道的狂野慶典。

　　但是，過去慶祝這節日的方式較為平和。習俗

是在新年一開始，由年輕人拜訪年長的親戚以表達敬意，那時，晚輩把帶有香氣的一小碗水輕輕倒在長輩的手上，並且祝賀他們來年能快樂健康。人們相信這水能洗掉過去一年所有不好的事情。長輩則會拍拍晚輩的頭給他們祝福，有時也會給點錢。

有些家庭還遵循這種安靜的儀式，只是將程序變的更為簡潔。但這些年來潑水已經成為慶祝潑水節的主要方式。其實，由於體認到這個習俗受歡迎的程度，政府已經將此國定假日從一天延長為三天；在北部的清邁省，每年度的慶祝活動現在甚至會持續一整個星期。泰國這個節慶意味最濃的假日不只變得比以前更加濕答答，時間也變得更長了。

1. F

邏輯 在本段第一句的最後面提到了 some unusual sights，這也是本段所要談論的主題。在第二句提到鄉下地區的兒童們對人們潑水的情況，而 (F) 選項則提到在城市裡人們互相潑水的景象，這兩者合起來剛好呼應了下一句所提到的 all over the country。

用字 除了本題的前一句和 (F) 選項中都有提到 throw water 之外，在下一句的最後面也提到 soak one another with water，這是 throw water at anyone/people 所造成的結果，因此可以確認這三個句子在意義上是具有連貫性的。

重複 在前一句中提到了 throw water，而在 (F) 選項中也重複提到 throw water，這暗示我們這兩句之間具有密切的關係。

2. D

邏輯 本段在說明人們為何會在泰國傳統新年 Songkran (潑水節) 互相潑水的原因。而在本題的前一句提到了在 Songkran 期間，每個人都會全身濕透，而這也使人聯想到與水有關。(D) 選項中提到了 lots of crowds, water guns, and wet streets，這都是與「水」有關的，而且也讓人聯想到大量群眾一起狂歡的場面，因此符合 Songkran 的慶祝意義，在邏輯上是連貫的。

代名詞 在 (D) 選項中的代名詞 It，所指涉的對象就是前面所提的 Songkran，因此是重要的答題線索。

重複 在前一句裡提到了 celebrate 這個字，而在 (D) 選項裡則提到了 celebration (慶典)，雖然詞性不同，但都是由同一個字所衍生出來的，可視為是同一個字的重複使用。作者利用此種重複關鍵字的方式，使語氣產生連貫性，這也成為我們答題時要尋找的重要線索。

3. A

邏輯 由本段的主題句可以看得出來，雖然前面提到了潑水節已經變成一個歡樂的節日，但是這個節日在過去的慶祝方式是更和平的，而這也正是本段的談論主題。(A) 選項中提到了 the custom，也提到了年輕人拜訪年長的親戚。而在下一句中則提到年輕人拜訪年長親戚時要做的事以及這兩者之間的互動情況，可見 (A) 選項所談論的主題與本段一致，且在事件發生順序上早於下一句，符合此處的時間邏輯。

換句話說 在 (A) 選項中，作者提到了 pay their respects，而在下一句裡則提到了 wished them happiness and good health，這兩者的說法雖然表面上不同，但是所表達的意思是很接近的，可以視為是換句話說，也是在答題時的重要線索，由此可知 (A) 是此處的正確答案。

重複 在 (A) 選項中和下一句中都重複提到了 younger people/relatives 以及 their older relatives，因此可以確認 (A) 選項與下一句所談論的主題一致，在語意上是連貫的。

4. C

邏輯 如同第 3 題中提到的，本段的主題是泰國傳統新年的慶祝方式，而且從本段的內容可以得知，慶祝方式主要是由 younger people 去拜訪 their older relatives，並祝福他們。而在 (C) 選項中則描述了這些 older relatives 在接受祝福之後也會祝福年輕人們好運、甚至是給一些錢。此敘述符合本段的主題，且由 (C) 選項中提到的 responded 一字，可以推測得知此處所描述的是發生在年輕人祝福年長親戚之後的情況，在時間邏輯上也符合本段的描述，因此可以得知是正確答案。

重複 在 (C) 選項中提到的 older relatives 和 the younger ones，在前兩句中都有提到，因此我們可以確認 (C) 選項所描述的情況和主題與本段相符合。而作者也利用重複重要人物的方式，使本段的語意產生連貫性。

5. B

邏輯 在前一句提到，由於潑水節實在太受歡迎，所以泰國政府已經把這個國定假日從一天延長到三天。而在 (B) 選項中也提到，泰國北部的清邁省的慶祝活動甚至長達一個禮拜。這兩句的主題都是延長了潑水節的時間，正好呼應了本段最後一句的 growing longer，因此可以確認 (B) 選項為正確答案。

用字 在前一句裡用了 extend (延長)、(B) 選項的 lasts (持續)、以及下一句裡的 growing longer (變得愈來愈長)，它們都表示了類似的概念，是判斷正確答案的重要線索，也清楚地暗示了這三句所談論的主題是一致的。

在本篇題目當中，只有 (E) 選項沒有被選到。該選項的內容描述了如果讀者有機會在潑水節期間到泰國，務必要參與這個慶祝活動。這是一種類似於呼籲讀者做某件事的句子，一般而言，這樣的句子會出現在整篇文章的最後面或最後一段，以當作文章的結尾。然而，本篇文章的最後一段只有一個題目，也就是第 5 題，而且從上下文所探討的主題來判斷，主要是在討論潑水節的慶祝時間延長，並沒有鼓勵讀者去泰國體驗潑水節的暗示，因此 (E) 選項並不適合成為此處的答案。

Round 15

翻譯

　　熱帶雨林覆蓋地表大約百分之七的區域，主要分佈於赤道附近，它分佈於南美洲北部的大片區域，以及中美洲、非洲、東南亞等地，是終年溫暖溼潤之地。雨林地區的平均年雨量在八十英吋 (兩千公釐) 到驚人的四百英吋 (一萬公釐) 之間，而均溫則大約在攝氏二十四至二十七度左右。

　　雨林以多種方式促進我們星球的福祉，首先，它們循環全球的氧氣、氮氣和二氧化碳，這樣有助於調節地球的溫度；它們提供許多人類和動物棲地，事實上，雨林存活著地球上百分之五十的動植物種類，當中有一些是在他處無法生存的物種；雨林也提供我們木材、枝條、乳膠、松脂、軟木、樹膠、染料、油料、食物、藥材、樹脂等資源。

　　不幸的是，由於對這些物資的需求日益增加，造成了一個嚴重的問題：雨林正快速萎縮。其他原因還包括大範圍清除雨林以供農業用途。雨林以每分鐘二十七英畝的驚人速度被摧毀，且每天有一百三十七種動植物滅絕。專家表示，不到五十年，全球很大部分的雨林都會消失，如果這是真的，那麼身為未來守護者的我們，是不是應該盡一切可能來確保不要讓這樣的事發生？

1. B

邏輯　　在第一句裡提到，熱帶雨林佔了約百分之七的地球表面，而且主要出現在赤道附近。而 (B) 選項提到這些地區涵蓋南美洲大部分的北部區域、中美洲、非洲、以及東南亞。而這些地區都是位於赤道附近，因此可以確認 (B) 選項所敘述的內容，是針對上一句進行說明，而其邏輯的安排是依循著「廣泛籠統→具

體明確」的次序，因此可以確認 (B) 選項為正確答案。

用字　　在本題的前一句和下一句裡面都有提到 area 這個字，而在 (B) 選項裡雖然沒有直接提到這個字，但是從內容可以判斷得知，(B) 選項裡所提到的也都是屬於和 area 有關的概念，因此可以看出這三句的談論主題是相同的。

代名詞　　(B) 選項中的代名詞 They，所指涉的對象就是前一句裡提到的 tropical rainforests。而下一句裡的代名詞 These，所指涉的對象就是 (B) 選項裡的「a large portion of the northern part of South America …」。因此，我們可以看出這三句之間有密切的關係，後兩句裡的代名詞所指涉的對象都在上一句裡，形成環環相扣的緊密關係，而這也是答題時的重要線索。

2. F

邏輯　　在下一句裡用了一個很常見的轉折詞 in fact，意指「事實上」。當作者使用這個轉折詞時，通常會有下列兩種情況：一種是用來提出與前面相反或是不同的意見或論點；而另一種則是先提出一個較為廣泛籠統的論點，然後藉由這個轉折詞，進而針對該論點提出較為具體的論述。而此處正是後面這種情況。在 (F) 選項中提到，熱帶雨林為許多人類和動物提供避難所。這裡提到了 many 這個字，是屬於比較模糊的概念，而下一句則用 In fact 開頭，進一步說明了有高達百分之五十的植物和動物品種生活在雨林之中。「fifty percent」就是針對 (F) 選項中的「many」這個概念進一步提出具體說明，因此我們可以確定此處答案為 (F)。

代名詞　　在 (F) 選項中的代名詞 They，很明顯地與前一句的主詞 They 是指相同的事物，也就是本段第一句裡的主詞 rainforests。若能辨識出這樣的相關性，則不難找出這三句之間的連貫性。

3. A

邏輯　　在前一句提到，地球上約有百分之五十的植物和動物品種生存在熱帶雨林當中，而 (A) 選項中則提到，有些物種甚至無法生存於其他地方。此處的 anyplace else 所指的就是除了熱帶雨林以外的地方，因此可以看出這兩句之間的關聯性。除此之外，我們也可以明顯地看出，(A) 選項中的敘述內容是針對前一句的內容做進一步的延伸和強調，因此可以確認 (A) 選項為正確答案。

重複　　在前一句和 (A) 選項中，species 這個字重複出現，就是一個很重要的答題線索，暗示這兩句之間具有密切的關聯性。

4. D

邏輯　　由前一句的內容可以看出，該句所探討

的主題是造成熱帶雨林快速縮減的原因，而 (D) 選項中提到的「大規模清除熱帶雨林」，也是造成熱帶雨林消失的原因，表示這兩句之間具有高度的相關性。

重複 在尋找本題的正確答案時，最重要的線索，就是在本題前一句和 (D) 選項中重複出現的 cause。而且在前一句中提到了 the cause，在 (D) 選項中提到 other causes，語意上很明顯是承接上一句而來。除此之外，前一句提到了熱帶雨林正在快速地縮減，而 (D) 選項中則提到了熱帶雨林的大規模清除，這兩者所提到的現象是類似的。因此，我們可以從上述兩個線索來確認 (D) 選項為此處的正確答案。

5. C

邏輯 在下一句的最後提到 do everything possible to make sure it won't happen。依語意邏輯來判斷，既然作者提醒讀者們要盡力阻止這件事的發生，代表這一定是件不好的事，雖尚未發生，所以還有機會去挽救。而在 (C) 選項中提到的「專家認為大部分的雨林可能會在不到 50 年的時間內消失」這件事，就正好符合這個條件，因此可以確認 (C) 選項為此處的正確答案。

代名詞 在下一句裡面提到的代名詞 this，以及最後面提到的代名詞 it，所指涉的對象都是 (C) 選項裡的 a large portion of the world's rainforests will be gone in less than 50 years 這件事，如果能夠辨識出這個重要的線索，就能找出正確答案。

在本篇題目中唯一沒有使用的選項是 (E)。在 (E) 選項中提到熱帶雨林也有助於減低溫室氣體的比例，由句意來判斷，本句所談論的主題應該是熱帶雨林對於人類或環境的益處，而在本篇文章當中，只有第二段的主題與此相同，因此 (E) 選項這個句子最有可能出現在第二段裡面。然而，不論是第 2 題或第 3 題，其前後句子都沒有提到與溫室氣體有關的任何關鍵字或是線索，因此我們可以判斷 (E) 選項無法當作這兩題的答案。

Round 16

翻譯

安樂死，是經由深思熟慮後，為已經沒有康復希望的人所執行的生命終結，因此我們也可以稱它為由醫生協助的自殺。反對安樂死的人主張，無論如何，好死不如賴活，而且不管醫生或是親屬，沒有人有權結束他人的生命；不過近年來，贊成安樂死的人數一直在增加。有幾個國家已進行立法，准許出於自願的安樂死，比方說一九九六年，美國聯邦法院已取消許多州對於「醫生協助下自殺」的禁令。

贊成安樂死的主要論點在於，安樂死為那些遭受難忍之痛或是已經病入膏肓的人帶來解脫。支持安樂死的人表示，這些病人理應擁有選擇死法和時機的權利。安樂死讓他們有機會能夠帶著尊嚴死去，不必繼續活在悲慘絕望之中。因此，根據這些贊成「醫生協助下的自殺」者的看法，讓不醒人事以及垂死的人靠著生命維持系統存活下去，不但沒有意義且相當殘酷，更浪費了寶貴的醫療資源。

顯然大家對安樂死都有自己堅持的看法，反對者認為生命寶貴，甚至連政府也沒有權利決定結束生命的方法；另一方面，贊成者認為這是由病患及家屬、醫生來決定的事情，但目前似乎尚無定論，爭議還會持續下去。

1. C

邏輯 本段主題句先提到了 euthanasia 的定義，而 (C) 選項則提出了安樂死的另外一個名稱，也就是由醫生所協助的自殺，這兩句雖然說法不同，但可以得知都是在談同一件事，因此在邏輯上是密切相關的。

用字 在 (C) 選項中的 suicide 與前一句裡提到的 ending the life of a person、以及下一句的 to end the life of another person，都是指終結某人的生命，在意義上密切相關，使這三句在語意上產生連貫性。

代名詞 由前後句意來判斷，可以得知 (C) 選項中的代名詞 it 就是指前一句與下一句裡的 euthanasia (安樂死)，因此是一個重要的答題線索。

重複 在 (C) 選項和下一句裡都有提到 doctor，也提到由醫生來協助終結另一個人生命，故可確認這兩句所談論的主題一致。

2. E

邏輯 在前一句提到支持安樂死的人數有逐漸上升的趨勢，而下一句則出現了很重要的轉折詞 For example。在使用這個轉折詞時，通常會在前面先提出一個較為廣泛的論點，然後再利用此轉折詞來舉出較為具體的例子，以強化自己的論點。在下一句中提到發生在美國的情況，因此可以反推本題的句子應該和各國的情況有關。在 (E) 選項中提到了 several countries，剛好符合了邏輯上「廣泛籠統→具體明確」的次序，且這兩句的主題也都和各國立法允許安樂死有關，因此可以得知 (E) 選項為此處的正確答案。

用字 (E) 選項中的 several countries，和下一句的 Unite States 都和「國家」有關，可視為相關線索。而 (E) 選項中的 legislation (立法) 和下一句的 federal courts (聯邦法院)、lift bans on . . . (解除對於…的禁令)，具有高度的相關性，均可視為解題的重要線索。

3. B

邏輯 本題的句子是本段的第一句，因此應是主題句，決定了本段的主題與走向。從本段的內容來判斷，此段在討論支持安樂死的觀點與理由。而 (B) 選項的內容中出現了支持安樂死的論點，此為重要的線索，這表示 (B) 選項的敘述正好符合本段的主題，且 (B) 選項的後半段提出一個廣泛的論點，適合作為主題句，故可知 (B) 選項為正確答案。

用字 (B) 選項中提到的 pain、ill 等字，和下一句裡的 patients 具有高度的關聯性，使句意產生連貫性，故為重要答題線索。除此之外，在 (B) 選項中的 in favor of 和下一句中的 supporters，在意義上亦具有高度相關，也是可多加利用的線索。

代名詞 在 (B) 選項中的 those，所指涉的對象為下一句提到的 these patients。

4. D

邏輯 前一句提到，安樂死的支持者認為病患應該有權利選擇死亡的方式和時間。(D) 選項則提到這樣一來，可以讓病患有尊嚴地離開人世，而不必一直承受痛苦。由邏輯來判斷，(D) 選項是前一句的內容所欲達到的目的，兩者具有明確的因果關係，因此可以確認 (D) 選項為此處的正確答案。

代名詞 在 (D) 選項中的代名詞 them，所指涉的對象正是上一句裡所提到的 these patients，使其語意一致。而在 (D) 選項中的另外一個代名詞 this，所指涉對象則是 these patients should have the right to choose how and when to die 這件事，由此可以看出前一句和 (D) 選項之間具有高度關聯性。

5. A

邏輯 本段第一句提到人們對於安樂死這個主題有強烈的意見或看法。此處作者用了 strong 這個字，暗示了正反兩方的意見不合且有很多爭議之處。接下來作者提到了反對者的意見，而最後一句還提到這個爭議會繼續下去，暗示正反兩方將會繼續爭論不休。而 (A) 選項的句子提了安樂死支持者的意見，與本段第二句形成強烈對比，剛好呼應了第一句的 strong views，以及最後一句的 the argument will continue 的說法，因此在邏輯上是合理的答案。

轉折詞 在 (A) 選項中的 on the other hand 是一個常見的轉折詞，在使用此轉折詞時，代表作者要提出一個與前面互相對立的論點，因此常常是答題時可以尋找的關鍵線索。以本題而言，在前一句提出反對者對安樂死的意見，而 (A) 選項後面則提出支持者的意見，因此完全符合 on the other hand 這個轉折詞的用法與涵義。

在本篇題目當中，只有 (F) 選項沒有被選到。該選項的內容提到有超過百分之六十的美國人支持安樂死。這樣的敘述內容是相當具體明確的，而且也提到了「美國」，在整篇文章中有提到美國的地方，就在第一段的最後一句，因此乍看之下會覺得應該是第 2 題的答案。然而，在第 2 題的下一句，也就是第一段的最後一句，一開頭就用了 for example 這個轉折詞，表示該句話的前一句應該是提到了一個較為廣泛的概念，所以才必須用 for example 這個轉折詞來提出較為具體明確的答案。但是 (F) 選項的內容已經相當具體明確，也沒有更進一步說明的必要，因此在該選項的後面不應該再使用 for example 這個的轉折詞，因此可以判斷 (F) 選項不適合作為第 2 題的答案。

 Round 17

翻譯

　　二○○三年八月底是六萬年來火星最接近地球的時候，這顆紅色的星球成了世人關注的焦點。天文學家一度認為火星上存在著高度的文明。而今科學家愈來愈了解火星，已經斷定這顆佈滿了岩石而且冷冰冰的星球顯然無生命跡象；但另一方面，更深入了解火星後又促使我們思考另一個課題：人類有朝一日能否在火星上定居？

　　科學家指望火星是因為它和地球相似的程度超出其他行星，舉例來說，兩者都有季節性的天氣型態，而火星的一天只比我們地球的一天長一點點；另外，火星也有大氣層，只是不像地球的那樣濃密溫暖。從表面來看，許多人相信在遠古時代火星有大片面積是被水所覆蓋，但某種原因造成水從表面消失，只有在兩極地區還存在大量的冰，儘管如此，不少科學家認為火星曾經具有生物圈也就是生命能欣欣向榮的環境。

　　科學家正在思考改造火星，以使其能再次適合生命居住的可能性。他們必須釋放氣體進入大氣層，將它增厚與暖化，這樣就能造成溫室效應，留住太

陽的熱氣。溫度升高能使極區的冰帽溶化，轉變成水，只要有水生命就能生存，植物也會開始生長。假如這些都能成真，火星最終就能變得適合居住。部分科學家認為在西元三千年的時候，人類移居火星的夢想就會成真，但其他人對此感到懷疑。

1. B

邏輯 在本題的前一個句子裡，作者提到了天文學家曾經相信火星上存在著有智慧的生命形體。在這個句子裡用了 once (曾經) 這個字，而且時態也用了過去式，暗示本句所提到的是之前的狀況，但現在則是完全不同的情況。在 (B) 選項中提到，現在科學家比較瞭解火星，也知道火星上面沒有生命。由句意來判斷，(B) 選項的敘述是前一句的合理延伸，也符合前一句所暗示的相反情況，因此為合理的答案。

換句話說 (B) 選項中提到了 know Mars better，而在下一句中則提到 a deeper understanding of Mars，這兩者是以不同方式在說同一件事，是使這兩句連貫起來的重要線索。

重複 在上一句、(B) 選項、以及下一句當中都重複提到了 Mars，可見這三句在探討的主題是相同的。而前一句中提到的 Martians、(B) 選項中的 lifeless、以及下一句提到的 live，都和火星上的「生命」這個主題相關，因此也是確認這三句在意義上的連貫。

2. D

邏輯 本段的主題句提到，比起太陽系中任何其他的行星，火星與地球更加類似。這是一個廣泛的論點，因此我們可以推測作者接下來會提出更具體的證據來支持這樣的論點。而在 (D) 選項中提到，地球和火星都具有季節性的天氣型態、而且火星的一日也只比地球的一日長一點點而已。這樣的敘述正是描述兩者之間的相似性，因此在語意邏輯上是合理的安排。除此之外，下一句還提到火星上也有大氣，這也是很具體的相似處，因此可以判斷此處的邏輯次序是「廣泛籠統→具體明確」，故 (D) 選項為此處的正確答案。

轉折詞 (D) 選項中的轉折詞 for example 是很重要的答題關鍵，作者經常會利用這個轉折詞來針對某個論點提出更為具體的證據。而作者在前一句提出了一個較廣泛的論點，故需要在此處以 for example 提出明確的證據。此外，下一句的 what's more 也是常見的重要轉折詞，用於提出類似的證據或論點。由此可知，作者在此利用 for example 和 what's more 這兩個轉折詞，針對火星和地球的相似處提出了數個具體的證據。

3. F

邏輯 在前一句裡提到，許多人相信火星表面過去有許多地方是被水所覆蓋的。在敘述此種情況時，作者是用「過去式」來表達，而且還強調是 in the ancient past，因此在邏輯上可以推論，這應該是暗示現在火星上可能找不到水了。(F) 選項中提到了火星上的水因為某種原因而已經消失，這是一個很重要的語意線索，因為符合了前一句話的暗示，在邏輯上是吻合的。

重複 在前一句與 (F) 選項中都重複提到了 water 這個字，因此可以確認這兩句在談論相同的主題，換句話說，作者利用 water 這個字來達成這兩句的連貫性。

4. E

邏輯 從這三句的邏輯關係來判斷，可以看出這是一種「因果關係」的陳述，本題的前一句是造成 (E) 選項的原因，而相對於下一句，(E) 選項則是原因，下一句是所造成的結果。也就是說，這三句是環環相扣的，因此可以確認 (E) 選項是此處的正確答案。

用字 在 (E) 選項中的 greenhouse effect (溫室效應) 和 heat (熱能) 是極為重要的關鍵字。由於全球暖化日漸嚴重，因此使得 greenhouse effect 一詞而廣為人知，因此 (E) 選項中的 greenhouse effect、heat 兩個字，和前一句的 warm、以及下一句的 higher temperature 具有極為密切的關聯性。換句話說，因為這些詞彙的關係，所以使得這三句之間產生了語意的連貫性。

5. C

邏輯 從本段的主題句 (第一句) 可知，本段所談論的主題是火星是否有能適合人類居住，而在本段的前半部分已經提到了使火星變得適合人類居住的一些方法，像是使大氣層變厚、留住熱能以使火星上的冰融化成水，而 (C) 選項的內容則提到，如果真能如此的話，則火星就可能變得 habitable (適合居住)。由此可知，(C) 選項除了表達前面數個句子的內容所要達到的目的，也呼應了本段的主題句所要探討的事物，因此在邏輯上是合理的安排。

同義詞 在 (C) 選項中的 habitable 一字，其涵意就等同於本段主題句中提到的 suitable for life，因此可以視為是同義字。除此之外，(C) 選項中的 habitable 這個字，也就是前一句所提到的 life can exist，因此可以確認 (C) 選項在語意上是承接了前一句而來的。

在本篇題目當中，只有 (A) 選項沒有被選到。在閱讀過 (A) 選項的內容後可以發現，該選項所談論的主題是科學家想要找出未來可以在火星殖民的方

法。在本篇文章的三個段落中，只有第三段的主題與此相似，因此可以判斷 (A) 選項比較有可能是出現在第三段中。然而，第 4 題和前後兩句有強烈因果關係，談論的主題是溫室效應以及使火星升溫，顯然與 (A) 選項的內容不合。至於第 5 題，前面已經明確地討論過各種讓火星適合人類居住的具體方法，而 (A) 選項的內容則是一個比較廣泛的概念，也就是幫助人類殖民火星的方法，與此處所提到的具體細節不符，所以不能當作此處的正確答案。

 Round 18

翻譯

雖然世界上有許多不同宗教，大部分似乎都有特殊的宗教節日或其重要的一段時程。對伊斯蘭教來說更是如此，事實上，其宗教節日為一整個月。這個月叫齋戒月，對穆斯林來說是所有節日中最神聖的。

齋戒月不在固定的日期開始，這是由於它是陰曆的一部份所致。這意味著每年慶祝齋戒月的時間都不一樣。然而，齋戒月每年都不會變的是其長度。它通常為期整整三十天。

穆斯林在齋戒月都做些什麼？他們會做幾件事情，但最主要的是齋戒，健康的成人尤其如此。這意味著從黎明到黃昏都不吃不喝。在齋戒月，大部分穆斯林會在黎明前吃一頓封齋飯。然後，晚上會吃開齋飯，停止齋戒。這幾餐通常會邀請賓客以及窮苦的人共享，在這之後清真寺可能會有晚禱。

在齋戒月，穆斯林也會盡力不動怒，還會趁這機會禱告、讀可蘭經、並幫助他人。他們相信在齋戒月應該要禮拜神，齋戒等行為則是要教導彼此耐心及同情心。事實上，齋戒是伊斯蘭的五功之一。

齋戒月對穆斯林來說無庸置疑地是一個非常重要的節日。齋戒自然是其一大部分，但對許多穆斯林來說，齋戒月給他們反省人生、更理解神的機會。

1. E

邏輯 作者在本段中所採用的邏輯次序，是「廣泛籠統→具體明確」，也就是由較大範圍縮小到較小範圍的寫作手法。本段中所使用的順序如下：「每個宗教都有神聖的節日→伊斯蘭教中有一整個月的神聖月份→這個月份的具體名稱為 Ramadan (齋戒月)」，因此可以確認 (E) 選項為此處的正確答案。

重複 作者在前一句中提到了 special holy days，而在 (E) 選項中則提到 an entire holy month，甚至連下一句也提到了 the holiest of holidays，其中不但重複了 holy 這個形容詞，並仔細閱讀前兩句，就會觀察到，這裡的 holy days 和 holy month 幾乎是同義詞。換句話說，作者利用這些詞彙來表達這三個句子之間的連貫性，這也成為在答題時可以特別注意的重要線索。

2. B

邏輯 在前一句提到，齋戒月並沒有固定的開始日期，而 (B) 選項中提到，齋戒月每年的慶祝時間都不一樣。由語意分析可以得知這兩句之間存在著因果關係，也就是前一句是「原因」，而 (B) 選項則是「結果」，因此可以確認 (B) 選項是正確答案。

換句話說 在前一句裡提到的 no fixed starting date for Ramadan (齋戒月沒有固定的開始日期)，與在 (B) 選項裡的 it is celebrated at different times every year，雖然說法不同，但是兩者所表達是同樣的意思，而作者則利用此種方式使這兩個句子產生連貫性。

代名詞 在 (B) 選項中的代名詞 This，所指涉的對象是前一句裡的 There is no fixed starting date for Ramadan。而在 (B) 選項中的另外一個代名詞 it，所指涉的對象當然就是前一句中提到的 Ramadan 了。由此可以看出這兩句之間的關係是相當密切的。

3. F

邏輯 從本段的第二句中得知，在齋戒月中最重要的事情就是 fasting (齋戒、禁食)，而從接下來幾句的內容可知，fasting 正是本段所討論的主題，而這個主題則與「飲食」有關。(F) 選項中也提到了與飲食有關的事，因此符合此處的主題。除此之外，(F) 選項中提到了在黎明之前先吃一餐，而下一句則提到在夜晚來臨時再吃一餐，這兩句除了都在描述齋戒間期間的用餐習俗之外，兩者之間也有很明顯的時間次序，也就是「黎明→夜晚」，因此更加確認 (F) 選項為此處的正確答案。

重複 在前一句裡提到了 eating，而在 (F) 選項裡也重複提到了 eat 這個字，因此可以得知 eat 是這兩句的關鍵字彙。

4. D

邏輯 前一句的後半段提到了伊斯蘭教徒把齋戒月當成是個好好禱告的機會，而 (D) 選項前半段也提到大家相信，齋戒月是個敬神的時間，代表兩句之間有前後呼應。除此之外，(D) 選項後半段提到了 fasting 的重要性和意義，而下一句則針對 fasting 再做更進一步的強調，因此可以看出這兩句之間也有互相呼應的情況，故可知 (D) 選項為正確答案。

用 字 在前一句中的 pray (禱告)，和 (D) 選項中的 worship (禮拜、敬神) 具有高度的相關性。同樣地，在前一句中提到的 help others，也和 (D) 選項中的 compassion for others (對他人懷有同情心) 具有高度的相關性，因此可以確認這兩個句子之間有密切的關聯性。

重 複 在前一句以及 (D) 選項當中都重複提到 Ramadan，可視為一個輔助線索，而更重要的是作者在 (D) 選項和下一句裡，都重複提到了 fasting 這個字。由這兩個字分別重複出現於前一句和下一句當中，可知 (D) 選項是銜接前後兩句的句子，並使這三個句子產生連貫性。

5. C

邏 輯 在 (C) 選項中的 without a doubt，是一個重要的轉折詞。當作者在使用這個轉折詞時，通常會在前面的段落或句子裡提出充分的陳述或說明，然後再用這個轉折詞帶出結論。在此已經是最後一段，作者在前面的一到四段中已經充分說明了 Ramadan 這個節日的習俗及對穆斯林的重要性，所以在此以 Without a doubt 這個轉折詞來帶出「Ramadan is a very important religious holiday for Muslims」這個結論，是非常適合的，因此可以確認 (C) 選項為此處的正確答案。

代名詞 在下一句裡所提到的代名詞 it，所指涉的對象正是 (C) 選項中的 Ramadan，因此可以作為輔助的答題線索。

重 複 在 (C) 選項提到了 for Muslims，而在下一句裡也提到了 for many Muslims，此為是作者刻意重複的重要詞彙，以達成兩句之間的連貫性。除此之外，在 (C) 選項和下一句裡也都重複提到了 Ramadan，這也可以當成輔助性的答題線索。

在本篇題目中唯一沒有使用的選項是 (A)。在 (A) 選項中提到有些伊斯蘭教徒認為，他們可以利用此種方式來瞭解他們的真神曾經經歷過多少的苦難，依照句中的 suffered 這個字與整篇文章的內容來判斷，(A) 選項中提到的代名詞 this 應該是指 fasting，如果 (A) 選項為答案之一的話，那麼在它的前面必定要先提到 fasting 這件事，才會有指涉的對象。根據這個來判斷，(A) 選項唯一有可能出現的地方，就在第三段中的第 3 題，因為在第 3 題的前面有提到 fasting 這件事。然而，由於在第 3 題的下一句有一個轉折詞 Then，表示第 3 題的答案與下一句之間有時間次序的先後關係，而 (A) 選項中卻沒有提到任何與時間有關的線索，因此我們可以確認 (A) 選項並不是第 3 題的答案。

Round 19

翻譯

你喜歡嘻哈嗎？現在有很多人都喜歡嘻哈，可是你可能會讓驚訝，並沒太多人知道嘻哈的起源和歷史。

據說，嘻哈誕生於 1970 年代紐約最貧困的幾個地方。當時，非裔及拉丁裔美人的青少年想發展出某種專屬於他們生活的東西。一些人在迪斯可舞廳和街頭派對當 DJ 播放歌曲。這些 DJ 用雙唱盤將兩片唱片「混音」並讓節拍延續不停。最後，一些人開始跟著 DJ 的節拍饒舌，這些人開始被稱為「MC」或「饒舌歌手」。

嘻哈音樂的第一首暢銷曲是 1979 年的「Rapper's Delight」，而對許多美國人來說，這是他們第一次聽到饒舌。嘻哈繼續在 1980 年代走紅，但仍以紐約市及美國西岸為中心。之後幾年，嘻哈音樂會傳遍美國，先至加州，在那裡 Ice T 和 NWA 獲得成功。之後，Outkast 等團體讓嘻哈音樂在南方站穩腳步，Eminem 和 Kanye West 在中西部讓嘻哈音樂獲得成功。

今日，嘻哈在全世界都很流行，包括台灣。在許多國家，年輕人將嘻哈的基本架構拿來改造並融入他們自己的生活和文化。舉例來說，台灣的一位 MC 可能會用台語饒舌，講他可能面對的挑戰。

雖然嘻哈起源於美國，現在，它絕對屬於全世界。

1. D

邏 輯 本段在討論 hip hop (嘻哈) 的由來。在第一句裡提到，hip hop 在 1970 年代誕生於紐約市中一些窮困的地區，而在 (D) 選項中除了用 at that time 這個轉折詞來接續前一句之外，其中所提到的 Africa-American and Latino teenagers，則是美國社會中較弱勢也較貧窮的族群，因此也呼應了前一句提到的 poorest areas 的概念，故 (D) 選項為此處的正確答案。

用 字 在 (D) 選項一開始時，作者提到了 At that time，一般而言，當作者要使用這個片語時，在前面的句子裡面一定會先提到過去的某個時間點，而在前一句裡提到 in the 1970s，因此我們就可以確定，(D) 選項裡的 at that time 所指的就是 the 1970s。

代名詞 在下一句裡所提到的代名詞 some，其指涉的對象就是 (D) 選項裡的 African-American and

Latino teenagers (非裔與拉丁裔美國青少年)。作者利用代名詞使這兩句產生關聯性,而這也是我們可以去尋找與利用的線索。

2. F

邏輯 在本題的前一句、(F) 選項,以及下一句之間具有明確的時間順序,也就是「些非裔或拉丁裔美國青少年開始去當 DJ 放音樂→他們播放一種特殊不間斷的音樂→有些人開始跟著節拍唱饒舌歌曲」,此可以看出 (F) 選項確實是此處的正確答案。

重複 在尋找本題的答案時,最重要的線索就是重複出現的關鍵字。在前一句裡和 (F) 選項中都重複提到 DJ 以及 record 這兩個字,而在 (F) 選項和下一句裡都重複提到了 beat (節拍),代表作者用這三個重複出現的關鍵字來串起這三個句子,使這些句子產生語意的一致性與連貫性。

3. A

邏輯 在前一句裡,作者提到 hip hop 第一首暢銷曲目出現於 1979 年,而在 (A) 選項中則提到,hip hop 在 1980 年代時受歡迎的程度日益增加,作者在本段的三句話是依照時間順序的邏輯來描述 hip hop 的發展經過,故 (A) 選項為正確答案。

重複 在前一句、(A) 選項,以及下一句裡都重複提到了 hip hop,因此可以看出這三句都是以 hip hop 為中心主題。

4. B

邏輯 本段的主題是 hip hop 在美國的源起與發展過程。作者是按照事件的時間先後次序來描述,但是從第三句開始,還加入了地理的層面,也就是 hip hop 原本只侷限在美國的紐約市,但後來擴散到全美國,而作者也依照擴散的地區次序來描述,其順序為「New York City、America's East Coast→California、West Coast→the South、the Midwest」,由此可以看到 hip hop 慢慢擴散到全美國的趨勢,因此也可以確認 (B) 選項為正確答案。

用字 在本題的前兩個句子中,都提到美國地區的名稱,像是 New York City、America's East Coast、California、the West Coast 等等,而在 (B) 選項中也提到 the South 以及 the Midwest,因此可以確認 (B) 選項與前兩句之間有密切關聯性。除此之外,在前一句裡提到一些知名的饒舌歌手,像是 Ice T 和 NWA,而在 (B) 選項裡也提到了其他成功的饒舌歌手或團體,如 Outkast、Eminem、Kanye West 等,換句話說,這兩個句子的主題和描述方式非常類似,而這也是重要的答題線索。

5. C

邏輯 前一句提到 hip hop 目前在全世界都廣受歡迎,而 (C) 選項中則提到年輕人擷取了嘻哈的基本結構,並且將它改編為符合他們自己的生活與文化,這一句為關鍵線索,因為在下一句裡,作者用 for example 這個轉折詞來針對這一句的內容提出在臺灣的具體例子。換句話說,這三句的敘述次序正好符合了「廣泛籠統→具體明確」的順序,因此我們可以確認 (C) 選項為此處的正確答案。

用字 在前一句裡提到了 all over the world,而在 (C) 選項裡則提到了 in many countries,這兩個詞彙的意義相近,因此可視為重要的答題線索。

重複 在前一句和 (C) 選項裡都重複提到了 hip hop,而在 (C) 選項和下一句最後,都重複提到了 culture 這個字,因此可以確認作者利用這些重複的字來達成這三個句子之間的連貫性。

> 在本篇題目中唯一沒有使用的選項是 (E)。在 (E) 選項中提到嘻哈音樂已經變成一種文化,而且饒舌歌手喜歡自己寫歌詞來反映社會,由這樣的敘述內容來判斷,(E) 選項所談論的主題應該是偏向於描述 hip hop 的現狀。在本篇文章中,第一段先引出 hip hop 這個主題,第二段描述了 hip hop 的起源,第三段描述 hip hop 在美國受到歡迎的發展過程,第四段提到 hip hop 目前在全世界的現狀,最後一句則是提出總結。因此 (E) 選項最有可能出現在第四段當中,也就是 (E) 選項可能是第 5 題的答案。然而,在 5 題的前後兩個句子當中,都沒有提到與饒舌歌手自己寫歌詞有關的細節,而且在下一句裡提到的 culture 指的是各地不同的文化,並不是指 hip hop 自己已經成為一種文化。因此 (E) 選項並不適合當作第 5 題的答案。

Round 20

翻譯

　　我們是否從新聞媒體接收了對時事的客觀觀點?許多的媒體,例如電視公司和廣播電台,都是營利事業。為了生存,他們需要客戶的廣告收入,而廣告客戶要的則是大量的觀眾。而這種現實情況,在呈現新聞時,容易助長用拉攏觀眾的方式來報導新聞。

　　「壞事傳千里」,而壞事也正好吸引觀眾。想想

看，為什麼新聞的開頭往往是震驚人心或駭人聽聞的頭條，離不開恐怖炸彈攻擊、火災、水災等新聞？這是「壞消息的偏好」，但同時也提高了收視率和廣告的收入。

「你聽說最新消息了嗎？」我們都想要聽到最新消息。這是「時間偏好」。閃現過電視螢幕上的「即時新聞」字眼，總是能使我們固定在座位上；而在他們說「別轉台」的同時，我們也收看了一分鐘左右黃金時段的廣告。

名人訴訟案和性醜聞的報導能夠驚爆成充滿戲劇性的「新聞」，非常適合做為連續劇並能抓住觀眾的頭條。這是「新聞敘述的偏好」，讓新聞有連續劇的感覺。緋聞纏身的總統會下台嗎？那名搖滾巨星是否犯下性侵害的罪行？有罪還是無罪？請收看下一節的新聞快報！

另一句古老諺語是這麼說的：「沒消息就是好消息。」但對新聞媒體來說並非如此。他們無時無刻都必須創作新聞，而且他們有強烈的動機以特定的方式描述這個世界。也就是說，我們實際從新聞中得到的消息是經過選擇之後的影像，而非實際發生事件的真實寫照。

1. C

邏 輯 前一句提到，新聞媒體一切都是生意。公司企業都是以營利為目的，才能生存下去，而 (C) 選項中提到這些公司必須有廣告商的收入才能生存，在語意上符合此處的邏輯論述，因此是正確答案。

用 字 在前一句裡提到的 businesses，以及在 (C) 選項裡提到的 income (收入) 具有密切的關聯性，可確認 (C) 選項和前一句之間確實有密切的關係。

代名詞 在 (C) 選項裡的代名詞 they，所指涉的對象就是前一句裡的 a lot of news media，以達成語意的連貫，因此是重要的答題線索。

2. A

邏 輯 簡單瀏覽文章的整體架構，就可以得知本文分成五段，第一段提出一個廣泛的概念，也就是在新聞中有各種 biases (偏見、偏差)，接著第二到四段分別針對三種不同的 biases 進行更深入的描述，而最後一段則是總結。在第二段提到第一種 bias，從第一句可得知，本段是在討論負面新聞，也就是新聞報導喜歡以恐怖攻擊或是各種災難為頭條，以吸引觀眾，而這個主題正是 (A) 選項中提到 bad news bias，其目的正是 (A) 選項中提到的 boosts ratings and commercial income，因此 (A) 選項為此處的正確答案。

重 複 在本段的主題句中就已經提到 bad news，而 (A) 選項則重複提到 bad news，達成前後呼應、強化本段主題的效果，由此可知此為重要的答題線索。

3. E

邏 輯 本段繼續討論另外一種 bias，也就是 time bias。根據本段前兩句的描述，人們都想要知道最新的消息，所以新聞報導也投其所好，讓人們能知道最新消息。而在 (E) 選項中提到了 Breaking News，意旨「即時新聞」，通常是報導最新的、或是剛發生的新聞，所注意的正是「時間」這個觀念，符合本段的主題 time bias，因此可知 (E) 選項為正確答案。

4. F

邏 輯 本段所討論的又是另一種 bias。根據第一句的說法，新聞媒體會把某些事件炒作成像連續劇一樣，以吸引觀眾的注意力。而 (F) 選項中提到 giving the news a soap opera feel，正好用來描述此種做法，soap opera 意旨「連續劇」或「肥皂劇」，其中個別的一集稱為 episode，而這個字正好出現在這一段的最後一個字，因此可以視為前後呼應。

用 字 本段第一句裡提到 dramatic stories、serial，和 (F) 選項中的 soap opera feel、以及最後一句的 episode 等字，都和此段主題有關，因此為重要的答題線索。

5. D

邏 輯 在前一句的前半段提到了一句俗諺 No news is good news，但是句子後半段則表示，這句俗諺並不適用於新聞媒體。而 (D) 選項中提到，新聞媒體必須 make news all the time，就像是在針對前一句話進行更深入的說明一樣，因此我們可以看出這兩句之間具有密切的連貫性。

用 字 在 (D) 選項中的最後面提到 in a certain way (以某種特定的方式)，而下一句則提到 selective image (選擇性的意象)，這兩者之間也具有關聯性。更確切地說，當新聞媒體以「某種」方式來呈現這個世界時，就會以某種標準來篩選或過濾新聞事件，因此最後呈現在我們面前的，就是經過「選擇」之後新聞，所以我們可以看出，(D) 選項和下一句之間具有因果關係，因此可以確認 (D) 選項為本題的正確答案。

代名詞 在 (D) 選項中的代名詞 they，所指涉的對象就是前一句最後的 new media，因此達成語意上的連貫，是重要的答題線索。

在本篇題目當中，只有 (B) 選項沒有被選到。在閱讀過 (B) 選項的內容後可以發現，該選項的內容是

指人們通常沒有察覺到這些新聞偏好，因此容易受到它們的影響。這樣的敘述曾出現在兩個地方：一是在第一段中，當作作者提出的主要論點，並在接下來的文章裡詳細說明；二則是在最後一段，當作整篇文章總結。由於在第一段裡，biases 這個字第一次出現就是在最後一句，後面已經沒有其他句子。而 (B) 選項中的 news biases 前面還有一個 these，表示前面必然有先提過 news biases 這個概念。但第 1 題的位置是在最後一句的前面，所以顯然 (B) 選項不是第 1 題的答案。而在最後一段裡，第 5 題的前後既沒有特別提到 news biases，更沒有提到這些 biases 所造成的影響，所以也和 (B) 選項的內容主題不符。因此，(B) 選項也不能當作第 5 題的答案。

🟦 閱讀測驗－題目篇

Round 1

翻譯

當動物變成寵物的那一刻起，他們就具有其他身分，再也不是動物了。他們搖身一變成了小狗道格拉斯、小貓凱薩琳、兔子拉菲、小蛇姍卓，寵物取了名字之後，他們就立刻成了我們的同伴、玩伴和朋友，簡而言之，他們變的幾乎和人類沒什麼兩樣。

眾所皆知，寵物帶給主人許多好處。小狗道格拉斯不只是小孩的玩伴，還能讓小主人學會負責任，在小孩幫道格拉斯洗澡或餵食的同時，他也學到別人是可以依靠他的。當然，寵物對於年紀稍長的主人也是貢獻良多。對老年人而言，寵物打破了孤立的藩籬，甚至還有人說寵物能讓年長者身體健康，每天和貓狗去散步對他們的健康可說是妙用無窮。

想想寵物帶給我們的一切，那我們回報他們給我們的好處也就不足為奇了，這在我們視他們為人類的時候尤其明顯。以日本女士 Noriko Uchiyama 為例，她每個月都去泡溫泉，但假如她邀你同行，你可得三思了。為什麼呢？因為狗狗小碰的緣故。小碰跟她一起去泡溫泉時會很緊張，不過牠非去不可，因為牠的毛正在脫落，據 Noriko 女士的說法，小碰皮膚掉毛的問題只要去泡溫泉，放鬆一下就能治癒。

Noriko Uchiyama 並不是個與眾不同的寵物主人，世界各地的主人都將他心愛的動物「人性化」了。他們在寒冬時節給兔子拉菲穿上衣服，到了萬

聖夜將小貓凱薩琳打扮成一條熱狗；有些狗甚至還進行整容手術，好讓耳朵直立突出；還有寵物持有自己的護照和主人一同旅行，也難怪當今的寵物主人反對「主人」這個字眼，他們還比較希望被稱做寵物的「守護者」。

1. A

⊕ 本題在考主旨大意，可使用略讀，快速掃過每一段的主題句。

⊕ 本題解題關鍵在於第一段的最後一句：In short, they are almost humans. 這裡的 they 指的正是寵物，可以得知對寵物的主人來說，這些毛小孩已經被像人類一樣地對待。文章中最後兩段也提出許多佐證，故答案選 (A)。

⊕ 選項 (B) 提出寵物需要很多錢和時間來照顧，並無觸及到寵物被 humanized 的重點。選項 (C) 則提到寵物提供主人愛與陪伴，雖然在第二段有提到，但並非全文的重點。選項 (D) 提到寵物被給予許多有創意的名字，雖在第一段有提到，亦非全文的重點，作者只是藉著這點來導入文章的大意。故答案為 (A)。

2. B

⊕ 本題在考代名詞 him 所指涉的字為何，通常該字會出現在此一代名詞的前方。

⊕ 本句 When the child gives Douglas a bath or a meal, he's learning that others can depend on him. 中，him 所指的名詞可能有 Douglas 和 the child，根據文意 others can depend on him 可以猜測 him 指的是這個孩子，因為孩子在照顧寵物時可培養責任感，所以別人 (寵物) 可以依賴他，故答案選 (B) The child。

3. D

⊕ 本題在考單一細節，利用瀏覽的技巧快速在文章中找到關鍵字，並細讀前後文字就可找到答案。

⊕ 本題的關鍵字為 besides companionship (除了陪伴以外) 寵物還可以給老人什麼樣的好處？從第二段的 physically fit 和 do wonders for their health 等可知寵物對老人「身體健康」的好處，故答案選 (D) wellness。

⊕ 選項 (B) Responsibility 其實是在第二段前半提到對孩子的好處，故並非答案。而選項 (A) 和 (C) 並沒有在文章中特別被提到。

4. A

⊕ 本題在考多個關於 Pon-chan 的細節，故瀏覽上下文找到 Pon-chan 出現的段落後，再逐一比對選項就可快速找出正確答案。

⊕ Pon-chan 出現在文章的第三段，選項 (A) 指出牠每週都去 spa，和文章中 but he absolutely has to 這句相符，表示 Pon-chan 每週都和牠的主人去 spa 因為他必須要去，故答案選 (A)。

⊕ 選項 (B) 指出 Pon-chan 喜歡去 spa，但是文中提到他對去 spa 這件事感到緊張，可以判斷此選項錯誤。選項 (C) 提到 Pon-chan 在掉牙齒，事實上文中只有提到他掉毛這件事 (his fur is falling out)，可知此為錯誤選項。選項 (D) 說到牠的皮膚問題已解決，但是文中只有提到 Pon-chan 的主人相信 spa 能改善牠的皮膚問題，並沒有提到是否真的有達到此一效果，故選項 (D) 亦為錯誤選項。

Round 2

翻譯

　　午夜時分，你走在紐奧良市法語區的波旁大街，身旁擠滿了人群。他們載歌載舞，飲酒作樂，其實大多數的人都已經醉了。樂隊從旁經過，演奏著音樂。衣飾誇張亮麗的人從花車上向你拋灑糖果、塑膠串珠和銅板…歡迎你來到全球最盛大的免費表演既熱鬧又墮落的「狂歡星期二」。

　　紐奧良是美國路易西安那州的第一大城。由法國殖民者於西元 1718 年建立，他們帶來了狂歡星期二的傳統。這個節日的起源可以追溯到古代，當時的人們慶祝冬天結束以及春天開始。春天是再生的時節，動物從冬眠中甦醒過來，植物冒出新芽，樹木也長出了新葉。基督教徒保留了這個節日並加以改良，賦予它宗教的色彩。狂歡星期二 (Mardi Gras) 的法文原意是「油膩星期二」，是基督教信仰中「四旬齋」開始前的最後一天。四旬齋為期四十天到復活節為止，這段期間必須齋戒、禱告與宗教冥想。這就是為何路易西安那州的法裔居民在四旬齋開始前的一個星期盡情享受的原因。他們大吃大喝，狂歡無度，因為他們知道在「油膩星期二」的午夜，一切的狂歡活動都得停止。

　　原本只是路易西安那州法裔居民之間單純的宗教慶典，而今成為全球盛事。交通與通訊設施改善後，人人都能參與並享受狂歡星期二。狂歡星期二的名聲與人氣是因為它的獨一無二。在美國其他地方你都無法體驗像這樣的奇景。

1. D

⊕ 本題在問作者在一開始使用何種手法來描述此節慶，因此詳細閱讀作者第一段的描述，可以看出作者描寫人們半夜在 New Orleans 慶祝的場景，由此可以判斷答案為 (D)，作者是從某一個特定場景 (a specific scene) 切入。

⊕ 選項 (A) 為節慶的歷史，這點在第二段才被作者提到，不是作者「開始」講述的點，故不是正確答案。選項 (B) 提到節慶的意義和選項 (C) 提到節慶的特別與獨特，這並非作者一開始描寫節慶的方式，故都為錯誤選項。

2. C

⊕ 本段在考文章的最佳標題，同學應善用略讀的技巧，從各段落的主題句快速找到文章的主旨。

⊕ 第一段的主題句在最後一句：That is the greatest free show on earth: Mardi Gras.。第二段的主題句為第一、二句，點出 New Orleans 和 Mardi Gras 的歷史淵源。最後一段的主題句則是在第一句：What started out as a purely regional celebration among the French in Louisiana is today a world-famous event.。從這三部分可以看出來本文在講 Mardi Gras 在紐奧良的慶祝方式，故選 (C) 為正確答案。

⊕ 選項 (A) New Orleans 的歷史只有在文章第二段提及，並非重點。選項 (B) Fat Tuesday 是節慶中的某一天，也是一個出現在第二段的細節，也非重點。選項 (D) 則是指 Mardi Gras 在世界各地的不同慶祝模式，文章並沒有提到，故非正確答案。

3. A

⊕ 本題在考上下文的字義，作答技巧是把四個選項都帶進原文比對，看哪個最符合上下文。

⊕ 句子後半段作者有提到 they eat, drink, and party to excess，表示 Louisiana 的法國人在 Lent (四句齋) 開始前會大吃大喝和無盡止地開派對，這就是 live it up the week 的意思，所以最適合的答案為 (A) make the most of it，表示充分利用這瘋狂的一週。

⊕ 選項 (B) put an end to it 為結束的意思；選項 (C) come up with it 為提出、想出之意；選項 (D) cut down on it 為減少的意思。上述皆不適合帶入上下文。

4. A

⊕ 本題在考如何從結論中推敲出正確答案，因此關鍵在於最後一段的內容。

⊕ 文章最後一段主要在講因為其獨特性，再加上大眾運輸的改良，讓路易斯安那州的紐奧良成為享受 Mardi Gras 最佳的地點，並從文章最後一句 In no other place in America can you experience such a spectacle 可以推論出 (A) 為正確答案。

選項 (B) 所提到的宗教層面在最後結論並沒提到。選項 (C) 的說法並末在文章中提及。選項 (D) 所提到的 celebrities 在文中也並未提到，故為錯誤選項。

Round 3

翻譯

你喜歡聽音樂嗎？許多人喜歡聽音樂取樂。但你知道其實音樂也可能可以增進你的學習能力嗎？

根據近期的幾個報告，音樂在學習上可以有很大的作用。史丹佛大學的一項研究指出，聽音樂可以幫助聆聽者更專注。在高度集中的狀態下，人們更容易吸收新資訊。另一項約翰·霍普金斯大學的研究亦有同樣的結果。新資訊若搭配上特殊的節奏或押韻，則會更加符合研究的結果。一位名為 Chris Brewer 的作家相信音樂可以讓學生更有意願學習。舉例來說，歡樂的音樂可以刺激學生學習新事物，而古典音樂則可以幫助他們專心讀書或寫作。

此外，學習如何演奏樂器可能對全面的學習有更大的影響。事實上，西北大學的研究發現音樂訓練可以增進談吐、注意力長度，甚至外語技能。根據這項研究，大腦接觸音樂時，它能夠更快速、容易地適應、改變。而且，這項研究發現，受過音樂訓練的學生與沒受過任何音樂訓練的學生相比閱讀能力更好、詞彙量更大。這些學生在學習一種不同的語言時也更會運用陌生的聲音模式。

所以，如果你真的想增進你的學習能力，可以考慮聽音樂或甚至學習如何演奏樂器。顯然，音樂似乎可以是一種非常有效的工具。

1. A

◉ 本題在考作者對「音樂幫助學習」的態度，在瀏覽文章時需細細體會作者的立場，並從用字遣詞中找到線索來判斷。

◉ 作者在文章第一段提出了音樂也許可以幫助學習的論點，而後瀏覽全文時會發現作者在第二段和第三段提出一些學者的研究，來告訴讀者音樂確實對學習有幫助，並且在最後一段明確地告訴讀者 It seems clear that music can be a very powerful tool，從此可以判斷作者的態度是相當正向 (positive)，故答案選 (A)。

◉ 選項 (B) negative (負面的)、選項 (C) neutral (中立的)、和選項 (D) conservative (保守的) 皆為錯誤答案。

2. C

◉ 本題在考「統整」的能力。可快速略讀第二和第三段，找出各個主題句，便可得到解答。

◉ 本題在考音樂的哪兩個方面能幫助學生學習。第二段作者提出了三個佐證，第一是 Stanford University 做的研究，第二為 Johns Hopkins University 做出的研究，第三則是 Chris Brewer 的看法。這三者都在強調聽音樂對學習的幫助；第三段的主題句「learning how to play a musical instrument can have an even bigger effect on overall learning.」，作者直接點出學習樂器也能幫助學習。因此，可以總結為聽音樂和彈奏樂器這兩方面，故選 (C)。

◉ 選項 (A) 和 (B) 裡提到的閱讀音樂論文在文中並未提及。文章中也沒有提出作曲可以幫助學生提升學習能力，故 (A)(B)(D) 皆為錯誤選項。

3. D

◉ 本題在考有關 a Northwestern University study 的細節，可快速略讀第三段後，和選項比對即可找出答案。

◉ 文章第三段第二句提到 musical training can improve speech, attention span, and even foreign language skills，直接點出音樂對學習語言有所幫助，最後一句作者也提到學生在學習不同語言時會比較會習慣新的發音模式，故和選項 (D) 所表示的「音樂會幫助學生學習外語」之意相同，故為正確答案。

◉ 選項 (A) 提到不適合的音樂對學生學習有負面效果，此點在文章中並沒有提到。選項 (B)「音樂能幫助焦躁不安的學生安靜下來」和選項 (C)「音樂能讓學生在吵鬧的環境中專注」，文章中都未描述此論點，故 (A)、(B)、(C) 皆為錯誤選項。

4. C

◉ 本題在考多重細節。瀏覽全文找到關鍵字會發現選項皆落在文章第二段，逐一比對後即可找到正確答案。

◉ 文中第二段後半段提到 Chris Brewer 相信聽音樂能幫助學生提高學習意願，此一敘述符合選項 (C)，故此為正確答案。

◉ 選項 (A) 與文中 Stanford University，提出的論點「聽音樂能幫助學生專注並提升對知識的吸收」不相符。而 Johns Hopkins University 則表示「聽音樂能幫助記憶」，和選項 (B) 中的提升專注力不符。而 upbeat music 能幫助學生學習新的事物和選項 (D) 提到讓學生分心也不符合。

Round 4

翻譯

　　你有因為你面對的某些挑戰或困難而感到擔憂或緊張嗎？如果有的話，你就體驗過壓力。壓力可能讓你不太舒服，而近期的研究已發現長期的壓力也可以很危險，因為它可以對一個人的健康造成很壞的影響。

　　壓力始於一種自動反應，它讓最早期的人類能在生死關頭自保，如面對掠食者時。增加身體的心跳率及能量讓人可以應付危及生命的處境。一些人稱之為「戰鬥或逃跑」反應。

　　然而，我們現在很少碰上到我們祖先碰上的問題。但是，我們的身體仍然繼續用相同的方式應對。因此，我們由於現代社會中的挑戰，如考試及格、付帳單，或在學校或職場與人相處，而感到壓力。

　　短期來講，壓力通常是令人不快的。然而，長期來看，壓力可能對我們的健康非常不好。當壓力持續很長的一段時間就會被稱為「慢性壓力」，它可以導致疲勞、頭痛，甚至某些疾病，如阿茲海默症。它也被認為與肥胖及憂鬱症有關。

　　幸運的是，我們可以採取一些手段來處理壓力。第一種手段是單純的深呼吸，因為它可以幫助你很快地冷靜下來。你也可以專注於當下，不去思考過去或未來，並試著想起你所感激的事物，藉此以正確的觀點來看你碰到的問題。

　　畢竟，壓力存在於我們的生命中，所以我們應該盡力確保壓力不會對我們的健康造成負面影響。

1. A

◎ 本題在考文章出處，故可以透過閱讀主題句來判斷文章屬性，並找到答案。

◎ 第一段的主題句，點出長期的壓力對健康有負面影響。第二段的主題句，提出壓力來自於人們對危險威脅的反應。第三段的主題句則提到現在社會的壓力來源雖然和以前不同，但表現的反應卻是相同的。第四段提到壓力對健康的影響，第五段為如何處理壓力。綜合來看，壓力和健康是此一文章的重點，故選 (A)。

◎ 選項 (B) 的飲食指南和選項 (C) 誠徵個人健身教練的廣告和上下文不符。選項 (D) 雖然可能會有類似內容出現在百科全書，百科全書比較不會使用提問來作為開頭，且百科全書不會提到 recent studies 這樣的內容，本篇文章比較有可能出現在報章雜誌中，故選項 (D) 為非。

2. C

◎ 本題考文章中對 fight-or-flight response 的定義，可快速瀏覽文章並找尋此關鍵字，便可找到答案。

◎ 關鍵字 fight-or-flight response 於文章中第二段，閱讀上下文後，可知 fight-or-flight response 指的是人在面對生命危險時 (life-or-death threat)，身體為了自保所產生的反應，如心跳加速等。此一定義符合選項 (C) 的描述：How our body reacts to a life-threatening situation，故此為正確選項。

◎ 選項 (A) 提到的短期和長期壓力和選項 (B) 慢性的壓力會導致疾病以及選項 (D) 處理壓力的方法，都不是此處對 fight-or-flight response 的定義。

3. D

◎ 本題在考長時間處在壓力下可能會產生的影響，利用瀏覽的技巧找出關鍵字，仔細閱讀上下文並比對選項就可找到答案。注意題目有改變遣詞用字；需選出文章「沒有」提到的選項。

◎ 文中提到 long-term stress 所產生的負面影響有 fatigue (疲累)、headaches (頭痛)、Alzheimer's disease (阿茲海默症) obesity (肥胖) 和憂鬱症。並沒有提到選項 (D) 的睡眠不足 (sleep deprivation)，故 (D) 為正確答案。

◎ 選項 (A) 的 tiredness 就等於 fatigue，選項 (B) 的 overweight 等於 obesity，選項 (C) 的 pain in the head 等於 headaches，皆為文中提到的影響。

4. A

◎ 本文在考作者寫作的目的，需要對全文有徹底的瞭解才能找出正確答案。

◎ 本文提到了壓力對早期人類的影響，而現代人也有壓力，並更進一步地闡述壓力對健康的影響和處理壓力的方法，由此我們可以看出作者對壓力做出了全面的介紹與解釋，故答案選 (A)。

◎ 選項 (B) 提到的「研究」在文章中並沒有多加著墨，故為非；作者並沒有提到適度壓力帶來的好處，雖壓力是一把雙面刃 (double-edged sword)，但此一描述並不符合文章的重點，故選項 (C) 為錯誤選項；選項 (D) 提到遠離壓力的健康生活方式，但作者並未多加描述，作者只有說明處理壓力的方法，故為錯誤選項。

Round 5

翻譯

　　對業餘運動員來說，有機會能在奧林匹克運動會與他人一較高下是件令人興奮的事，倘若他們夠

快或夠壯，甚至有可能贏得獎牌，為自己的國家帶來無上的榮耀與關注。

　　不過在某些情況下，一旦發現獲勝的運動員靠著禁藥才得到勝利，那份自豪與榮耀就會轉變為恥辱與難堪。東窗事發後，獎牌遭到沒收，運動員會被禁賽一段時間，也可能終生禁賽。

　　有時候，運動場上使用禁藥純粹是意外，舉例來說，賽跑選手可能因為頭痛或感冒而服用藥丸，裡頭也許含有違反奧會規定的成分，不過也有些情況是運動員明知這成分是不許可的，但他們還是服用了該藥物。

　　有個使用禁藥的著名例子是發生於一九八八年在南韓舉行的奧運，在當時的奧賽中，加拿大籍的班・強生在一百公尺的賽跑項目打破世界記錄，一舉拿下金牌，但當一項檢驗結果顯示他先前使用過禁藥後，不僅金牌遭到沒收，他也立刻成為加拿大的恥辱。加拿大政府對這起案件進行調查，因而促成了運動禁藥方面更嚴格的規定與檢驗。

　　為什麼運動員會冒著被查獲的風險而使用禁藥呢？因為他們為了贏得勝利，承受很大的壓力，或者對自己的表現不滿意，又或者猜想對手也在使用禁藥，而且認為自己必須如法炮製才有獲勝的機會。

　　為了提高獲勝的機會而服用禁藥非但不對，也很危險，服用某些藥物可能會危害運動員的健康。雖然大多數運動員都知道因服用禁藥而賠上運動生涯和健康不值得，但有些人仍然明知故犯。

1. A

◉ 本題在考文章的大意主旨，略讀每一段的主題句後，即可找出正確答案。

◉ 第一段點出業餘的運動員都想參加奧運，第二段則點出最重要的一句「But in some cases, that pride and glory turn to shame and embarrassment . . .」，點出使用禁藥是件可恥的事。第三段提到運動員用禁藥有時是意外，第四段舉出運動員用藥的案例，第五段則提出運動員服用禁藥的理由。綜合來看，可判斷此文章主旨為運動員使用禁藥以贏得獎牌，故答案選 (A)。

◉ 選項 (B) 指出奧運非常競爭，難以贏得獎牌，故為錯誤選項。選項 (C) 提出藥物上癮是現代社會的嚴重問題，完全沒提到運動競賽，也為錯誤選項。選項 (D) 提到運動賽事中作弊是很常見的事，但做弊的方式有很多，禁藥的使用只是其中一種，故為錯誤的選項。

2. B

◉ 本題在考字義，可從關鍵字的上下文判斷。

◉ 關鍵字 banned 出現在第一段最後一句，句子中的 that 指的是前方運動員使用禁藥被發現的事，當被查出使用禁藥時，他們的獎牌就會被沒收，而這些運動員理也所當然地會被暫時或永久禁賽，根據上下文可以看出來 ban 是禁止的意思，與選項 (B) 的 Not allowed (不被允許) 意思接近，與 (B) 為正確答案。

◉ 選項 (A) Not invited (未受邀請)，表示運動員不再被邀請參與運動賽事，並未符合 ban 的語意。選項 (C) 的 Encouraged 則剛好相反。而選項 (D) Replaced (取代) 亦和文意不符，運動員是被禁賽而非取代，故為錯誤選項。

3. C

◉ 本題在考與 Ben Johnson 有關的細節，略讀全文並找出介紹 Ben Johnson 的段落，即可找出正確答案。

◉ 選項 (C) 提到他在 1988 年的奧運比賽中贏得獎牌，但因為發現使用禁藥而沒收獎牌，與文章的描述符合，故為正確選項。

◉ 選項 (A) 提到他在 1988 年贏得金牌，並且留有此金牌，與文章描述抵觸，故為錯誤選項。選項 (B) 提到他代表美國參與 1988 年奧運，但文章第四段第二句表示他為加拿大人，且最後一句也提到加拿大政府為此展開調查，可以判斷 Ben Johnson 是代表加拿大參加奧運並非美國。選項 (D) 提到調查後，證實 Ben Johnson 使用禁藥，但文中事實上並未直接提到此一細節，只有說到他的獎牌被沒收，且加拿大政府開始使用更嚴格的規定和更嚴謹的禁藥測試，故此一選項亦為錯誤。

4. B

◉ 本題需要對全文有徹底的理解，並用邏輯推理出正確答案。

◉ 第一段主旨為贏得奧運是非常光榮的事。但第三段卻表示運動員肯冒著被抓的風險使用禁藥。第五段又說到運動員若不使用禁藥就有可能不會贏得比賽，因為他們認為對手也都有使用。最後一段也指出：使用禁藥會危害運動員的生涯，但是部分的運動員仍選擇使用禁藥作弊。綜合看來，選項 (B) 中的「儘管使用禁藥有風險，運動員仍嘗試使用禁藥」較符合以上說法，故答案選 (B)。

◉ 選項 (A) 提到運動員不再使用禁藥 (a thing of the past)，剛好與文意相反，故為錯誤選項。選項 (C) 提到運動員使用禁藥的原因是因為不清楚使用禁藥的危險，此一選項與最後一句的文意剛好相反。選項 (D) 提到各國政府應該攜手合作打擊禁藥的使用，與此相關的內容在文中完全沒有被提到，因此也非正確選項。

Round 6

翻譯

　　愛爾蘭這個國家歷經幾世紀激烈的政治鬥爭，所以若說他們的文化以歡樂的音樂、舞蹈和優美的文學著稱，而人民也是出了名的樂觀友善，你可能會感到很驚訝。

　　早在九千年前左右，愛爾蘭島就有人定居，不過在兩千多年前塞爾特人入侵時，才帶來了文化上最重大的影響。塞爾特人統一全島的語言 (愛爾蘭語，也就是蓋爾語)，雖然大多數人講的是英語，不過愛爾蘭語仍是愛爾蘭的官方語言。五世紀時，聖博德將基督教信仰傳到島上，而今日，約有百分之九十五的人口是天主教徒，而聖博德節是最重要的國定假日。最近幾個世紀以來，愛爾蘭和英國的激烈衝突不斷。英格蘭於十七世紀掌控愛爾蘭之後，到一九二一年該島分割成南北兩部分之前，爭取獨立的行動時有所聞。

　　儘管一九九八年簽定了和平協定，愛爾蘭北部的政治鬥爭卻沒有中斷過；不過當大家想到愛爾蘭人，就會想到音樂、舞蹈、說故事、文學、和酒吧等。每個城市和村莊都至少有一間酒吧，當地居民聚集在那裡聆聽現場的音樂演出，並且和鄰居碰面；酒吧裡的音樂是塞爾特民謠，主要的樂器通常是小提琴、錫笛、鼓和風笛。愛爾蘭口傳故事的根源也相當久遠，是以仙女和身材矮小的妖精為主角。多年來文學上的傳承日漸發達，愛爾蘭目前因幾位英國文學史上最優秀的作家而聞名，葉慈、喬伊斯、王爾德只是其中的三位。

　　撇開政治戲碼不談，愛爾蘭是塊文化豐富的土地，能為你帶來歡樂且歡迎你的造訪。

1. C

🔎 本題在考文章最佳標題，可使用略讀的技巧，找出每一段的主題句，綜合推理就可以找到本文的大意，選出文章最好的標題了。

🔎 第一段就直接點出 culture 和 people，明顯的表達出主旨在於人與文化。第二段的開頭提到了愛爾蘭的文化始於兩千多年 Celts 入侵時，可推測本段主要在講文化的演進。第三段的主題句為「when most people think of the Irish they think of music, dancing, storytelling, literature, and pubs」，表現出愛爾蘭數種文化形式。文章最後一句話再次點出愛爾蘭豐富的文

化，因此可以判斷出來本文最佳的標題為 (C) Irish Culture。

🔎 選項 (A) 為愛爾蘭的音樂和文學，雖然也是愛爾蘭的文化，但文中有提到其它的文化形式，如宗教等，故 (A) 為錯誤選項。選項 (B) 為愛爾蘭的紛爭，雖然文中有一再提起，但主要都是拿來與愛爾蘭多采多姿的文化做對比，非文章的重點，故 (B) 也為錯誤選項。選項 (D) 的 Saint Patrick Day 在第二段被提及，但只是文中的小細節，非文章的重點，因此不適合用來當文章標題，所以選項 (D) 也是錯誤的。

2. D

🔎 本題主要考文章中的細節，哪一個外來文化「沒有」影響愛爾蘭，可以使用瀏覽的技巧掃過文章，找出關鍵字，閱讀上下文即可找出答案。

🔎 掃過全文可以發現選項 (D) The Vikings (維京人) 完全沒有在文中出現，因此可以判斷 (D) 為答案。

🔎 文中提到 Saint Patrick 把基督教帶到島上，使得現今愛爾蘭人信羅馬天主教的比例高達 95%，故選項 (A) 提到的羅馬天主教有影響愛爾蘭文化。另外，文中也提到英國在十七世紀時占領了愛爾蘭，從那時開始影響了愛爾蘭文化，故選項 (B) 並非正確答案。文中有明講 Celts 是最早影響愛爾蘭文化的人，故 (C) 選項也非正確答案。

3. D

🔎 本題在考多重細節，故使用瀏覽技巧，將選項 (A) 到 (D) 逐一檢視，並透過找出選項中關鍵字然後去比對文中上下文的方法，即可找到正確答案。

🔎 從文中第二段可知大部分的愛爾蘭人會說英文並有 95% 的人口的信仰為羅馬天主教，而羅馬天主教正是基督教的分支之一，故 (D) 為正確答案。

🔎 選項 (A) 的關鍵字為 the 5th century，但文中並沒有直接提到愛爾蘭文化從何時開始，所以五世紀這時間點是錯誤的。選項 (B) 為英國人從 17 世紀開始就一直控制愛爾蘭，這邊要注意選項 (B) 使用的是現在完成式，表示一直以來愛爾蘭都受到英國控制，到現在還是，但此選項是錯誤的，因為文中第二段最後一句提到 on-again, off-again 的情況，表示統治的情況並沒有一直持續，且後面也提到 1921 年後，愛爾蘭就獨立了。選項 (C) 提到 1998 年的和平協議後，Ireland 就一直很和平，但第三段則提出「the political struggle continue」，可得知仍有政治不安，故不是完全的和平，因此為錯誤選項。

4. A

🔎 本題在考第三段的大意，最快速簡單的方法就是閱

讀本段第一句，也就是主題句，就可以找出答案了。但為了不要掉入陷阱，建議還是快速讀過段落。

◉ 主題句為「The political struggle continues in the north ...」。該句點出本段重點在 music、dancing、storytelling、literature 和 pubs；往下仔細閱讀可以發現本段的重點是在音樂和文學，故選 (A) 為正確答案。

◉ 選項 (B) 提到的 leprechauns 出現在第三段，但是只是一個小細節；選項 (C) 提到的政治不安只有在主題句提到一下，但完全沒有出現在本段內文裡，故不是本段大意；選項 (D) 提到愛蘭爾最棒的作家則是出現在本段的最後一句，但只是一個小細節，並非大意，因此也非正確答案。(B)(C)(D) 三個選項都只是段落中出現一次的小細節，並不是段落大意，所以做答時需要小心不要因為看到關鍵字出現就急著選為正解。

Round 7

翻譯

要了解一個國家或文化，起碼得先知道它大概的歷史；要了解西方文明，就要知道一場發生在三千兩百年前左右的一場戰爭。怎麼說呢？因為這場為期十年的特洛伊戰爭大大地影響了西方歷史與文學的發展。了解過去，即便是傳說故事般的歷史記載，對於了解現在也相當重要。

西元前十二世紀，在地中海的東岸興起了特洛伊城邦，其國王普利安和他兩個兒子巴里士和海克特英明地領導國家，他們最主要的敵人是獨自發展城邦的希臘人，史實的部分僅止於此。然而，傳說通常摻雜著事實與虛構。希臘人相信世界為人神共居(之處)，不過這些神有能力介入人間的事務，而且經常如此。據古希臘最偉大的作家荷馬記載，有位女神答應巴里士能擁有世上最美麗的女子，而那女子恰好是海倫，而且恰好嫁給一名希臘人。在女神的協助之下，巴里士前往希臘劫持了海倫，將她帶回特洛伊。不管是浪漫主義者或是史學家都能猜到接下來的發展，也就是希臘人展開入侵特洛伊的行動，想奪回海倫。

十年過去了，雙方仍然僵持不下，最後，希臘人想到一個辦法。他們建造一隻巨大的空心木馬，裡頭裝滿了士兵，然後將木馬留在特洛伊城門口，假裝離去。特洛伊人認為這匹馬是個禮物，於是帶回城裡頭去。那天晚上，希臘士兵悄悄爬出馬腹，打開城門讓等在外頭的同袍進來毀掉這座城。獲得

這項勝利後，希臘人成為地中海無庸置疑的統治者。

荷馬在《伊里亞德》和《奧德塞》中寫到特洛伊戰爭，這兩部作品是早期的西方文學。希臘文化之後也大大影響了羅馬人以及之後的歐洲人和美國人。這就是為什麼想了解西方文化源頭，就得先約略熟悉特洛伊戰爭，事實和虛構的部分皆然的原因。

1. A

◉ 本題在考作者寫作的目的和原因，此類題型需對文章有完整的了解，才能找出正確答案。

◉ 文章的本文雖然主要在講 Trojan War 的故事，但作者在全文開頭和結尾都有提到為什麼認識 Trojan War 很重要；第一段內文的「Because the ten-year Trojan War greatly influenced the development of Western history and literature.」直接說到十年期間的特洛依戰爭深深影響了西方文化和文學。文章最後一段作者也提到「This is why understanding the cultural roots of the West ...」，作者認為不管是故事中的 Trojan War 或是史實中的 Trojan War，都對西方文化很重要，因此可以推斷作者寫這篇文章的目的或原因是因為 Trojan War 在西方文化的重要地位。

◉ 選項 (B) 提到的希臘邊境、選項 (C) 這是人類史上最長的戰爭、和選項 (D) 這是新的戰爭形式，都是文章中沒有提到的點，故皆為錯誤選項。

2. B

◉ 本題在考單一細節，找到題目中的關鍵字，利用瀏覽的技巧就可以快速找到答案在文中的位置，並仔細閱讀上下文，即可作答。

◉ 本題的關鍵字為 Homer's writing 和 what triggered the war。掃過文章後，可以發現答案出現在第二段「the Greeks began an invasion of Troy to recapture Helen」，由此可知希臘人發起戰爭的原因是 Helen，因為 Paris 綁架了 Helen，所以希臘人才進攻，故選 (B)。

◉ 選項 (A) 希臘人想得到 Troy 的土地，可能是史實上此戰爭發生的原因，第二段第一到第三句有提到 Greece 想發展自己的 city-state，不過這屬於史實，不是 Homer 寫的內容，故此為錯誤答案。選項 (C) 提到的 feud 是長期不和的意思，文章中完全沒有提到，故此為錯誤選項。feud 雖為較困難的單字，但是因為正確答案很明顯，所以並不會影響正確選擇。選項 (D) 指的是希臘人和特洛伊之間的宗教不合，文中也沒有特別提到，故不是正確選項。

3. D

◉ 本題在考推理和暗示，但是必須針對一句話做出推理。仔細閱讀四個選項並比對這句話，即可選出答案。

◉ 本句「Legends, however, often mix fact with fiction.」的意思為流傳已久的傳奇故事常常是 fact (事實) 和 fiction (虛構) 的結合。選項 (D) 提到的 Trojan War 雖然是神話故事，但其實是真正發生過的戰爭，剛好符合這句話的意思。此外，本句話出現在文章中第二段第五句，隔開了史實和神話故事。

◉ 選項 (A) 提到我們無法確定 Trojan War 是否為真實事件，但是文中的確有提到發生的原因，所以此一選項為非。選項 (B) 提到 Homer 是確實地記錄歷史的歷史學家，但文中並未提及此事且 Homer 所寫的作品為事實和虛構的結合，故判斷此為錯誤選項。選項 (C) 提及特洛依戰爭的故事完全是捏造出來的。此陳述為非，因為特洛伊戰爭還是有部分史實，並非完全捏造。。

4. B

◉ 本題在考單一細節，找到題目中的關鍵字，並在文章中比對上下文，即可找到答案。

◉ 題目的關鍵字為 plan，在考希臘人久攻城牆不破，想出來的計劃 (plan) 為何？此一關鍵字出現在第三段，可知接下來的文章發展會細講這個攻城計劃。而這個計劃便是使用巨大的木馬，內藏士兵，並偽裝為禮物送到 Troy 城內並襲擊。此一計劃的描述與選項 (B) 相符，故可判斷選項 (B) 為答案。

◉ 選項 (A) 為給每位士兵一匹馬、選項 (C) 為向宙斯 (Zeus) 祈求協助，而選項 (D) 為建造木造的要塞，但在文章裡都沒有提到，因此這三個皆為錯誤選項。

Round 8

翻譯

時尚的世界裡有幾個大名鼎鼎的人物，如 Calvin Klein、Karl Lagerfeld 和 Vera Wang。然而，過去二十五年間時尚界最重要的人物之一，是 Marc Jacobs。

Jacobs 出生於 1963 年的紐約。Jacobs 的父親在他七歲時過世，令人遺憾，母親又與別人交往並改嫁，這位小男孩度過了一段苦日子。幸運的是，Jacobs 後來與祖母同住，和祖母過起安穩的日子。他的祖母總鼓勵他要有創意、要嘗試新事物。他十五歲時就在服飾店工作，還說服服飾店讓他設計毛衣。

這些設計作品幫助 Jacobs 進入德高望重的帕森設計學院。之後，他贏得數個獎項。他畢業於 1984 年，之後隨即開始設計他的第一個時裝系列。Jacobs 迅速成為 Perry Ellis 的首席時裝設計師，以他的年紀來說，這是不小的榮譽。雖然他在 Perry Ellis 獲得獎項和好評，Jacobs 最後還是離開 Perry Ellis 開創自己的時裝系列。

Marc Jacobs 這個品牌很成功，但在 1997 年，Jacobs 決定要同時擔任 Louis Vuitton 的創意總監。之後數年，Jacobs 的作品會為他贏得多項榮譽，包括年度男裝設計師和年度配件設計師。現在，Jacobs 不僅有數家店面，還有自己的香水和配件。

顯而易見的，在時尚世界裡，Marc Jacobs 是當今活躍的設計師中最重要的幾位設計師之一，他在將來數年也很有可能會在時尚界有強大的影響力。

1. C

◉ 本題在考文章的大意，可使用略讀的方法，讀過每一段的主題句，綜合理解後，便可以判斷出文章的大意，找出正確的選項。

◉ 第一段的最後一句，作者直接點出本文的重點是 Marc Jacobs。第二段主要在討論 Marc Jacobs 的早期生活；第三段的主題句則提到他進入設計學校唸書，可猜測本段主要在講他做為設計師的人生；第四段則提到他品牌的成功，最後一段說到 Marc Jacobs 是時尚產業的重要人物。綜合來看，可以判斷本文在講 Marc Jacob 的人生以及他成功的故事，所以選項 (C) 為正確答案。

◉ 選項 (A) 時尚品牌 (designer brands) 非正確選項，因為本文主要在講 Marc Jacobs 這個人，只是順帶提到品牌而已。選項 (B)Marc Jacobs 的童年時期只有在第二段被提及，因此也非全文主旨。選項 (D)Marc Jacobs 的才華雖然是文章重點之一，但是比起選項 (C)，這個選項沒有提到他的早期人生、求學和創業經過，故 (C) 為正確答案。。

2. C

◉ 本題在考多重細節，找出每個選項的關鍵字，並在原文中找到位置，仔細閱讀與比對，便可找出正解。

◉ 題目已經把範圍縮小到 Marc Jacobs 的早期人生，因此可以直接閱讀第二段並比對 4 個選項。選項 (C) 提到他的祖母扶養他長大，並激發了他源源不絕的創意，與文中的第二段第三、四句，他父親過逝，母親再嫁而祖母養大他，並培養了他的設計才華的陳述相符，因此選項 (C) 為正解。

選項 (A) 提到他母親在他七歲時去世，事實上去世的是他的父親。選項 (B) 提到父親在他十歲時離開他，但其實是他母親離開他，且沒有提到時間點。選項 (D) 提到十六歲時 Marc 在服飾店工作，而第二段倒數第二句說到他是在十五歲時開始在服飾店工作的，故此也非正解。

3. A

本題在考事情發生的順序，需找到題目中的關鍵字，再回原文中找出時間點，並按時間順序排列就可找到正確答案。

四個選項中出現的關鍵字有 Perry Ellis、Marc Jacobs、Louis Vuitton，瀏覽全文後，可以找到 Perry Ellis 出現在第三段第三行，這是在 1984 年他剛畢業時工作的地方。Marc Jacobs 這個關鍵字因為是設計師的名字，也是品牌的名字，但出現在文章太多地方，若順著剛才 Perry Ellis 的地方讀下去，可以發現在第三段最後的地方提到他開始自己的品牌，並在第四段第一句直接點出品牌叫 Marc Jacobs，可以知道 Marc Jacobs 出現在 Perry Ellis 之後；Louis Vuitton 出現在第四段第一句後半，時間點是 1997 年，Marc Jacobs 同時為 Louis Vuitton 工作，因此我們可以判斷出選項 (A) 為正確順序。

4. A

本題在考作者的態度，在瀏覽文章時需細細體會作者的立場，並從作者的遣詞用字中找到線索來幫助判斷。

本題在考作者對 Marc Jacobs 的態度，仔細閱讀上下文時，可以發現作者將他與世界知名時尚設計師齊名，如文章開頭提到的 Calvin Klein、Karl Lagerfeld 等。再加上各段不停地提到他的設計才華以及他所得到的各種設計獎項，結論提到在未來的幾年他還是會影響著時尚業，從這幾點可以看出作者對 Marc Jacobs 的態度是正面讚許的，故選 (A) approving 做為答案。

選項 (B) 為不讚同的意思，與作者態度相反。選項 (C) 為不感興趣的，但很明顯作者相當有興趣，因此不是正確答案。選項 (D) 為中立 (neutral) 的意思，作者其實很讚許 Marc Jacobs，完全沒提到他哪裡做不好的地方，故沒有中立平衡的內容，因此選項 (D) 亦非正解。

 Round 9

翻譯

　　不用說，地球的雨林很重要。這些大型的自然區域可以在世界各地找到，尤其是在南美洲、非洲，和亞洲，而且它們據說是地球百分之五十以上的物種的家。雨林也是我們許多重要現代藥品及醫療用品的一個主要來源，而且它們是氣候變遷和全球暖化的要角。不幸的是，最近的報告指出全世界的雨林現在正以令人擔憂的速度消失。

　　信不信由你，專家說每天正有差不多八萬公頃的雨林被摧毀。因此，每天有差不多 135 種植物、動物，和昆蟲消失。某些專家說，每年總共有五萬種左右的物種因為全球雨林的快速毀滅而消失。

　　簡單來講，雨林大多在世界上較窮困的開發中地區，那些地區的人正極力拓展至新的地方。此外，商業活動，如伐木、耕作、放牧，和採礦，在這些地區持續增長。令人難過的是，這常意味著大型的雨林區域現在正被清除掉以讓出空間給這些人和活動。

　　不過，一些科學家對未來仍有希望。他們指出雨林的某些地方現在已受保護並很有可能會至少存活到 2030 年。然而，另一些科學家就不這麼樂觀了。他們指出，依目前的毀滅速度，世界上所有雨林會在 100 年左右消失。這很顯然地會是我們地球的一大災難。

　　毫無疑問，世界各處的雨林很重要，且它們正在消失。所以，我們顯然應該對此做點什麼——立刻！

1. A

本題在考文章的主旨大意，可使用略讀的技巧，快速讀過每段的主題句，加以分析，便可以找出文章的大意。

文章第一段的第一句點出雨林的重要性，但本段最後一句點出全文的主旨：Unfortunately, it has recently been reported that the world's rainforests are now disappearing at an alarming rate.。第二段則提出數據佐證大量雨林及物種正在消失；第三段主題句 Why are the rainforests being cut down? 點出消失的原因；第四段為科學家的看法；最後一段則再重申雨林不停在消失的事實。綜合看來，全文的主旨在講述雨林的消失以及雨林需要保護，故選 (A) 為正確答案。

選項 (B) 提到雨林孕育了世界上超過一半的物種，雖然此一細節為正確的，但這不是全文的主旨。選項 (C) 提到氣候變遷正在破壞地球，但文中並非提及，故非正確答案。選項 (D) 提到經濟發展破壞了雨林，確實為第三段提到的雨林消失的原因，但只是文章眾多段落的其中一個，故也非正解。

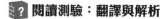

2. C

◎ 題目問的重點為每年雨林中物種消失絕種 (die out) 的數量，雖文中沒有用到 die out 此片語，但能找到同義詞 disappear (消失)。因此可以知道每年有約 50,000 種物種消失，故答案選 (C)。

◎ 選項 (A) 的 50 出現在第一段中間，指的是地球上超過 50% 的物種住在雨林；選項 (B) 的 135 出現在第二段第二句，指的是物種「每天」消失的量，而非每年；選項 (D) 的 80,000 出現在第二段第一句，指的是每天有 8 萬公頃的雨林消失，也非正確選項。

3. B

◎ 本題在考單一細節，利用瀏覽的方法，仔細閱讀上下文便可找到答案。

◎ 本題在問雨林大量消失的原因為何，而第三段主要在探討雨林消失的原因，因為開發中國家為了商業發展與進步，大量砍伐雨林的樹木，導致雨林快速消失，此敘述與選項 (C)「人類為求發展所以犧牲雨林」的敘述相符。

◎ 選項 (A) 提到因極端氣候造成雨林消失，這或許是依據邏輯或常識我們會選擇的原因，但是文章中並沒有提到極端氣候造成雨林消失，反而是在第一段後半提到氣候變遷是雨林消失的「影響」之一，故非正確選項。選項 (B) 提到雨林生態系統的不平衡為雨林消失的原因，但只有在第二段提到因雨林的消失造成物種消失，故非正解。選項 (D) 提到因為降雨量減少，但文中完全沒有提及，故為錯誤選項。

4. B

◎ 本題在考推論或暗示，通常需對全文有徹底的瞭解才比較好作答，四個選項均仔細閱讀，並在文章中找到相關的字、詞或句子。

◎ 文中第四段，句子的結構 some scientists . . . other scientists 就暗示了至少有兩派的看法，第一派的看法是雨林已受到保護，至少可能到 2030 年。而另外一派的看法則是不太樂觀的，認為雨林在未來一百年左右會消失，因此可判斷科學家對雨林的未來並沒有共識，故答案選 (B)。

◎ 選項 (A) 說到雨林對人的生存並非必須，但在文章中第一段提到雨林非常重要，且若雨林消失將會是一個大災難 (disaster)，故此選項為非。選項 (C) 提到政府在盡最大努力保護雨林，但文章中完全沒提到此點。選項 (D) 則提到雨林在一百年內會消失在地球上，文章雖然有提到這一點，但也有提到另一派的科學家有不同看法，因此這個說法不一定正確，故非正確選項。

 Round 10

翻譯

　　若在腦海描繪世界各地的森林，我們通常會想到的是平靜、安逸、充滿高聳的樹木及翠綠的植物的地方。然而，世界各地的森林年年都會變成某種狂暴、危險之物——森林大火——的肆虐之處。事實上，森林大火，有時又被稱為野火、森林火災，每年會發生數千次，並摧毀自然界數百萬公頃的土地。

　　野火有幾種不同的成因。閃電是許多場野火的成因，尤其多在乾燥少雨的地區。這也許不大令人意外，研究報告指出，每年地球都被雷擊超過三十億次，且大多發生在偏遠地區，這意味著發生在這些地區的野火更不容易撲滅。

　　不幸的是，還有許多野火是由人類造成的。露營者和登山者常不小心引起野火，通常是因為他們忘記熄滅營火，或用不恰當的方式熄滅營火。有些營火則是由於人們燃燒垃圾所引起。根據幾個案例，野火還會由我們稱為「縱火犯」的廢罪者刻意引起。

　　大部分野火擴散迅速，尤其是在乾燥、多風的地區，這意味著盡可能快速做出應變是很重要的。消防隊員通常使用大量的水撲滅野火，但有時候也必須用其它方法，如藉由移除樹和植物製造防火道。

　　雖然野火對森林及人類來說可能極具破壞性，它仍有一大作用。野火摧毀老舊或甚至死亡的植物和樹，讓新的植物和樹能在原地生長。它也讓不可或缺的養分回到土壤。

　　明顯地，野火仍會是自然界中重要的腳色，所以我們應盡力理解它。

1. A

◎ 本題在考本文的最佳標題為何，此類型的題目需對全文有所瞭解才能做答；但可利用略讀技巧，找出每段的主題句，綜合分析後，便可以找出文章的大意，做出最佳標題。

◎ 文章第一段最後一句提出 wildfires (野火) 每年發生數千次，催毀許多土地；第二段主題句提出野火發生的原因有很多。第三段主題句則提及很多時候野火是人為的。第四段講到野火蔓延的很快，第五段則是提到野火破壞性很強，最後一段為結論，說明我們應多加瞭解野火。綜合來看，本文主要在介紹野火的各種面向，故選 (A) A Closer Look at Wildfires。

◎ 選項 (B) 野火發生時該做和不該做的事，在文章中並沒有特別提到，因此不是正確答案。選項 (C) 提到的縱火犯和野火在文章中第三段最後一句有提到，但只是一個細節，因此不適合當作標題。選項 (D) 提到撲滅野火的方法，在第四段有提到，但這是其中一個段落，因此也不適合當成標題，故 (D) 非正解。

2. A

◎ 本題在考代名詞的指涉，代名詞所指涉的字、詞或句子通常位在代名詞的前方，因此往前讀可以最快找到答案，並將可能的答案代入代名詞後順讀，即可知道是否正確。

◎ this 的前一句為「Wildfires often spread very quickly, especially in dry, windy areas」，意思是野火通常在乾燥和強風的地方會蔓延地很快。首先，句子中的名詞 wildfires 和 areas 都為複數，故不會是正確答案。再來就是整句話表示野火的撲滅或控制需要立即反應，可以得知 this 指涉的是出現在其前方的整句話，故答案選 (A) 野火很快就會失控。

◎ 選項 (B) 指出野火常常是人為造成的、選項 (C) 指出消防員需要快速反應、選項 (D) 指出野火對森林和人類都俱有破壞性這件事，都和 this 前方這句話意思不符，故皆非正確答案。

3. D

◎ 本題在考單一細節，找出題目的關鍵字，並且掃瞄全文找出關鍵字出現的段落並仔細閱讀，便可以找到正確答案。

◎ 題目在問野火的好處。掃過全文，可在倒數第二段找關鍵字「they do serve an important purpose」，提到野火的重要性，野火讓新植物有空間成長，也讓營養物回到地上。選項 (D) 提到野火讓營養物能被放回地上，符合文章內容，故此為正確答案。

◎ 選項 (A) 中出現的閃電在第二段有提到，指電擊在森林中常會造成森林大火，沒有說到野火讓閃電不會擊中同個地方兩次，故此為錯誤選項。選項 (B) 提到的 fire breaks 出現在第四段最後一句，是消防員撲滅野火的方法之一，並非野火會帶來的好處。選項 (C) 提到野火幫助人們開展森林覆蓋的地方，這一點在文中並未提及，亦為錯誤選項。

4. C

◎ 本題在考細節，需要找出文章「沒有」提到的野火形成的原因。

◎ 文章第二段和第三段都在說明野火發生的原因，因此需仔細讀過這兩段才能找出作者「沒有」提到的原因。選項 (C) 提到的香菸在文中並未被提及。所以此為

正確答案。

◎ 選項 (A) 提到的閃電 (lightning) 在文中第二段第二句有提到是野火的原因之一，故非正確答案。選項 (B) 提到沒人看顧的營火 (unattended campfires) 在第三段第二句有提到，露營的人和健行的人常常會升了火後，卻沒有好好熄滅這些火，故在文中有提到，所以非正確選項。選項 (D) 提到的垃圾焚燒，在第三段的第三句有提到人們有時因為燒垃圾造成野火，故此也為錯誤選項。

Round 11

翻譯

　　大部分人都從哪找到新資訊？在過去，媒體——電視、電台，和雜誌——通常是許多人最重要的資訊來源，尤其是即時新聞和世界大事。在許多國家，尤其是民主國家，大家常常想當然地認為媒體應該呈現公平、不偏頗的新聞，因為人們常常根據這些資訊投票選擇他們的領導人。不幸的是，儘管媒體內許多人盡了最大努力，一種叫做「媒體偏見」的現象已經出現。

　　一般而言，媒體記者應該盡可能呈現公正持平的新聞報導。然而，這不會一直發生，且媒體偏見會以幾種不同的方式出現。舉例來說，記者可能會省去事件的某一方面或忽視某些事實。這叫做「故意忽略偏見」。記者也可能會採用傾向同一特定觀點的「專家」或「觀察家」。這叫做「消息來源偏見」，它常在記者試圖找到願意給出符合特定報導的發言的人時發生。當只有特定事件被報導，而其它事件被遺漏，叫做「事件選擇偏見」。類似於此，當特定事件被給予更多重視和大標題，或是出現在報紙頭版或新聞頭條，則叫做「版面安排偏見」。而如果新聞事件或政府政策只有一家說法，沒有其它任何意見或看法，這可能會成為「內容闡釋偏見」。

　　當然，媒體的職責就是呈現給大眾清楚、不偏頗的報導。然而，當他們無法做到這點時，識讀——並公諸於眾——媒體偏見就是大眾的責任。

1. A

◎ 本題在考文章最佳的標題，可使用略讀技巧，快速閱讀各段落的主題句找到文章的主旨，便可判斷出何為最佳標題了。

◎ 第一段最後一句提到全文重點 media bias (媒體偏好)，第二段主題句「However, this does not always happen, and media bias can occur in several different ways.」，點出媒體偏好有不同方式，最後一句再提出結論，可以得知本文主要在談論 media bias，因此選項 (A) 是最佳標題。

🎯 選項 (B) 新聞自由在文章並無多說，反而提到媒體不公正的現象。選項 (C) 公正報導是作者多次提到媒體要做的事，但並非文章要探討的事。選項 (D) 事實或虛構在文中並沒提到，故為錯誤的。

2. **B**

🎯 本題考通篇文章的大意，這類型的題目需要對全文有徹底的了解，才能幫助判斷答案。

🎯 本文分為三段，第一段為引言，第二段是全文重點，而第三段為結論。第二段第二句為主題句，提到 media bias 有不同型態，並在後方的支持句中提出了不同的媒體偏好，包含了 bias by omission、bias by selection of sources、bias by story selection 等各種不同的形式，可知此篇文章欲條列出各種 media bias 的類別，故選 (B) 為正確答案。

🎯 選項 (A) 提到談論媒體是可以相當有偏好的，這類文章可能會以很極端的例子來證明，而非本文仔細分析偏袒的類別，故選項 (A) 為較不適合的答案。選項 (C) 提到教育大眾如何不要被誤導，但文中並沒有仔細說明這點，故非正確選項。選項 (D) 提到比較現今和往日的媒體，但文章只有在第一段開頭稍微提到今昔之比，並未在文中進一步探討，故為錯誤選項。

3. **D**

🎯 本題考細節，因為文章中列出了多種媒體偏好的類別，這一題主要測驗同學是否完全理解類別的定義與差異，需對第二段有徹底的了解才能選出正確答案。

🎯 題目說到媒體只報導政府政策 (government policy) 有多好，卻完全沒有提到其它不同觀點，掃過第二段後，可在最後一句找到 government policy，仔細閱讀後，可瞭解作者對 bias by spin 的描述完全符合題幹的敘述，故可判斷 (D) 為正確答案。

🎯 (A) bias by selection of sources 指的是媒體只選用支持同一看法的專家，與題幹敘述不符。選項 (B) bias by story selection 指的是媒體只報導部分，而不談及其它內容。選項 (C) bias by placement 指的是媒體對偏好的報導給予較大的標題，或放在顯目的位置。

4. **D**

🎯 本題考單一細節，使用瀏覽的技巧，找出題幹關鍵字在文中的位置，仔細閱讀上下文就可以找出正確答案。

🎯 本題問「為什麼特別在民主國家更需要公正公平的媒體」，關鍵字為 democratic，掃過全文能發現第一段

就可以看到 democracies，仔細閱讀上下文後，可以知道因選民會受媒體偏好的資訊影響而選出不理想的領導人。對應選項後，可以知道選項 (D) Because people choose their leaders using the information from the media (人們憑藉來自媒體的資訊來選擇領導人) 為正確答案。

🎯 選項 (A) 為越多自由越多責任、選項 (B) 民主國家不太管束他們的媒體和選項 (C) 媒體的資金影響選舉，這三個選項文章中皆無提到。

 Round 12

翻譯

　　當代醫學確實達成許多了不起的成就。比方說，許多傳染病已經滅絕或獲得控制，再也無法進行人與人間的擴散。不過，有另一大類的疾病卻不斷增加，這些疾病稱做文明病，已開發國家的人民因為生活習慣不健康而為之所苦。

　　主要的文明病有心臟病、中風、某些種類的癌症、第二型的糖尿病和肺病。這些疾病是由於飲食偏差、體重過重、缺乏運動和抽菸所造成的。在已開發國家，飲食偏差通常是指一個人攝取過量的脂肪，而水果、蔬菜和穀類卻攝取不足。據估計，只要飲食能更健全，即可預防約三分之一的癌症。其他疾病大多數與飲食偏差、缺乏運動兩者有關。食用超過身體消耗的熱量會導致體重過重或是肥胖，也可能造成心臟病、中風以及第二型的糖尿病。最後，抽菸會造成肺部疾病、心臟病和中風。生活中其他造成文明病的因子包括酒精、藥物使用以及壓力。

　　這些疾病是全球醫療保健系統的龐大負擔，而情況預計將更形惡化。二〇〇三年的時候，每年有四百萬人死於吸菸相關的疾病，而根據估計，這項數字每年增加三百萬。世界衛生組織表示，每年有三百萬人的死因和體重過重有關，預估到了二〇二〇年，更將攀升到五百萬人。

　　文明病是致命的殺手，我們不能留待科學來治療。不過，好消息是，只要選擇更健康的生活方式，我們本身就能加以預防。

1. **A**

🎯 本題考文章的大意，回答此類題型，可使用略讀的技巧，讀過每一段的主題句之後，再綜合分析出文章的大意，便可找出正確答案。

文章第一段最後一句提出：These are called lifestyle diseases, and are suffered by people in developed countries as a result of unhealthy lifestyles.，點出是生活型態的不健康造成文明病。第二段的主題句提出這些疾病包括了心臟疾病、中風、某些類型癌症等疾病。第三段主題句提到這些疾病對各國的健保系統帶來很大的負擔，而最後一段呼籲我們要儘快想辦法處理這個現況。綜合來看，可以推斷出文章的主旨在講述 lifestyle diseases (生活型態疾病) 是現代社會一個嚴重問題，故選 (A) 為正確答案。

選項 (B) 提到生活型態疾病是一個我們難以應付的問題，與文章主旨不合，文章最後一句提到我們選擇健康的生活型態就能預防這些疾病。選項 (C) 提出健康的飲食幫助人們不會得到這些生活型態的疾病，雖然文中第二段有提到 poor diet 是生活型態疾病的原因之一，但這只是細節並非通篇文章大意。選項 (D) 提到超重是因為吃太多和太少運動的結合，也是第二段的細節。

2. D

本題考細節，使用瀏覽的方法掃過全文便能找出文中提到哪些 lifestyle diseases。

掃過全文後，可以發現第二段第一句提到了許多疾病，包括 heart disease、stroke、cancer、diabetes 和 lung disease，因此馬上可以判斷出選項 (A)(B)(C) 皆在文章中有被提到，只有選項 (D) 高血壓在文章並無提及。

3. B

本題考推理和暗示，要求我們針對一句話做出推理，仔細閱讀四個選項並比對這句話，即可找到答案。

題目要求我們依據 "we cannot wait for science to cure them" 這句話推理作者的意思為何，此句話出現在最後一段第一句，上一句提到生活型態疾病是奪走性命的殺手，而下一句則表示我們能選擇過健康生活來避免這些疾病。以此可判斷作者想告訴我們現代醫學還無法有效治療這些生活型態疾病，因此我們應儘快想辦法改善生活習慣。此與選項 (B) 的說法相符，故選 (B)。

選項 (A) 提到我們應該投注金錢和努力來找出治療方法，但並不是作者想要強調的重點，作者更強調改善生活習慣。選項 (C) 提到我們要更有耐心等待治療方法被發明，這也與作者的意思相悖。選項 (D) 提到我們需要更好的健保體系來幫助人們，文中有提到這些生活型態疾病對健保體系帶來很大的負擔，因此要改的是人們的生活習慣，而非健保體系。

4. A

本段為測驗字義，作答時可將四個選項都帶進原文比對，看何者最符合上下文。做答的線索也可在前後文找到，不妨把句子前後一起仔細閱讀，能選出最正確的答案。

eliminated 出現在第一段第二句，本句在舉例說明現代醫學的神奇，許多病可以被根除 (eliminated)，或是受到控制，讓傳染力大幅下降。選項 (A) wiped out 此一片語為完全摧毀的意思，剛好符合上下文的意思，故為正確答案。

選項 (B)spread out 為散開的意思、選項 (C)opened up 為打開的意思、選項 (D) wound up 為結束的意思，皆與文意不合。

Round 13

翻譯

斯里蘭卡是位於印度正南方的島嶼，宗教以佛教為主，當地仍奉行許多民間習俗與佛教以外的宗教活動，「鬼之舞」即是其中一例，基本上，這項舞蹈的目的是要驅除惡魔、疾病或霉運。

該舞蹈是由數名舞者與鼓手來進行，他們全是來自社會底層且精通此道的人。不過一開始會先在苦主的住家前面搭建三座供神鬼暫歇的場所，這些用棕櫚葉搭成的建物是要獻給魔鬼、神祇和惡靈的，接著舞者試著將這些神靈請出為祂們蓋好的新住所，引導至儀式進行的區域。在鼓手瘋狂敲打的同時，男性的舞者進行一連串充滿力量與動感的舞步以鼓動神靈，過程可能持續好一段時間，因此有時也會休息，休息的過程當中其他的舞者可能為圍觀的民眾帶來魔術表演，或是其他的餘興節目。

之後來到儀式的高潮，舞者戴上面具並讓造成苦主生病或煩惱的邪靈附身，這些神靈從祂們借來的軀體當中向觀眾介紹自己，訴說造訪此地的原委，在此同時，主祭者開始質問、威脅祂們，有時候主祭者甚至還可能獻上金錢或其他的贈禮，要求祂們放過苦主。

這項習俗可能在佛教之前就存在了，但斯里蘭卡的鄉間仍奉行不悖，佛教與其他主流宗教一樣，接納並適應各地習俗信仰中的重要元素，藉此加強與當地居民的聯繫，但如此一來也使得斯里蘭卡的佛教與西藏、泰國、中國或是日本的佛教產生極大的差異，姑且不論這對於全球佛教界的一致性具有什麼意義，斯里蘭卡「鬼之舞」這一類的儀式的確可說是豐富多彩而迷人。

1. C

◎ 本題考文章的主題為何，可使用略讀的技巧，快速讀過每一段的主題句，綜合分析找出文章的主題。

◎ 文章第一段最後一句是主題句，講到 devil dancing 是斯里蘭卡趨邪的一種舞蹈。第二段主題句為第一句，提到 devil dancing 是由社會較低階級的舞者和打鼓的人所執行的，第三段最主題句為第一句，講到 devil dancing 表演到最高潮處所發生的事，最後一段第一句提到 devil dancing 和斯里蘭卡佛教的關係做為結論，可以綜合看出本文的主題是 devil dancing，故選 (C)。

◎ 選項 (A) 的佛教和選項 (B) 的斯里蘭卡是雖然在文中常常出現，但斯里蘭卡是 devil dancing 這習俗的所在地，而佛教是斯里蘭卡的主要宗教，但為了在地化，也融合了當地民俗信仰，但都不是文章最重要的主題，因此皆為錯誤選項。選項 (D) 的邪靈是 devil dancing 表演要趨走的東西，也非文章主要題裁，因此也為錯誤選項。

2. D

◎ 本題考代名詞的指涉，代名詞所指涉的字、詞或句子通常位在代名詞前方，因此往前閱讀可以最快找到答案，並可將答案代入代名詞檢視文意是否通順，便可知道是否正確。

◎ 本題的代名詞為關係代名詞 which，此關代出現在文章第二段最後一句，關代常指涉前方的先行詞，但此處關代 which 前方為介系詞 during，因此需往前尋找先行詞。which 後半句說到其它的表演者會表演魔術等，而前方最接近的名詞為 breaks，套入 which，表示在中間休息時段會有其它的表演，為合邏輯的文意，故答案選 (D)。

◎ 選項 (A) dance routines 指的是舞蹈動作，在舞蹈動作中有魔術表演並不合理。選項 (B)drumming 打鼓，雖然合理但前方並無 drumming 做為先行詞。選項 (C) 的魔術是在關代後方，不太可能為 which 的先行詞，且文意上也不通順。

3. A

◎ 本題考細節，找出題目中的關鍵字後，瀏覽全文找出關鍵字的所在位置，仔細閱讀上下文後，比對四個選項，便可找出答案。

◎ 題目的關鍵字是 climax (高潮)，瀏覽全文後可發現 high point 為同義的字詞，出現在第三段第一句，仔細閱讀後可以得知在表演最高潮時，舞者帶上面具被邪靈附身，並且和旁觀者對話，此一敘述符合選項 (A) 的描述，故 (A) 為正解。

◎ 選項 (B) 提到鼓者用力快速擊鼓來使邪惡興奮是出

現在第二段中間，為舞蹈表演的一開始。選項 (C) 提到在受害者房子門口立起小型建物也是出現在第二段的部分，是 devil dancing 開始前就會完成的事。選項 (D) 提到牧師開始吟誦咒語驅邪，雖然牧師驅邪是對的，但在文中牧師並非唸咒語，因此這個選項也不正確。

4. B

◎ 本題測驗推理與暗示，針對最後一段關於佛教的內文做推理，仔細閱讀最後一段並比對題目的四個選項，便可找到正確答案。

◎ 最後一段作者提到 devil dancing 在斯里蘭卡有久遠的歷史，比佛教還早。佛教傳到斯里蘭卡時還需要適應當地習俗，這也是為什麼各地的佛教多多少少有些差異，不全然相同，此一大意與選項 (B) 提到的因為和當地文化融合的關係佛教在各地有所不同的意思相符合，故此為正解。

◎ 選項 (A) 提到佛教在傳到不同國家時沒有做太多改變與最後一段文意不符。選項 (C) 提到在這些地區佛教非主要宗教，這一點在文章中並無直接提到，但根據內容我們可以判斷佛教在這些地區為主要宗教。選項 (D) 提到佛教與各地習俗不同，甚至被禁止，與最後一段大意悖道而馳的。

Round 14

翻譯

　　太陽能板正變得越來越流行，產業內或住家內皆同。這正幫助節省電能使用、減少汙染，並增長我們對太陽能科技的可能性的理解。這領域的最新發展之一，是「薄膜」太陽能板的應用。

　　這種類的材質極薄、極為柔韌，因此，它們可以被彎曲，讓它們被加進有趣又精巧的新建築設計中。薄膜太陽能片可以被應用在幾乎任何表面上，包括金屬、塑膠、紙，或屋面材料。從設計的角度看，沒有其它太陽能物料比它用途更廣。它們處在開發階段已久，但從研究到製造間花了差不多二十年。目前存在三種薄膜板：非晶矽 (用於隨身計算機)；碲化鎘 (便宜，但碲的供應有限且鎘有毒性)；和銅鋼錶晒 (CIGS)。其中，CIGS 的公司吸引到大量的投資者資金。這種物料很有效率，而且，雖然它很難掌控，仍被預測將在 2020 年前成為主流。能源開發公司現在持續地試圖減少每瓦能源的成本，而這些能源要成功必須與化石燃料相比較。無論技術再怎麼進步，也要買得起，不然就無法廣泛被採用。

在開發低成本、高效率的太陽能物料的競賽裡，薄膜太陽能板是個值得關注的解答。許多人砸重金投資它們的開發，而中國是這個領域的領先者。它們在居住建築及商業建築設計上越來越被接受，意味著未來成長的正向趨勢。市場毫無疑問地有旺盛的需求，需求來自營造商和那些想要自家有有效率的綠色能源的人。希望我們很快就能看到它們變得更容易取得。

1. A

◎ 本題考文章出處，可以透過閱讀主題句來判斷文章屬性，並找到答案。

◎ 第一段的主題句為最後一句，提到一種新型、叫做 thin film 的太陽能板。第二段的主題句為第一句，提到這種太陽能板很薄且能彎曲，可以應用在創新的建築設計上。最三段的主題句提到這種太陽能板可能是未來低費高效能太陽能板主流。綜合看來可以判斷本文是在介紹新種的太陽能板，因此答案選 (A) 科學雜誌。

◎ 選項 (B) 為室內設計雜誌，太陽能板一般裝置在室外屋頂上，所以這個選項是錯誤的。選項 (C) 是回收的小冊子，文中並沒有提到回收的概念。選項 (D) 是醫學期刊，內容通常會與醫學相關，因此也是錯誤選項。

2. A

◎ 本題考代名詞的指涉，代名詞所指涉的字、詞或句子通常位在代名詞前方，因此往前讀可找到答案，並將可能的答案代入代名詞檢視文意是否通順，便可知道是否正確。

◎ 本題所考的代名詞 they 出現在第二段中間，由此代名詞所引導的句子：They have been in development for a long time, but it has taken about twenty years to move from research to manufacturing.，本句意思是這些東西研發很久了，從研究到製造花了二十年。往前找複數名詞，最靠近的就是 roofing materials、thin film solar sheets，architectural designs 等字，逐一代入，可以發現 thin film solar sheets 最符合上下文，表示這種多用途的太陽能板研發花了更多研發，故正確答案選 (A)。

◎ 選項 (B) 的傳統太陽能板並無出現在代名詞前方。選項 (C) 鋪屋頂的建材並不是研發的重點，在前文提出只是為了突顯 thin film solar panels 可以搭配任何建材使用，來強調多功能性，並非指研發鋪屋頂的建材。選項 (D) 的太陽能板公司離代名詞有點距離，且太陽能板公司是公司不是科技，不能被研發。

3. C

◎ 本題考細節，找到題目中的關鍵字後，瀏覽全文找到位置，並仔細閱讀上下文後即可找出答案。

◎ 本題考何者為未來最主要的 thin film 太陽能板，關鍵字為 main，在原文中對應的相關字為第二段後半出現的 dominant，雖然不是同一個字，但字義相近，皆指主要的或主流的意思，這裡指的是 CIGS 在 2020 年會成為主流的 thin film 太陽能板，故答案選 (C)。

◎ 選項的 (A) 和 (B) 為第二段所介紹的另外兩種 thin film 太陽能板，amorphous calculators 被用在做計算機，cadmium telluride 便宜但數量有限且 cadmium 有毒，文中也無提到它們的未來。選項 (D) 的化石燃料非太陽能板，只有在第二段提到能源發展時被提出來比較而已。

4. A

◎ 本題考與 thin film 太陽能板未來有關之細節，瀏覽全文找出每個選項中關鍵字的位置，並一一比對，即可找出正確答案。

◎ 選項 (A) 的關鍵字為 affordability 和 solution，在最後一段第一句有提到 low cost 和 solution，仔細閱讀後可判斷這句提到這種太陽能板是低費用高效能的，所以可以判斷此選項為正確答案。

◎ 選項 (B) 提到美國為 thin film 太陽能板的龍頭國家，關鍵字 leading country 出現在最後一段第三句，作者提到 China is a leader in this area，中國才是龍頭並非美國。選項 (C) 提到這種太陽能板在商業上的廣泛應用近程仍不太可能達成，commercial 為關鍵字，出現在最後一段第四句：Hopefully, we will see them become more readily available soon. 可以判斷此選項錯誤。選項 (D) 提到這種新式太陽能板比傳統太陽能板製造較多污染，關鍵字 pollution 只出現在文中第一段，作者比較太陽能發電比傳統發電方式製造較少污染，此外並無做其它比較。

 Round 15

翻譯

昔日的船員描述他們聽到溺斃水手的鬼魂聲，巨大的呻吟咆哮、大哭大叫的喧鬧聲從海面下傳來；今日的船員依舊聽到這樣的聲音，且知道他們聽的是鯨魚的歌唱聲。會唱歌的鯨有好幾種，不過歌聲最繁複而優美的要算是座頭鯨 (又名大翅鯨) 了。這些歌聲是具有高度結構的集合，包含高音、低音和

中音，時間通常維持二十到四十分鐘，旋律一再重覆，可以持續數小時之久。這些是情歌嗎？很多研究人員如此認定。

只有雄性座頭鯨才唱歌，可能是要吸引母鯨或是警告其他雄性不得靠近。演唱這些歌聲可能是要展現牠們適合做為配偶。座頭鯨可能會證明牠能歌唱多久、音量有多大或是能閉氣多久。牠們秋天從冷水海域往溫水地區迴游繁殖與過冬時，雄性座頭鯨的歌唱便開始了。接近繁殖季節時，他們的歌唱時間和頻率都會增加，隨著繁殖季的結束，歌聲也變小了。

世界不同海域的座頭鯨所唱的歌都不一樣，但在同一群的團體裡頭，所有雄性唱的歌都一樣。繁殖季進行的同時，歌聲雖然只有小幅變動，但是經常發生，可能是加入了新的細節，或者省略某個拉長的低沉嗚咽聲。歌唱內容改變時，所有鯨魚都唱新版本。令人驚訝的是，即使是和團體分隔遙遠的鯨魚也會唱著更改後的樂曲。科學家追蹤一頭在夏威夷離開群體游往日本的座頭鯨一直唱著牠們族類的歌，即便是離開夏威夷海域之後才發生的變動也完全一致。

生物學家不斷研究座頭鯨的歌唱，以期解開牠們意圖的謎團，以及更進一步了解這種迷人歌唱家的生活。

1. B

◉ 本題考大意，善用略讀的技巧，快速讀過每一段的主題句，綜合分析後可找出正確答案。

◉ 第一段的主題句出現在文章中間，提到座頭鯨 (Humpback whale) 會唱出最美最複雜的曲調；第二段的主題句提到只有雄性座頭鯨會唱歌，目的是吸引異性或驅趕走其它求偶競爭者。第三段提到座頭鯨的歌曲有區域性，最後一段則為結論指出科學家仍會持續研究座頭鯨唱歌之謎。綜合來看，本文主要講述座頭鯨唱歌的習性，故選項 (B) 為正確答案。

◉ 選項 (A) 文章並無強調座頭鯨的交配季，故非正確答案。選項 (C) 水手的海的故事只是全文的一個引子，並不是文章的重點。選項 (D) 提到不同品種之鯨魚唱的歌，文中主要專注於討論座頭鯨而非各種不同品種之鯨魚。

2. C

◉ 本段考上下文的字義，可把四個選項分別帶進原文比對，看何者最符合文意。

◉ 本段主要講述座頭鯨唱歌的細節。第二句提到牠們所唱的歌會隨季節慢慢變化，但是同一群座頭鯨所唱的

曲調都是一樣的。中間部分提到若是座頭鯨中途離群，所唱的歌仍然會和牠所屬的鯨群變化一致，根據上下文判斷 variations 指的是 changes，意思為離群的座頭鯨仍會唱出在牠離開後群體曲調的變化，選項 (C) 的 changes 代入後文意合邏輯，故為正解。

◉ 選項 (A) 意外、選項 (B) 暫停和選項 (C) 的謎都不合上下文邏輯。

3. D

◉ 本題考細節，瀏覽文章找出題目關鍵字的位置，比對後即可找到答案。

◉ 題目的關鍵字為 fitness，雄性座頭鯨如何藉由唱歌來展現體健。掃過文章後，可在第二段第二句找到關鍵字 fitness，閱讀上下文後可以發現因為唱歌讓雄性座頭鯨展現自己能唱多久、多大聲，以及可以憋氣多久。選項 (D) It shows how long a humpback can hold its breath. 符合文中的描述，故為正確答案。

◉ 文中並無提及選項 (A) 邊唱歌邊游泳的速度、選項 (B) 能唱出最美歌聲、及選項 (C) 歌聲吸引到的雌性座頭鯨數量。

4. B

◉ 本題考多重細節，每個選項都需仔細閱讀，並利用瀏覽的方式在文中找到上下文，比對後即可知何者正確。

◉ 選項 (B) 提到座頭鯨就算離開自己的鯨群仍能唱出一樣的曲調，此一細節出現在第三段中間：Amazingly, even humpbacks that travel far from the rest of their group will sing the revised song. (座頭鯨即使遠離自己的鯨群，仍能唱出修改後新版的歌曲)，可判斷選項 (B) 為正確答案。

◉ 選項 (A) 提到座頭鯨唱出的歌曲是即興的音符，此選項與第一段第四句相悖：These are highly structured collections of notes of high, low, and intermediate pitch, which typically last from 20 to 40 minutes. ，指出他們所唱的歌曲是很有結構性的。選項 (C) 提到座頭鯨唱歌的目的是要嚇退敵人，文章第二段第一句提到唱歌的目的是要警告其它雄性座頭鯨的，並非嚇退敵人。選項 (D) 提到生物學家已解開座頭鯨唱歌之謎，但文章最後一段提到生物學家們仍會繼續研究座頭鯨唱歌的目的 (purpose)，故可知此為錯誤選項。

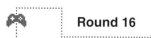

Round 16

翻譯

每顆在夜空閃爍的恆星都有其壽命。而很湊巧

地，在發光發熱了數百萬年後，在恆星的臨終時刻終於來臨時，它們用一聲巨響作結束。以下是事情經過。當一顆恆星變得過於龐大且積蓄多於它能夠釋放的能量時，恆心的中心，即其核心，開始塌縮。當核心終於達到密度最高、質量最大的時候，就無法繼續塌縮，垂死恆心的能量在一場爆炸中被釋放。在此過程中，大量的熱和光，甚至比太陽的光還亮，可以被觀察到。天文學家將此稱為一顆恆星變成超新星。

恆星變成超新星時，作為其毀滅的標記的巨大爆埃讓大量的塵埃湧出太空。這種「宇宙塵」由組成恆星的元素的原子所組成，如氧和碳。它們一冷卻，零散的原子就鍵結在一起。宇宙塵的每顆粒子直徑大概只有一公分的千分之一，但塵埃形成的雲會隨著它遠離爆炸持續擴張。較大塊的物質雖然會在超新星爆炸中永遠被摧毀，但宇宙塵可以承受此強烈的衝擊波的證據已經出現。

為了更了解宇宙，使用先進設備的科學家已在研究黑洞陰影下的宇宙塵，黑洞有強大的引力。據報告，有一朵在一萬年前的超新星爆炸形成的塵埃雲擁有足夠做出七千顆地球大小的行星的物質。而事實上，目前已證實來自爆炸的恆星的宇宙塵其實是新的恆星和行星的組成的來源。

1. B

◎ 本題在考文章的主題，利用略讀的方法，先觀察標題，之後找出每一段的主題句，仔細閱讀這些主題句，綜合分析後便可以判斷出何為文章的主題了。

◎ 標題上寫到了宇宙塵 (cosmic dust)；第一段的主題句提到天空的恆星都有壽命，並在最後一句提到恆星死亡時的大爆炸被稱為超新星 (supernova)；第二段的主題句提到這巨大的爆炸會送出大量的宇宙塵；第四段主題句提到科學家利用先進的科技來研究黑洞是如何影響宇宙塵的。綜合看來，本文的最主要要探討的主題是宇宙塵，故選擇 (B)。

◎ 雖然文章開始提到恆星爆炸時被稱做為超新星，但這其實是為了帶出文章重點宇宙塵用的，所以選項 (A) 和 (D) 都不是正確答案，選項 (C) 的黑洞則只有出現在最後一段，也不是全文的重點。

2. B

◎ 本題在考單一細節，找到題目中的關鍵字後，瀏覽全文找到關鍵字所在，仔細閱讀上下文便可找出正確答案。

◎ 題目問恆星的生命何時結束，關鍵字為「life end」，

瀏覽文章後可以發現第一段第二句有提到 for stars to die，往下讀便可以找到恆星何時開始死亡的。When a star gets too large and has built-up more energy than can be released, the star's center, known as the core, starts to collapse. 這一句話便是作答的關鍵，當恆星太大，累積太多能量，恆星開始塌陷，這就是恆星死亡的開始，由此我們可以判斷出選項 (B) When a star has more energy than it can handle (當恆星有太多能量時) 為正確答案。

◎ 選項 (A) 提到恆星沒有能量與文章中的說法剛好相反、選項 (C) 提到恆星互撞和選項 (D) 當恆星被黑洞吞噬，在文章中都沒有提到，故這三個選項都是錯誤的。

3. C

◎ 本題為數字題，主要在考分數的辯讀，分數一般分子寫成一般數字 (one, two, three 等)，然後再寫分母，以序數表示 (third, fourth, fifth…等)，當分子大於一時，分母加上 s。

◎ 題目問宇宙塵直徑多長，瀏覽全文可以發現第二段第四句有提到：Each particle of cosmic dust measures only around a thousandth of a centimeter across，所以可以得知一顆宇宙塵粒子的直徑為 a thousandth 公分，這是 1/1000 centimeter 的意思，所以答案選 (C)。

◎ 選項 (A)1000 centimeters 英文寫作 one thousand centimeters，選項 (B)1/7000 centimeter 英文寫作 one seven-thousandth centimeter，選項 (D) 1/10000 centimeter 英文寫作 one ten-thousandth 都不是正確選項。

4. A

◎ 本題在考推理與暗示，要求針對全文最後一句話做出推理，仔細閱讀四個選項並比對這句話，即可找到答案。

◎ 文章最後一句話寫到：And in fact, it is now known for sure that the cosmic dust that comes from exploding stars is actually the stuff that new stars and planets are made of. 恆星爆炸後產生的宇宙塵事實上會組成新的恆星和行星，此一概念就如同選項 (A)，恆星的死亡事實上是新的恆星和行星的開始，所以此為正確答案。

◎ 選項 (B) 的意思是宇宙塵會造成恆星壽命終結於大爆炸中，選項 (C) 的意思是宇宙大到無法用現用科技測量，選項 (D) 新的恆星和行星因為體積小，不會爆炸死亡，這三個選項均與文章最後一句不符或無關，所以都是錯誤的。

Round 17

翻譯

數千年來，農作物經過選擇性的培育，目的是要生產出成長更快、口感更佳、更能抵抗害蟲的食物，整個過程漫長而不精確。而今，科學家透過基因工程，有能力大幅加速這個過程，他們還可以選擇想要的物種特性，不管是取自於他種植物，甚至是動物身上，再將掌管該特性的基因轉植到目標作物。如此一來，科學家已經可以創造出含有額外維他命 A 的稻米，成長更快且更美味的蔬菜，甚至是自己能產生驅蟲物質的馬鈴薯。科學看似在打造更美好的明天，不過有時候外表是會騙人的。

創造或使用基因工程食物的確有風險和危險，對環境和人體健康造成的短期結果或許不明顯，但改造後的植物可能流落到野外而變成「超級雜草」，有些可能排擠原生植物而造成物種滅絕，有些食物則可能在某些人身上造成過敏反應。最近在老鼠身上的試驗發現，經由基因工程所製的馬鈴薯會減弱牠們的免疫系統，並且造成體內的器官萎縮，相同的事情會不會發生在人類身上呢？

雖然基因工程食物的發展在某些方面看起來前景大好，但風險和揮之不去的未知數卻令人不勝其擾。至少這些新食物的長短期影響都應加以廣泛測試，包括對於環境的影響，以及食用之後對於人類和動物健康的影響。基因工程可說是把上帝的權柄交到人類的手中，但恐怕這個權利以及隨之而來的責任，卻不是今日的科技水準足以承擔的。

1. D

◎ 本題在考多重細節，仔細閱讀四個選項，找出關鍵字，利用瀏覽的方法在文章中找到相應的地方，比對後便可知道哪個選項在文章中「沒有」被提及。

◎ 選項 (D) 提到基因改造過的食物會造成癌症，這說法在文章中並沒有出現，文章中只有提到可能會對人的健康造成影響，因此選項 (D) 為正確答案。

◎ 選項 (A) 提到基因改造的植物可能會成為超級野草，關鍵字 super weeds 可以在第二段第三句找到，讀過上下文便可知道選項 (A) 是文中有提到的，故非正解。選項 (B) 提到基因改造的植物會完全取代原本沒被改造過的植物，關鍵字 original 在文章中第二段第四句可以找到，作者說：Others may squeeze the original plants out of existence. (會讓原本的植物消失)，所以此

選項錯誤。選項 (C) 提到基因改造食物會減弱我們的免疫系統，關鍵字 immune systems 在第二段到數第二句可以找到，仔細讀過本句可以得知基因馬鈴薯在老鼠實驗上有此效果，故對人體也可能會減弱免疫系統，可知此也並非正確答案。

2. C

◎ 本題在考代名詞的指涉，通常所指涉的字、詞或句子會在此一代名詞前方。

◎ 代名詞 they 出現在文章中第一段中間：They are able to select specific traits that they wish, whether they are from a different plant or even animal, and transplant the gene responsible for that trait into the target plant，代名詞前方的複數名詞有 traits 或再往前的 they，和 scientists 等。句子開頭的 they 指的是 scientists，意思表示科學家能夠選出他們想要的特定特色 (traits)，而題目問的 they 指涉的便是這些特色，後半句作者有說明科學家能選擇任何他們要的特色，然後移植基因到他們要的植物中，藉此得到這個特色，故答案選 (C)。

◎ 選項 (A) 和 (B) 提到的動植物是出現在代名詞 they 之後，故不是答案。選項 (D) 的基改食物嚴格來說也沒有出現在前方，只有出現 G.E.，所以也不是正確答案。

3. A

◎ 本題在考句義，仔細閱讀前後方的英文，可以猜測句子的意義，再從四個選項中挑選最接近的，即為答案。

◎ 上一句說 It looks like science is creating a better tomorrow，作者表示基因改造食物看似會給我們更美好的明天，接著馬上用連接詞 but 轉折語氣，可以得知下面應是說到基因改造並不好，因此答案選 (A) The truth may not be as it appears to be. (事實可能不如表面的美好)。

◎ 三個選項都不符合上下文的文意，故非解答。題目中的 deceiving 為欺騙的意思，因此三個選項都有提到謊言，但是如果不拘泥於單一詞彙的意思，而是配合上下文的理解，就可以避免因單字受到混淆而誤答的狀況。

4. A

◎ 本題在考作者的態度，在瀏覽文章時需細細體會作者的立場，並從作者的遣辭用句中找到線索來幫助判斷。

◎ 作者在一開始提到基因改造食物的好處與原因，但第一段最後一句馬上使用 but 轉折，並提到 looks can be deceiving；第二段作者更以 There are real risks and dangers 做為主題句開頭，並用了一整段說明基因改造植物、食物的缺點。第三段的主題句仍維持一樣，用了 disturbing (令人憂慮的) 來形容，最後一句也提到現今科技還無法應付基因改造食物可能帶來的危害。綜合看來，作者是相當擔憂的，所以答案選 (A) concerned。

◉ 選項 (B) 樂觀的、選項 (C) 中立的和選項 (D) 漠不關心皆不是作者的態度，所以都是錯誤選項。

Round 18

翻譯

　　說到未來，沒有人能精準預測。然而，大部分專家一致認為人工智慧會是其一大部分。 人工智慧常被簡稱為「AI」，簡單來講，就是機器的智能。換句話說，有了 AI，機器就能自己思考並自發行動以完成不同任務。AI 的使用例子包括可以理解人類言語，或是解釋大量複雜資料的機器。自駕車也是一例。

　　然而，有些人發出警訊警告我們 AI 的危險。明確地說，一些知名的科學家，如霍金博士認為，在 AI 和軍武的開發上我們必須非常小心謹慎。畢竟，一旦機器學會使用這些武器，人類就有可能無法控制機器。 雖然這聽起來可能像魔果終結者的劇情，有人擔憂這可能會成為現實。

　　有些人因為其它理由害怕 AI：它幾乎肯定會改變工作領域。直截了當地說，AI 讓機器能夠取代許多人類現在做的工作。事實上，有人預測，十年內將有半數以上的工作由機器完成。 對重複性高的工作或資料分析相關的工作來說更有可能如此。

　　不過，有些人相信人類可以適應 AI 並學習如何與機器合作。比爾蓋茲等領袖說，面對未來，人們必須集中在科學、技術、工程及數學領域尋找未來 AI 建立的機會。

　　當然，沒有人知道未來會發生的變化，但我們可以有把握地說 AI 會是其中之一。

1. B

◉ 本題在考文章最佳標題，可使用略讀的技巧，讀過每一段的主題句，綜合推理就可以找到本文的大意，並選擇出文章最好的標題了。

◉ 文章第一段作者提到人工智慧 (artificial intelligence) 一定是未來的一部分，第二段提到 AI 的定義，第三段則提到 AI 對人類的危險，第四段提到 AI 對人類的另一個危害，第五段用 yet (但是) 開頭轉折提到 AI 對人類不見得都是壞處，最後再總結。可以看出作者主要在講 AI 的發展和人類未來的關係，所以答案選 (B)AI and the Future。

◉ 選項 (A) 提到的 AI 和失業只是第四段的內容，不是全文的大意，應該不適合拿來當標題。選項 (C) 提到的 STEM 出現在第五段最後，表示 Science, Technology, Engineering and Mathematics，和主題 AI 沒有直接關係，所以也不是正確答案。選項 (D) 提到 AI 的危險，雖然文中大量著墨這一方面，但在第五段也有提到相反的見解，故不足以做為標題，所以是錯誤選項。

2. B

◉ 本題在考字義，但不是要求找出 The Terminator 的意思，而是希望我們能通過上下文讀出 The Terminator 指的是什麼，需仔細閱讀前後的文字，便可找出答案。

◉ 關鍵字 The Terminator 出現之處的後半句為：some worry that it may become a reality. (有人擔心這可能會真為事實)，這半句和前半作用使用 although 連結，表示前後有相反的意思，因此可以判斷 The Terminator 是 reality 的相反，再從四個選項中去挑選，可以找到答案 (B) 是科幻電影或小說，表示有一天人工智慧會像電影、小說描繪的那樣不受人類控制，甚至攻擊人類。事實上，The Terminator 指的是電影《魔鬼終結者》。另一個可以判斷的技巧是 The Terminator 在文中是斜體字，這格式通常用在書名和電影名等等。

◉ 選項 (A) 科學理論，選項 (C) 大規模破壞武器和選項 (D) 人工智慧實驗室不符合上下文文意，所以都不是答案。

3. C

◉ 本題在考單一細節， 使用瀏覽的技巧在文中找出 AI 機器的例子，比對四個選項即可找到答案。

◉ 題目要文中提出的 AI 機器的例子，掃過全文後可以在第一段找到一些例子，如能理解人類語言的機器，能處理大量資料的機器，能自動駕駛的車子等。比對題目四個選項可以找到 (C) A car that can drive itself 為正確答案。

◉ 選項 (A) 提到的 STEM 出現在第五段中，但作者並沒有提到 AI 可以取代老師教這些科目，故為錯誤選項。選項 (B) 機器寵物在文中也沒有被提到。選項 (D) 會下西洋棋的機器人也為錯誤選項，因為作者並沒有提到這類的 AI。

4. B

◉ 本題在考單一細節，找到題目中的關鍵字後，瀏覽全文找到關鍵字所在，仔細閱讀上下文便可找出正確答案。

◈ 題目的關鍵字 replaced by AI，在問未來最有可能被 AI 取代的工作為何，瀏覽全文在第四段 take over jobs，再往下讀可以看到作者說 repeated tasks or data analysis 的工作在未來最有可能被機器取代掉。比對四個選項，選項 (B) 提到 repetitive tasks (重複性高的任務) 為正確答案。

◈ 選項 (A) 提到需要準確性的工作、選項 (C) 需要力氣的工作和選項 (D) 需要邏輯推理的工作，雖然這三個選項依常識推理都有可能，但在文章中沒有被提到是未來最容易被取代的工作，因此都不是正確選項。

 Round 19

翻譯

　　由於全世界有數十億手機使用者，媒體的關注集中在這些電子設備可能引起的健康風險。此刻，一場爭論正在發生，爭論有關手機在打電話時使用的 RF (無線電頻率) 波的影響。

　　有些研究者認為這些 RF 波可能會致癌。它們讓體內的原子和分子震動。他們聲稱這會製造多餘的熱能，其可能會破壞身體組織。這可能會增加不尋常的細胞增長及癌症的可能性。然而，令一些人認為這是無稽之談，因為 RF 波不是如 X 光一類導致危險的波。

　　不過，世界衛生組織 (WHO) 對此仍很擔憂，並在 2011 年發布聲明，說高手機使用率可能伴隨罹癌風險的增加。然而，沒有足夠的統計資料及數據去證實雙方的論點，因為像癌症這樣的疾病可能要數十年成熟。

　　不過，手機已在兩個領域被證實有健康危險。第一個是道路安全。研究已顯示出邊使用手機邊開車大大增加交通意外的風險，尤其是在人們將手放開方向盤去使用手機時。第二個是細菌的擴散。人們去哪裡都帶著手機，包括廁所。手機表面可能變得細菌滿布，細菌在人們碰觸手機時可能會從皮膚進入人體。

　　人們現在必須考慮 RF 波的健康風險並對要如何使用他們的手機做出決定。他們可以採取預防措施，像將開機的手機遠離身體。他們可以縮短通話時間或多用傳統的室內電話。關於駕駛和使用手機，決定已經幫他們做好了，因為許多國家已制訂法律禁止在駕駛時使用手機。此外，每個人都應該留意，不時擦拭，讓手機保持清潔。

1. A

◈ 本題在考文章的大意主旨，可以藉用略讀的方法，綜合每一段的主題句來找出正確答案。

◈ 第一段最後一句提到對於手機使用的無線電波人們有不同的看法。第二段提到一些研究人員認為無線電波會致癌，但其它人不認為如此，第三段則提到世界衛生組織擔憂無線電波會對身體造成危害，第四段提到手機被證實真實存在的危害，最後一段第一句作者表示我們應該要自己判斷是否手機真的有害，並提出可以採取的預防措施。綜合來看，本文的大意應是選項 (A) 手機對我們的健康有害。

◈ 選項 (B) 提到 WHO 對過度使用手機感到擔憂只是文中一個小細節，並沒有對 WHO 的看法多加著墨，因此不是正確選項。選項 (C) 提到無線電波的危害需要更多證據，雖然文中有提到此一點，但作者還有提到無線電波以外的手機危害，因此此一選項不正確。選項 (D) 禁止手機的使用在文中完全沒有被提到，因此不是正確選項。

2. A

◈ 本題在考有關無線電波的多重細節，利用瀏覽的技巧在文中找到 RF 波的說明，比對四個選項便可以找到正確答案。

◈ 選項 (B) 提到無線電波是 radio frequency wave 的簡稱，出現在第一段最後一句括孤裡面，因此為正確答案。

◈ 選項 (B) 提到無線電波和 X 光一樣，掃瞄全文可以在第二段最後一句找到關鍵字 x-rays，仔細閱讀本句可以發現作者的意思是 RF 波和 x-rays 不一樣，x-rays 是危險的，因此選項 (B) 不是正確答案。選項 (C) 提到已經證實無線電波會致癌，掃瞄上下文找到第三段提到手機使用可能會提高癌症罹患機率，但再往下讀可以看到作者說：Yet, there are not enough statistics and data for proof either way, because diseases like cancer can take decades to develop.，因此可以知道資料數據仍不足以得到定論，所以選項 (C) 仍為錯誤的。選項 (D) 提到無線電波是所有電話都會使用的，但第一段最後一句提到手機撥打電話時才會發出無線電波，因此 (D) 也是錯誤選項。

3. C

◈ 本題在考單一細節，找到題目中的關鍵字後，瀏覽全文找到關鍵字所在，仔細閱讀上下文便可找出正確答案。

◈ 題目的關鍵字是 germs，問為什麼手機表面充滿細菌。瀏覽全文後，可以在第四段中間找到 germs，仔細閱讀上下文，可以讀到：People take their phones everywhere, including the bathroom. (人們走到哪手機

帶到哪，包括廁所)，這便是手機表面充滿細菌的原因，因此答案選 (C)。

⊕ 選項 (A) 人們不太清潔手機表面、選項 (B) 手機表面的製材容易藏污納垢、選項 (D) 人們常把手機借給別人使用，這三個選項都是文中沒有提到的，所以都不是正確答案。

4. B

⊕ 本題在考最後一段的大意，把最後一段仔細讀過後，便可以輕鬆地找到答案了，主題句可以幫助判斷。

⊕ 最後一段第一句作者提到：... make up their own minds about how they use their mobile phones，接著提出許多許多預防手機危害的作法，這便是本段的主旨，如何小心使用手機的實際做法，故答案選 (B) Steps that can be taken to prevent health risks caused by mobile phones. (避免手機造成的健康風險的做法)。

⊕ 選項 (A) 提到的手機使用是否致癌的爭議出現在第三段，選項 (C) 提到手機在日常生活的必要性，在本段並沒有特別提到，因此不是正確答案。選項 (D) 提到手機使用太多可能會有的許多危險是第四段的主旨，因此也非正解。

 Round 20

翻譯

　　目前，全球資訊網是大多數人偏愛的資訊來源。由於資訊的收集豐富且取得容易，只要手指輕輕一按，很多難以找到的資訊都立刻出現在電腦螢幕前！這能成真全靠現今搜尋引擎的神奇力量，而其中最多人用的就是 Google。不過，網路世界不是從以前就這麼輕鬆快意。

　　早期的網路根本沒辦法搜尋，Yahoo! 致力於記錄資訊，然後設計了網頁分類，並且放在網路上。有了這個分類法後，人們才能首次搜尋網路。這項發展相當重要，也難怪很多人誤以為 Yahoo! 是搜尋引擎了！

　　電腦硬體價格下降加上連上網路更為容易，激發更多的人使用網際網路，而想要快速且有效率地找到資料的需求也越來越明顯。這促成網路上出現第一個真正的搜尋引擎 Lycos。從那之後，許多改良過的搜尋引擎紛紛投入市場，搜尋網路就變得更有樂趣了。

　　搜尋引擎的普及度提高後，其中有不少開始提供電子郵件、新聞、天氣預報、聊天室等服務。但

如此一來，它們反而就忽略了改進搜尋技術的需求。就在這段期間，有個名為 Google 的全新搜尋引擎於一九九九年九月加入市場。

　　Google 的創辦人賴瑞・佩吉和塞吉・布林起初是一同參與史丹佛大學的一項搜尋引擎計劃，他們從而發展出當今最知名的搜尋引擎。Google 之所以成功，其背後的主因在於強調優質的搜尋結果。當其他的搜尋引擎還滿足於準確率百分之八十的搜尋結果時，Google 的創辦人不但了解品質的重要，且努力不懈改善他們原本就已經很強大的技術和服務。

1. B

⊕ 本題在考文章的大意主旨，可以藉用略讀的方法，綜合每一段的主題句來找出正確答案。

⊕ 第一段的重點在倒數第二句，提到搜尋引擎改變了我們取得資訊的方法，而 Google 又是最受歡迎的搜尋引擎。第二段提到早期的網路，第三段提到網路的普及，第四段一開始的搜尋引擎提供搜尋以外的服務，第五段提到 Google 的開創，最後一段則提到 Google 如何持續其成功並壯大。綜合來看本文主要在搜尋引擎龍頭 Google 一路走來的成功，並用早期網路的發展做為引子。故答案選 (B)。

⊕ 選項 (A) 提到搜尋引擎的歷史只有符合文章前的引子，卻沒有提到後半的重點 Google，因此是錯誤的。選項 (C) 提到 Yahoo 和 Google，Google 雖然是文章重點，但 Yahoo 只有匆匆帶過不是主旨，因此 (C) 也是錯的。選項 (D) 提到搜尋引擎開始的一個迷思，這是出現在第二段的中間的一個細節內容，在略讀時不見得會察覺的到，不是答案。

2. C

⊕ 本題在考單一細節，找到題目中的關鍵字後，瀏覽全文找到關鍵字所在，仔細閱讀上下文便可找出正確答案。

⊕ 題目在問最早的搜尋引擎為何，關係字 first true search engine，瀏覽全文，可以發現文章第三段第二句 Lycos 後半有一模一樣的字樣，故可以判斷選項 (C) Lycos 是正確答案。

⊕ 選項 (A) 的 Google 是後來才出現的搜尋引擎，因此是錯誤的。選項 (D) 的 Googleplex 出現在文章最後一段，作者說 Googleplex 是 Google 在加州的總部，不是搜尋引擎，因此不是正確答案。選項 (B) 的 Yahoo 誘答性很高，文章第二段後半有提到 Yahoo 最早推出 web directory，讓人一直以為 Yahoo 是個搜尋引擎，

但事實上，第三段澄清真正的第一個搜尋引擎是正解的 Lycos。

3. **D**

◉ 本題在考有關 Google 的多重細節，每個選項都需仔細閱讀，並利用瀏覽的方法在文中找到上下文，比對後就可知道哪個細節是正確的了。

◉ 選項 (D) 提到 Google 有業界最聰明的人，這在文章中最後一句有提到 by hiring only the best，可以判斷 Google 雇用的人一定很傑出，故為正確選項。

◉ 選項 (A) 提到 Google 是由 Larry Page 一個人獨立建立的，掃瞄文章可以在第五段中開始找到 Google 的建立者有兩個人：Larry Page 和 Sergey Brin，故選項 (A) 為錯誤的。選項 (B) 提到 Google 是 NASA 的一個計劃，第五段第一句後半有提到 Google 是 Stanford 大學的計劃，因此 (B) 也是錯誤的。選項 (C) 提到 Google 的正確率高達 80%，掃瞄上下文，可在第五段最後一句看到 Google 的正確率不像其它搜尋引擎只有 80% 就滿足了，可以判斷 Google 的正確率更高，所以 (C) 也是錯誤的。

4. **A**

◉ 本題在考字義，作答時可以把四個選項都帶進原文比對，看哪個最符合上下文。通常做答的線索也都在前後文，不妨可以把句子前後一起仔細閱讀，可以幫助做出最正確的選擇。

◉ 本題考的片語 lay their hands on 出現在最後一段 The employees at Google are not only proving good at their mission to organize every bit of information they lay their hands on, but are doing it in style!，表示 Google 的員工不僅是在處理資訊很強，但且連做的方式也很講究，關鍵詞 lay their hands on 便是用來修飾資訊 (information) 的，將四個選項代入，可以發現選項 (A) 獲得 (obtain) 最符合上下文，因此選 (A)。

◉ 選項 (B) 傷害 (harm)、選項 (C) 控制 (control)、選項 (D) 監控 (monitor) 代入文句中皆不合上下文的邏輯，因此都不是正確答案。

英文歷屆指考超絕剖析&模擬實戰

★ 囊括近八年的指考試題，讓您熟悉題型、穩握趨勢。

★ 收錄四回模擬實戰，全真模擬指考題目，讓您身歷其境、累積經驗。

★ 詳盡試題剖析，逐題詳解有如名師在陣。

★ 解析本獨立成冊，參照方便，省時有效率。

指考秘技，戰無不勝⁺

本書特色：

 本書包含理論篇和題目篇。理論篇精闢分析文章架構，引導您學習如何抓出文章重點及關鍵字，讓您迅速瞭解文章結構、掌握答題技巧，剖析文章一把罩。

 題目篇收錄20則篇章結構和20則閱讀測驗文章，內容多元豐富，囊括各類題材，讓您熟練各類主題。

 解析本含全文中譯及各題詳解，授課、自學皆宜。

 學校團體訂購附8回贈卷。